WHEN I PASSED THE STATUE OF LIBERTY
I BECAME BLACK

'Harry Edward was a hugely talented athlete and an extraordinary man who fought all his life for justice and fairness in the face of repeated prejudice. His story is as powerful today as it was when he lived it and I urge everyone to read this book.'
Linford Christie, 1992 Olympic 100m Champion

'A fascinating historical document. Harry Edward had a sharp eye and an ever-busy pen. Unfailingly frank, humorous, always dignified and empathetic, Edward describes a world in flux, as seen by a Black hero no one really knows about – and everyone should.'
Hugh Muir, writer and editor at the *Guardian*

'The celebration of Britain's first Black Olympic medallist would merit its own narrative, but that was just the beginning of Harry Edward's race through life. His story deserves to be told and his experiences should remind us all that we are all equal both in and out of the sporting arena.'
Steve Cram, British track and field athlete

'Harry was empowered by his Olympic experience and truly lived the Olympic values. He fought injustice and for inclusion wherever he went. His story is an inspiration to us all and is as relevant today as it was fifty years ago.'
Joël Bouzou OLY, president of the World Olympians Association

'Harry Edward tells the story of a man who fought for justice in the United States – and the world over. His was truly an Olympic spirit.'
Katherine Mooney, author of *Isaac Murphy*

'Such a beautiful, engaging, fascinating book – and to think we had it here at the Amistad Research Center all this time. *When I Passed the Statue of Liberty I Became Black* is a wonderful contribution to the fields of sports and history. Kudos to Neil Duncanson for getting this memoir out into the world where it belongs.'
Lisa Moore, Amistad Research Center

'An engrossing account of the life of a remarkable man wrestling with a variety of racial and professional issues in the early twentieth century. It's as if his commitment to athleticism was reflected in the way he dealt with life's more important challenges.'
James Walvin, author of *The People's Game*

'Captivating. Edward's singular voice and extraordinary achievements should reach a wide audience.'
Simon Hall, author of *Ten Days in Harlem*

'America's original twentieth-century everyman turns out to have been a Black Brit from Berlin by the name of Harry Edward. In the fairer world he fought for, his incredible life story would have been heard long ago. This book is his final, posthumous victory.'
Tom Peck, writer at *The Times*

'This is a fascinating discovery, a real jewel which yields so many invaluable insights into the life of the truly remarkable Harry Edward, an Olympian in the sporting arena and beyond.'
Philip Barker, editor, *Journal of Olympic History*

'This is an incredibly important and beautifully constructed tribute to a proper hero. We are incredibly proud of Edward at the University of Westminster (home to the Polytechnic Harriers) and indebted to Neil Duncanson for his extraordinary labour of love in seeing this book finally realised.'
Guy Osborn, University of Westminster

WHEN I PASSED THE STATUE OF LIBERTY I BECAME BLACK

Harry Edward

Edited by Neil Duncanson

YALE UNIVERSITY PRESS
NEW HAVEN AND LONDON

For information about this and other Yale University Press publications, please contact:
U.S. Office: sales.press@yale.edu   yalebooks.com
Europe Office: sales@yaleup.co.uk   yalebooks.co.uk

Set in Freight Text Pro by IDSUK (DataConnection) Ltd
Printed in Great Britain by TJ Books Limited , Padstow, Cornwall

Library of Congress Control Number: 2023948653

ISBN 978-0-300-27097-6

A catalogue record for this book is available from the British Library.

10 9 8 7 6 5 4 3 2 1

CONTENTS

CONTENTS

1. Harry Edward in 1918.

INTRODUCTION
Neil Duncanson

Harry Edward had until now been forgotten. What robbed him of his rightful place in history was the simple combination of time, geographic displacement and, of course, the colour of his skin.

A few years ago, I was working on a new edition of a book about the men's Olympic 100 metre medal winners: this new edition would include brief sketches of all the Olympic medallists, not just the champions. I knew the name Harry Edward, but there wasn't much to go on – only a few entries in the record books. He'd won two medals in the sprint events at the 1920 Olympics, where he represented Great Britain. He was a three-times national champion at the 100 and 220 yards. Harold Abrahams, 1924 Olympic 100 metre champion and star of *Chariots of Fire*, described him as 'one of the greatest sprinters I ever saw'.

Then Harry Edward vanished from view.

There were none of the standard retrospectives, hardly a mention in any books of the time, no newspaper articles and not a single obituary to rely on. My research took me in a surprising direction. Although he had won medals and titles for Britain, curiously Harry Edward had been born in Berlin and spent most of his life in the United States.

More digging led me to the Amistad Research Center, in New Orleans, an independent repository for papers, books and materials relating to African-American culture.

All Harry Edward's papers were donated to the Amistad Center after his death. Nine large boxes contained scrapbooks and photographs, letters and documents, medals and certificates. But the greatest find was a complete, typewritten memoir that Harry had finished in the early 1970s and had taken around the publishing houses of New York and London – without success.

One New York literary agent had been particularly blunt:

Dear Mr. Edward:

You've led an interesting life – but I'm afraid the book doesn't seem to me too interesting. It just doesn't seem very lively. Perhaps part of this is due to so much of the book dealing with events in the past and also to a great deal of detail which doesn't, at this time, seem very important.

The manuscript sat untouched in its box for nearly fifty years, but the world changed around it – in ways that would have pleased and troubled Harry Edward. Today we can see that his memoir and perspective have tremendous value, to all kinds of readers.

Athletes are not known for their writing, but this is a compelling tale of an extraordinary life. Harry Edward was present at some of the most significant moments of the twentieth century, and not just as a passive observer. Every page reveals an almost *Zelig*-like journey through wars, the depression, the civil rights struggle, social upheaval and international affairs. Harry Edward met kings and presidents, orphans and refugees. Immensely capable at everything he attempted, he worked alongside W.E.B. Du Bois and Orson Welles. He faced injustice and bigotry; he challenged prejudice and intolerance; he never backed down – and he never stopped.

INTRODUCTION

This text follows Harry Edward's final manuscript, with American spelling, but includes some additions from earlier versions of his memoir, along with some of the rich visual archive included in the nine boxes donated to the Amistad Center.

1

DISCOVERY OF AMERICA

It was on a beautiful August afternoon in the year 1923 when I "discovered" America. As the good ship RMS *Franconia*, seven days out of Liverpool, sailed along the coast of Long Island, I, like many other passengers, filled out the various, required government forms. I recall how a British fellow traveler at my side burst out in pretended indignation: "It's an outrage for Americans to call me, an Englishman, an alien!"

The ship came to a halt in the Narrows between Brooklyn and Staten Island and took aboard a group of immigration and health officers of the Federal Government. Slowly the RMS *Franconia* steamed into the inner harbor and the Statue of Liberty came into view. It was then that I was called before the immigration officer. This conscientious official established that I was an alien, born in Germany, entering under the German immigration quota, that I had a valid British passport because I was born a British subject, that my vocational designation was "clerk," because I had not completed the final portion of the professional examination of a British Chartered Society akin to that of Certified Public Accountants. The immigration official observed my dark complexion, curly hair and recorded, furthermore, that I was a Negro. Thus it happened that I

2. Cunard's RMS *Franconia* at Liverpool Dock.

became black, a Negro, when passing the Statue of Liberty. The question of color had not affected me previously in any serious manner.

I came to the United States in response to an invitation by a sports promoter to take part in the Wilco Games, at the Yankee Stadium. In the preceding year I had won three British track championships in one day, namely the Amateur Athletic Association's Championships open to all-comers. These contests had preceded the modern cycle of the Olympic Games by more than a half-century and were regarded as World Championships. The AAA Championships of 1922 had been honored by the visit of HM King George V. Thus, it happened that I was called before His Majesty and congratulated by him. This event was recorded on photographs and films which were distributed throughout the world and especially in the United States to the sports-conscious American press.

3. Harry Edward is congratulated at Stamford Bridge in July 1922 by King George V, after winning the AAA Championship 100, 220 and 440 yards finals in less than an hour – a feat that will never be matched.

Upon my setting foot on the soil of the United States of America I learned very soon that among all the classifications given me, the designation "Negro" was the most significant. On my visit to Paris the year before I had been received at the airport by the secretary of the International Athletic Association, a deputy minister of health and officials of the sponsoring club with their ladies. At New York a clerk of the promoter perfunctorily sped me to the Harlem Young Men's Christian Association, which facilities proved to be quite a contrast to those of the Hotel St. Lazare, in Paris. However, I had been toughened by my experiences as a prisoner of war.

4. The declaration form for US citizenship that so typified
Harry Edward's life in the United States. Born, Germany; Nationality,
British; Race, African Black.

During World War I, I had spent three years and eight months as
a British prisoner of war in German prisons and in a German internment camp under exceedingly rough conditions. Therefore, the
lack of many comforts did not disturb me particularly. From my
base in the YMCA I decided to discover Harlem, then hailed by the
news media and in literature as "the Mecca of the New Negro." And
surely, I was a New Negro.

Negro Harlem extended at that time approximately from 126th
Street to 155th Street, from Fifth Avenue in the east to Eighth
Avenue in the west. 135th Street was regarded as the center of Negro
Harlem. Located there were the YMCA, the Negro newspapers,

4

Negro physicians and lawyers, real estate operators, beauticians, and undertakers. 125th Street was even then the up-town shopping center, having also several vaudeville, burlesque, and movie theatres. Businesses in that thoroughfare were exclusively in the hands of white merchants, organized in the lilywhite uptown Chamber of Commerce. In places of entertainment, with few exceptions, Negroes were directed to the balcony and barred from orchestra seats. In business establishments they were effectively excluded from employment as sales personnel and confined to functions as porters and maintenance workers. Many Negroes lived south of 125th Street, as well as in the peripheral areas west and east, while many white residents, especially store owners, were interspersed throughout the area.

However, at the time of my arrival, my eyes, ears, and mind were not attuned to racial differences, color, and color-shadings. Thus, when I met light-skinned, fair-haired, blue-eyed Walter White, then Assistant Secretary of the National Association for the Advancement of Colored People, it took mental effort to comprehend and believe his proud claim of belonging to the Negro race. My initial introduction to the new and strange world which surrounded my monastery-like room at the YMCA was aided by Lt. Roy Morse of the 369th Infantry Regiment, himself a former track athlete. He was the son-in-law of the publisher of the *New York Amsterdam News*. In this manner I met William Kelly, the paper's imaginative editor, Romeo L. Dougherty, a feature writer on sports and theatrical events, and J.W. Roger, a writer known for his iconoclastic column "From Superman to Man," an indefatigable researcher into racial myths. These gentlemen made possible my meeting a group of people regarded as leaders in Negro Harlem: Nail & Parker, Philip A. Payton, realtors; Alderman Fred Moore, owner of the *New York Age*, a weekly newspaper; "Bojangles" Robinson, who starred in a Negro Revue; Charles Anderson, Collector of Internal Revenue; Assistant Corporation Counselor James Watson; "Billboard" Jackson, theatrical writer; George Harris, leader of Harlem's Republican Club; Physicians E.P. Roberts and Ernest Anderson, whose wives gave loyal and devoted volunteer service to Harlem's Young Women's Christian Association. I was also honored to meet the hard-working and efficient secretaries of the two Harlem Y's [the YWCA and the YMCA]: Mrs. Cecilia C. Saunders and Mr. Henry K. Craft.

In those early days on the American continent I visited also some English members of my London athletic club, resident in New York City. They received me warmly and one of them arranged my having a rented room on upper Broadway close to Columbia University's South Field, the athletic field then located south of 116th Street, opposite the Low Library. There I had the visits of photographers and sports writers whose professional products appeared in stories published in the *New York Herald*, *The New York Times*, *The World*, *The Sun* and *The Globe*, *The Evening World*, *The Home News* (New York City had many newspapers then) announcing my appearance at the Yankee Stadium track meet. My name had been entered in the 100 yards, the furlong, and the quarter-mile races, over which distances I had won the AAA Open World Championships the preceding year. However, I failed to land among the first three in any of those events, on this my first appearance in America. Nevertheless, other invitations were extended to me to take part in athletic competitions organized by the New York Athletic Club and the Boston Athletic Club in the fall of 1923. When traveling to Boston by means of the old Dominion Line, via Providence, Rhode Island, I remember reading an article on the Heavyweight Boxing Championship fight between [Luis Ángel] Firpo and [Jack] Dempsey, held at the Polo Grounds with "20,000 fans in the stands." I was astonished. True, in August I had suffered from the unaccustomed, humid heat of New York City, but I could not imagine that an outdoor event attracted so many fans.

It took a little time to get used to "American English," especially the sports headlines of the *New York Daily News*, as for instance:

"Yanks, Sox split before 25,000." Lifts became elevators, petrol – gas, trolleys – streetcars, a bowler hat was called a derby. I had such a hat in those days, as well as a Mackintosh, a British raincoat. Thus attired, I presented myself to several businessmen of New York City to whom I submitted letters of reference given me by well-known London merchants. I was job-hunting with vigor for a clerical position, but to no avail.

2

SEARCHING FOR A JOB

Friends referred me to the office of the National Urban League, whose staff consisted of Eugene Kinckle Jones as executive secretary and six clerical assistants. They urged my seeing Attorney L. Hollingsworth Wood, founder and President of the National Urban League. It was a heart-warming experience to meet and talk to this cheerful and forthright Quaker, who had made the right of the American Negro to equal economic opportunities his life's work. After listening to the story of my business experiences in Europe he asked me to accompany him for the purpose of visiting some of his friends in their Wall Street offices. He presented me to them with a flowery description of my studies and accomplishments and asked them to provide a job opportunity for me. In one instance, a director of an insurance company threw up his hands and exclaimed: "Impossible!" Others accepted the request with calm. In one instance, a prominent coffee importer offered me a possible job in Brazil. I felt forever grateful to L. Hollingsworth Wood for this tangible evidence of his Christian commitment.

Two years later I met him again in Philadelphia at a conference of the Urban League. Hard at work with his usual cheerfulness and zest I asked him whether he did not grow tired and discouraged at times. He replied: "Oh, my dear Mr. Edward, this is the greatest joy of my life!" When relating this story to friends who had worked closely with him, they assured me that the remark was a true reflection of his inner feelings. The memory of the words and deeds of L. Hollingsworth Wood and of a few other white Americans were often the soothing balm on so many wounds inflicted by the bigotry in American society.

I learned that the renowned Wanamaker store promoted annually the Millrose Indoor Track Meeting held at Madison Square Garden, then located on the site of the present New York Life Insurance office building, near Madison Square. This meeting, I was told, always had a strong representation of Negro athletes, staff members of Wanamaker's department store. In my job search, I presented myself to the personnel director of Wanamaker's. He listened politely to the recitation of my qualifications and told me in a matter-of-fact voice that he could offer me only a job as elevator operator or porter.

While searching through the "Male Help Wanted" columns of *The New York Times* I spotted a vacancy which called for skills which I was able to offer with the utmost of confidence, skills which I had used successfully in a job in London. The advertisement read: "German and French correspondent for Import and Export House, typing required." There were no restrictions listed, such as "white" or "colored," or "under 40," customary in those days. Promptly I presented myself to the fee-charging employment agency, submitted my credentials, which included English, French, and German shorthand, and requested a referral for an interview with the employer. The employment agent gazed at me for a moment and said in a somewhat bombastic manner: "Oh, I am sorry, but I am looking for a typical American boy!" All my pleas for a try-out fell on the deaf ears of a prejudiced mind.

Foot-sore and soul-sore I began to realize that the doors to office jobs were closed to me. I became painfully aware that my meagre finances were rapidly declining. There was no income and living expenses were relatively high with my room on Broadway and food taken in restaurants. I discussed my plight with a young lady from British Demerara, now Guyana, who had opened a job placement agency on Sixth Avenue, near 46th Street, where scores of job agencies were situated. "Harry," she said, "you are too damned honest!" She continued: "If you want a job" (and we were discussing manual labor) "you must tell them that you have experience." She gave me the address of a small restaurant in the garment district where a vacancy existed for a dishwasher. In addition, she handed me a list of three restaurants she knew for their high labor turnover. I walked briskly to the restaurant and asked for the boss. He came from behind the counter and motioned to me to sit at one of the dozen tables, where he joined me. He asked me whether I had experience as a dishwasher, and with a voice ringing full of confidence and conviction I said: "Sure, I have." Then he queried: "Where?" Frankly I had forgotten the names of the places where I was supposed to have worked. Without being flustered in the least, I drew out of my pocket the slip with the names of my alleged, former employers and read them to the boss. It seemed he was not measuring my IQ, because he said I could start the next day. He showed me the kitchen, a narrow space behind a wooden partition, the tubs, and the boxes of soap powder.

I was there the next morning at the appointed time, put on my apron, got acquainted with the short-order cook, and learned from him the routine of the place. The rush period was, of course, lunch time. I washed most conscientiously the constant flow of dishes, cups, and saucers, washed them in hot water with lots of soap powder. I believe I was a good dishwasher. However, after a week my hands became painfully sore as the soap powder seemingly ate away my fingernails. I reduced the quantity of soap, but then the boss complained once or twice that the plates were not sufficiently shiny. Anyhow, I had something to eat, free of charge. So, I ate! It seemed that I consumed too many sandwiches and pies for the boss's liking, because after ten days he paid me off.

Then I heard that the docks paid well for longshoreman work, 53 cents per hour for longshoremen and 49 cents per hour for truckmen, with overtime at the rate of time and a half after eight hours of work. Dockworkers were not unionized at that time. I went to the docks dressed as usual in my British raincoat and derby and told the boss at the hiring office that an employment agency had sent me. He said that I should not pay a cent to any employment office, that he and he alone was the hiring boss. He instructed me to come back at 6 p.m. for the shape-up. The shape-up was the usual hiring method in those days at the docks, as well as at the entrance gates of factories. The men seeking work would form a semi-circle and the boss facing them would pick those he wanted. That evening the hiring boss at the dock called the low-numbered crews of eight who had worked the previous night, then new crews were made up and higher numbers given them. The number of crews depended on the volume of work to be handled. Each crew consisted of four longshoremen and four truckmen. Two longshoremen would be stationed in the railcar on the floating barge and two at a designated space on the dock. The former would load the crates of fruits or vegetables onto handtrucks, which the truckmen would trundle to the docks. There the two longshoremen would stack the crates by lot numbers. Circulating among the crews were "pushers" who would push the men to maximum effort and speed.

At the shape-up the hiring boss had spotted me in my derby and English raincoat and had hired me. He asked me whether I was a longshoreman or a truckman. I replied promptly that I was a longshoreman, having in mind the higher rate of pay. However, I soon learned that longshoremen worked almost continuously stacking those 50 pound crates, sometimes 6 feet high, while the truckmen could often lean on their handtrucks and rest. My muscles became very tired and sore after ten or eleven hours of slinging crates, so that I decided on my first night that I would henceforth be an experienced truckman.

There were other adventures during the early days of my discovery of America. For two weeks I worked as a laborer on a construction job in Brooklyn, several times as a car-washer in Brooklyn garages.

My first job as a car-washer was an ordeal. Having developed a boldness in claiming broad experience, I had assured the garage owner that I could wash and drive cars. In reality I had never driven a car and so I had to learn how to drive that very afternoon. Lt. Roy Morse had a car and he was kind enough to take me to the Harlem Speedway and teach me for one hour. First he drew a capital "H" on a paper and explained the standard gear-shift with its first, second, high gear, and reverse positions. Then he explained how to turn the ignition key, keeping the gear in neutral and to give gas, how to release the accelerator, shifting to first, then step up gas, release and shift to second, give gas again, and shift to third and high gear and accelerate. Well, I did drive the car over a short distance, perspiring under great nervous strain. That afternoon I learned by heart the procedure. When riding the subway to my new Brooklyn job I repeated over and over again: "Put gearshift in neutral, turn on ignition, give her gas, reduce gas, shift to first, give her gas, reduce gas, shift to second, give her gas, reduce, shift to third, give her gas!" I thought I knew it.

However, on the job, when wishing to put the first car from its parking space unto the washstand, the car refused to move, yet I had followed all the instructions. The boss came over and asked what the trouble was. I said naively: "It does not move." He looked inside and said: "Why don't you release the hand brake?" How was I to know? Nobody had told me. At about midnight, many customers arrived from their parties and theatre shows and left their cars in the passage until they spilled over into the entrance and the street.

12

I had to park them somehow to keep the entrance clear. Oh, how I did sweat that night, handling cars of all makes and trying to get them into their narrow spaces. I cannot remember how many cars I washed, but it was an exhausting experience. I lasted two nights on that job.

There were other car-washing jobs, but on my last job as a washer I was so efficient and well thought of by the boss that he assured me on my leaving that I could get my job back any time I wanted. However, I had procured a "steady" job, namely as a porter at the Aeolian Hall, one of the foremost concert halls of New York City. As a fringe benefit to my menial occupation I could listen to the New York Philharmonic and numerous instrumental and vocal concert artists. Thus it happened that I was present when George Gershwin and Paul Whiteman's band gave the original performance of *Rhapsody in Blue*, this broody, instrumental composition, irregular in form like an improvisation. It was so much like my struggles since passing the Statue of Liberty: irregular in form, like an improvisation and in a blue mood.

To stay or not to stay this side of the Statue of Liberty, that was the question, a question turned over in my mind numerous times. In London, England, I had been a cost accountant and French and German correspondent with merchants and manufacturing concerns. In Great Britain I was known to the sports fraternity as a seven-times track champion, who had captained many teams on goodwill tours on the European continent. In 1921 and in 1922 I had been honored with the "Best Athlete of the Year" Award, and the Polytechnic Institute had inscribed my name in marble on the Honor List of members who had made valued contributions to the school in sports or scholarships. From Europe I had viewed the United States of America as the land of hope for the peace of the world. President Wilson's Fourteen Points had stirred great hopes in the hearts of a large segment of mankind touched by World War I, "the war to make the world safe for democracy."

The prominence in sports that I had gained enabled me to participate in many concrete expressions of the "Peace Corps idealism" of that period, when youth sought to reach out to youth of other lands. In those days, too, there was a generation gap. The older generation longed for the peaceful, "good old days" and the political slogan expressing that sentiment was, both in Great Britain and in the United States: "Back to normalcy!" An American song of that period also sketched the divergent pulls of the post-war days:

> How y're goin' to keep 'em
> down on the farm
> after they've seen Paree?

I was reading voraciously in those days both large morning newspapers of New York City, namely *The New York Times* and *The New York World*, 2 cents per copy. I made a valiant effort to understand my environment and the problems of the day. And there were many problems. In the US Senate, Senators Norris, Wagner, Walsh, and LaFollette were thundering against the unrestrained manipulations of capitalists grown richer and more powerful by accumulated war profits. The Teapot Dome revelations [of uncompetitive tendering] disclosed how graft and corruption had reached into the president's Cabinet. Senator "Cotton Tom" Heflin of Alabama was the champion of white supremacy of the rural South and a violent and virulent anti-Catholic crusader. The nightriders of the Ku Klux Klan were burning crosses, flogging, and killing those of whom they did not approve. They exerted themselves also politically, capturing some city halls and state houses. In the Pennsylvania coal fields open warfare raged between the United Mine Workers of America, led by John L. Lewis, and the armed, private Coal and Iron Police of the mine owners. The civil right of workers to join a union was then still eleven years in the future. In those days of Prohibition, bootleggers and their syndicates corrupted many phases of public life, and their methods were even more ruthless than those of the Mafia today. My endeavor was to evaluate life in America with all the mentioned problems against life in Europe with its destructive nationalism and long history of wars. Into these considerations entered also the seeming American economic success stories of some of my friends from Great Britain, France, and the West Indies. There is no doubt that I underrated considerably the pervasiveness and depth of America's racial factor, in spite of my harsh experiences.

I had to decide whether to ask my wife and fourteen-year-old stepson to join me in accordance with our original plans, or whether I should return to Great Britain, admitting that my plans had been a failure. My wife was, however, anxious to join me, in spite of my evident inability to offer her an adequately secure economic base. She was a very talented dressmaker and hoped to supplement the family income. It was my good fortune to find and rent an upper-floor apartment in a conveniently located private house in Brooklyn, which I furnished with second-hand furniture. The landlord, living on the premises, was a congenial English family who had heard and read about my exploits on British cinder tracks.

The arrival of my wife and son was a happy occasion, beclouded by the thought that their passports carried only a six-month US visitor's visa, not an immigration visa. The Swiss immigration quota – and they had been born in Switzerland – was filled. It was my hope that I might overcome that legal obstacle, little realizing the difficulties and complexities of official procedures and red tape. The solution to this and other problems was a few months off.

When I was working as a longshoreman, L. Hollingsworth Wood, President of the National Urban League, had introduced me to a fellow Quaker, Paul J. Furnas, who was to exert a great influence on my life. Paul Furnas and a group of Quaker entrepreneurs were then planning to launch a corporation for the manufacture of felt-base floor covering. He asked me whether I would join their enterprise as a laborer, taking my chance with the progress of the company. I declared my willingness and even my eagerness, and thus started a happy association with Paul J. Furnas, Treasurer of Sandura Company Inc., Paulsboro, New Jersey, who became a wise counselor and friend. Paulsboro, in Gloucester County, where the plant was situated, had a few other industries, namely the Vacuum Oil Company and the Harrison Fertilizer Plant of Du Pont. The county was, however, predominantly rural. Its farmers employed extensively Negro migrant labor from Virginia at harvest time. The Klan was active and became visible occasionally when staging peaceful demonstrations against the Pope and Catholicism, which really meant against "foreigners," i.e. recent immigrants from Italy, a reflection also of the strong divisive feelings generated by the Sacco–Vanzetti [armed robbery and murder] case of that period. Paulsboro had a population of about 4,000, of whom about 15 percent were Negroes, mostly from Virginia. We were offered quarters on the company's property adjacent to the plant, a former ammunition factory. We painted and fitted up former dormitory space in the best way possible. My wife's adaptability and artistic talents added considerably to the transformation of bare rooms to comfortable living quarters. Many years of living under war conditions had taught her adaptability to various environments, to scarce food supplies, and to difficult working conditions. I, too, had felt the sharp pinch of necessity in those years of war and had learned some valuable lessons from life for living.

3

SUCKED INTO THE VORTEX
OF WORLD WAR I

World War I had fallen upon a psychologically unprepared world. Most historians agree today that Europe stumbled and blundered into that devastating conflict. On Sunday, June 28, 1914, when Archduke Francis Ferdinand of Austria was assassinated in Sarajevo, I took part in a sports meeting. I ran for the first time in the newly built Berlin Stadium, competing against German Olympic runners. I finished in second place behind the German sprint champion, but beat the German quarter-mile champion over the distance of 200 meters. After the race, Alvin E. Kraenzlein, the American coach engaged by the German Athletic Association in preparation for the scheduled Olympic Games of 1916, congratulated me. He was a renowned Olympic gold medalist, having won the 60 meters run and the 200 meters hurdles in the Games of 1900.

The Berlin sports meeting had been favored by bright, beautiful sunshine, and an enthusiastic crowd of spectators had enjoyed the races. Upon leaving the stadium, a pall of gloom settled upon the crowd as the assassination of the heir-apparent to Austria's throne became the dominant theme of conversation. However, the thought of an impending war was far from everybody's mind. I, too, could not imagine on that particular day, that four weeks later in Budapest

I would see the outbreak of World War I, and that I would witness in the first days of August the unfolding of a nation's mobilization for war in Berlin. Although I did not realize it at that time, my life's chapter of peaceful living in the circle of my family, of school and play had come to an end.

Life in Western Europe during the four decades preceding World War I had been a relatively good life. Europe had enjoyed nearly a half-century of peace. And a century of non-involvement in a major war. The application of steam power and electricity had vastly increased economic productivity and had provided an expanded labor market. International trade had grown rapidly and the search for foreign markets was supported by dynamic, colonial, expansionist policies of Europe's industrial nations. The "population explosion" of that period had found a safety valve in the migration of surplus population to the North and South American continents. Such, then, was the atmosphere in which I had grown up.

My father had come to Berlin in 1894 to work in some of the world-famous restaurants and cabarets as a trained waiter and

5. The earliest known picture of Harry Edward (aged three) taken around 1901.

receptionist-headwaiter. He was an impressive 6 foot 3 inches tall, had acquired a working knowledge of German, French, Italian, Czech, and Hungarian by his stays and work in various spas. Such language facilities were useful tools in the international restaurant and hotel trades. A native of Dominica, British West Indies, he had left home as a young man to work on ships as a cabin boy, then had joined the circus to see the world, and in this manner had reached Europe, where he had found work as an apprentice waiter. In contrast, my mother came from the sheltered environment of a strict Prussian family. She was the second oldest in a large family of five boys and two girls. Trained in the domestic arts, which included studies in music, she became eventually a teacher of piano.

My father and mother were married in Berlin's Church of England (Episcopal). The choice of that denomination may appear as a compromise between the upbringing of my father in the Catholic Church and of my mother's Lutheran faith. Her marriage to my father caused a stir in the staid and well-regulated family of my grandfather, then chief administrator of one of Berlin's railway freight yards, a senior civil servant. However, my mother was a mature thirty years of age and my father a tall, imposing, and handsome man, widely known. In his life my father left, undoubtedly, his imprint in the shaping of my character and future international work. His vocation brought him into contact with visitors from many countries. He invited many to our home, which often took on the atmosphere of an international center.

In those days my father enjoyed a relatively good income, and he believed in theory and practice to pass on wealth to his environment. Thus, when boarding horse-drawn buses it seems that all conductors knew my father. He always gave a tip in addition to the fare. Similarly, nearly all the waiters in famous restaurants greeted him affably. Father took me there to have some rare and most delicious, rich vanilla ice cream served in cool metal bowls, while he

6. The apartment where Harry was born, at 19 Willibald-Alexis-Strasse, a cobbled street in Berlin's Kreuzberg district, built in the 1890s and now in a protected area of historic buildings near the old Tempelhof airfield.

would peruse some foreign newspapers found on display-racks there.

My mother's piano brought music into the house, and I loved music. The visits of an organ-grinder, usually Italian-born, with his monkey were exciting events and we, children of the neighborhood, would follow him from yard to yard and help to collect for the organ-grinder paper-wrapped coins thrown from windows. When a military band marched down the street I could not resist marching with them at the very head of the band, down many, many streets to the palace or to the barracks. On such occasions I disappeared from my parents' sight for two hours or longer, until my weary feet would find their way home again. Both my sister Irene, four years younger, and I were brought up and confirmed in Lutheran churches. My parents settled in Berlin, where I was born. In good time I went to a public grade school and later to a school of secondary education. There is no doubt that my mother's larger family, of uncles, aunts, and cousins provided much of the emotional social security I enjoyed in my childhood.

At age fifteen I became very interested in athletics. I read extensively about the ancient Olympic Games and the excavations conducted by a German archaeological expedition at Olympia, Greece, site of the Ancient Olympics. I learned about Baron de

7. Harry Edward's Prussian family – a formal picture taken in Berlin, in October 1912, to mark the fiftieth wedding anniversary of Harry's grandparents. Harry's mother Maria Magdalena sits fifth from the left in the second row – next to her mother and father – while Harry (aged fourteen) peeks out from just behind the middle of the third row, and his sister Irene (aged ten) is sitting at the front.

Coubertin's efforts in bringing about a revival of the Games and the slowly growing interest in the modern cycle begun in 1896. Germany was scheduled to be the host to the Olympic Games of 1916, an event which did not take place because of the hostilities of World War I.

I joined the youth section of an athletic club in 1913 and entered that year in a track event restricted to youth under sixteen, and another limited to youth under eighteen years of age. Much to my surprise, I won the first mentioned and finished the other in third place. This success overcame the objections to track and field sports raised by my family and helped to establish me as a good track athlete in the eyes of my club members. Further successes in

8. On 3 August 1913, fifteen-year-old Harry Edward had his first competitive race against top-class national opposition: the 100 metres at the Asseburg Memorial meeting in Charlottenburg, Berlin. German champion Richard Rau (far right) pips Schoulze (left arm raised) and Harry, referred to in *Der Rasensport* as 'the negro' (third).

athletic competitions and the resulting publicity in sports papers helped to inflate the ego of this fifteen-year-old runner. Then, I happened to get beaten by a little-known, short athlete of another club. I expected some expressions of sympathy and regret from fellow athletes, but failed to get them. The coach came to me and said: "Harry, I am glad you lost – you were getting a swelled head." "Remember," he added, "the higher you float up in the air, the farther you will have to drop, the more it will hurt when you have to come down." I believe I learned this valuable lesson at an early age and that it contributed to the process of maturing, and under unfolding war conditions people tended to mature quickly.

Events seemed to move rapidly after the described happenings of June 28, 1914. The athletic competitions in the Berlin Stadium were written up at length in the sports columns of many European papers. Thus, it occurred that a telegram was received by my Berlin club inviting me to an international meeting in Budapest, scheduled for Sunday, July 26, 1914. We verified the authenticity of the invitation and wired for the telegraphic transmittal of traveling expenses for two persons. My mother insisted that the club's coach accompany me. No telegram arrived, and we were obliged to decide

9. On 10 August 1913, Harry Edward wins a German junior 100 metres title in 11.8 seconds.

10. On 31 August 1913, two British sprint eras collide in an international meet in Berlin. Despite injuring himself in a race in Cologne the previous weekend, Harry Edward entered the 100 metres to face England's 1912 Olympic star Willie Applegarth (on Harry's right). Harry Edward ran a close second to the old charger, but limped out of the final, which Applegarth duly won.

11. Harry Edward's last run at Berlin's new Olympic Stadium (built for the 1916 Games) on 28 June 1914, and a narrow defeat in the 200 metres by his old foe Richard Rau (far right). Rau, aged twenty-four, won in 21.6 seconds, with sixteen-year-old Harry Edward just a tenth of a second slower, making it one of his best ever 200 metre runs, in a time that would easily have won him the 200 metre gold at the 1920 Olympics.

whether to advance the railroad fare ourselves or to drop the matter, disregarding the verified invitation. We paid the fare out of our own pockets, took the Budapest Express out of Berlin on Friday evening, scheduled to reach the Hungarian capital on Saturday afternoon. We believed that after a night's rest I would be fit for Sunday's competitions. What we did not realize in the seemingly placid atmosphere was the fact that the wires had been pre-empted for urgent government communications, and that behind the calm surface a drama of serious proportion was being enacted, namely the futile diplomatic endeavors to prevent a world conflict. These conditions accounted for the delay in the transmission of all private telegraphic dispatches.

The athletic coach and I relaxed in our second-class compartment of the Budapest Express and were able to snooze a few hours. In the morning hours we passed through the mining area of Silesia, Germany, now Poland, and crossed the frontier to Austria, now Czechoslovakia. We were fascinated by the countryside which became hilly, wooded, broken by fertile fields. With the approach of the noon hour we became hungry and welcomed the announcement that the dining car was ready to serve meals. We moved forward in the train to the dining car and settled down to a satisfying dinner. We consumed it leisurely while enjoying the passing scenery, which had become mountainous and rugged. After a sitting of almost two hours we left the table and walked back through the train, but were unable to find our compartment where we had left our coats and valises. When we showed our tickets to the conductor, who spoke only Czech and Hungarian, and saw his agitation and gesticulation, we gathered that something was wrong. With the help of a passenger who spoke broken German we pieced together the facts. We were on the wrong train, rolling through the Carpathian mountains toward Transylvania. During dinner our car had been taken off at the junction of Žilina, where it had been attached to another locomotive to proceed southward to Budapest, while we in the detached front-part of the train were rolling eastward.

The conductor consulted his timetables and established that there was no junction ahead of us which would make a connection with Budapest. It was necessary to return over the same line to Žilina. We were advised to get off the train at the next stop, a small town in the Carpathians called Lipto San Miklos [Liptovský Mikuláš]. However, first we had to make our trip "legal" by paying the fare for that part of the journey not covered by our ticket, plus a fine for having traveled without a prepaid ticket. We learned at the station that the next train back would be a local one, due in five hours, and that the return trip would take four hours. We understood that at Žilina we could make a connection to Budapest, due to reach that destination on Sunday morning, the day of the sports meeting.

At Lipto San Miklos we carefully counted our money, greatly depleted by the unexpected expenses. We sent telegrams to the promoters of the sports meeting advising them of our delayed arrival and another wire to the station master of an intervening stop of our Budapest Express, requesting the conductor to take care of our belongings. After paying for the telegrams, we were broke, absolutely broke, stranded in a Galician village. We told the station master that we were unable to pay for the tickets for our trip to Žilina. He arranged with the conductor of the local train to let us ride as "blind passengers" in third class. After boarding the train we were invited into a second-class compartment by an Austrian sales representative, who proved to be a most interesting traveling companion and guide. He pointed out to us in the dusk and enwrapping darkness the various textile factories along the way, the number of spindles in each, and the special products of those mills.

It was late in the evening when we reached Žilina and were led by the conductor to the station master's office. There we were asked by a clerk to pay for the journey from Lipto San Miklos to Žilina, plus an extra charge for having made the trip without a ticket. This demand was repeated in German by the tall, handsome, young station master who had been summoned. He added calmly and emphatically that if we were unable to pay the amount he would be obliged to lodge us in the local jail. This took our breath away for a moment, but we were not speechless, as we pleaded eloquently to consider our obligation toward the Mayar Turn Club [actually the Magyar Testgyakorlók Köre], the foremost athletic club of Hungary, the promoter of the international sports meeting in Budapest. In support, we submitted the telegraphic invitation and copies of our wires, which the station master regarded as insufficient documentation. At the point when our case seemed hopeless the station master said: "I am a member of MTK (Mayar Turn Klub). I shall advance the money you owe, and you can reimburse me on your return journey." Well, we could have kissed that guy. He, with his red helmet and large blue cape, accompanied us to the waiting train for Budapest.

Our valid tickets for that route entitled us to second-class seats. The station master instructed the conductor to lock the compartment, so that we would be undisturbed and would be able to rest for the races the next day. Then he asked us at what hour we had eaten the last time. We told him honestly that it had been at noon of that day, and at that moment the watch showed 11 o'clock in the evening. He vanished to reappear with a large package under his cape. Out came two French loaves of bread, two salamis, and a number of red vegetables which I took to be tomatoes. The latter looked so inviting that I promptly bit into one only to come up gasping for air as I discovered that the tomato was a hot Hungarian paprika pepper. We thanked the station master most profusely and, needless to say, we honored our promise to repay him on our return journey.

Upon our arrival at Budapest's railroad terminal, we recovered our valises and topcoats, informed MTK by telephone of our arrival, and received instructions how to reach the stadium. The promoters provided me with a room in the club's quarters where I had a few hours' rest. The international track meet was a great success. The weather was clear and beautiful, the crowd large and enthusiastic. Two Americans were the star attraction: James C. Patterson, a college all-star from the University of Pennsylvania, in the sprints, and middle-distance runner Homer Baker, from the New York Athletic Club, who had won the English half-mile championship race a few weeks previously. I was successful in beating Patterson in the 200 meters, but lost to him over the 100 meters. In the 300 meters handicap I encountered the Hungarian champion Agost Szubert [Ágost Schubert]. Both of us were at the scratch mark. I beat him but failed to overtake the large field of handicapped runners. Yet, it seemed that the spectators were not disappointed with my perform- ance, because a group of young men lifted me onto their shoulders on my way to the dressing rooms, while the crowd gave lusty cheers.

However, the strongest impressions made upon my memory of those days were the excited groups of young people I saw parading in the main streets of Budapest in the evening, carrying Austrian flags and pictures of Emperor Francis Joseph, voicing emotion-filled epithets directed at Serbia and Serbians. World War I had begun.

Count Leopold Berchtold, Austria's foreign minister, had made ten demands on Serbia for suppression of anti-Austrian agitation. Serbia conceded all but two, which called for Austrian enforcement police inside Serbia. However, national emotions were running high and Austria demanded all or nothing. Imperial Russia regarded the hostile ultimatum against Serbia as a threat against herself. Germany backed Austria, while Britain, France, and Italy proposed mediation. In those days there was no United Nations, no League of Nations with their forums for mediation, arbitration, and legal actions. On that Sunday, July 26, 1914, Germany refused to join a conference of the large powers proposed by Britain's foreign minister. Two days later, Austria declared war on Serbia, setting in motion a chain of war declarations and mobilizations. Several young Hungarian athletes were swept along by the war hysteria, so vivid before my eyes. I learned that many had volunteered for enlistment in the Austro-Hungarian Army during the following days.

The return trip to Berlin was on schedule and uneventful. The news during those days was bewildering and ominous. A week after the Budapest events, I found myself in a crowd at the Schlossplatz in Berlin, in front of the Kaiser's residential palace, awaiting some news about the disturbing developments. The mood of the crowd was subdued and somber, in great contrast to the atmosphere I had encountered in Hungary's capital.

As I was a British subject resident in Germany, I wondered how the threatening war conditions would affect me and my first job as a clerk-bookkeeper with a coffee wholesale house and encroach upon the life of my family. These questions were soon answered by the visit of a representative of Germany's secret police. He asked a series of questions to fill out a complete dossier about us, namely my mother, my sister, and me. My father was in Budapest, where he had a summer job, which seasonal work he had followed for many years. In fact, my decision to travel to the Budapest sports meeting had been greatly influenced by my wish to surprise my father as a "famous athlete." He had not realized what impact my Berlin Stadium race had made on the sports community. Thus, during the two days we spent together I was able to bring him up to date on family matters and sports news as they had developed over the three months since his departure.

As the war progressed and Germany rounded up all male British subjects of military age, we were grateful for the fact that father had stayed in Hungary, where he remained free and unrestricted in his movements. Furthermore, he was able to send us some needed financial support.

In Berlin, the political atmosphere grew increasingly tense and threatening during the last week of July and the first week in August. On July 31, 1914, the German Government declared a *Kriegsgefahrzustand* – "condition of war danger." Mobilization for war, actual and psychological, was thrown into higher gear.

The British Embassy in Berlin was stoned, French Ambassador Jules Cambon was ill-treated, and the Hotel Adlon, where British and American newspapermen stayed, was besieged. British subjects without distinction as to age and sex were arrested and sent to the prison fortress at Spandau, where three decades later the Nazi leaders found guilty at the Nuremberg Trials were incarcerated.

In the fall of 1914, the British Government decided on interning German residents in Great Britain. Thereupon, the German Government, as a reprisal, immediately interned all British civilian men and locked them up in Ruhleben. When the British first captured a German submarine crew, Winston Churchill, then First Lord of the Admiralty, declared that the crew should not be treated as ordinary prisoners, but should be thrown into jails "like the felons they are" because of their inhuman acts. In reprisal, the Germans picked a number of captured British prisoners of war, twice the number, and clapped them into jails in Burg and Magdeburg. Selected were members of distinguished British families and although I did not belong to any elite, I too was drawn into the whirlpool of those strong, swirling human emotions so wide-spread in those early days of the war.

It was not long before I was called to our police precinct, where I was given identification papers and instructions to have them stamped twice each day. My movements were confined to a radius of 5 miles from my home. I followed those instructions closely. My twice-daily visits to the police station became a routine affair over the first seven months of the war, until one day, early in April 1915, a few days before my seventeenth birthday, I was detained at the precinct and asked by the police officer to take a seat. The scene is very clear in my mind to this day. I recall that the police officer whistled the "Funeral March" by Chopin. This prompted me to ask whether the news he had to tell me was really that bad. He quickly stopped and told me that a telegram had been received from police headquarters to place me under arrest. *Schutzhaft* was the term used, meaning protective custody. I was not allowed to go home or to my place of work. Eventually he sent a detective to my mother with my handwritten note explaining the circumstances and requesting a small handbag with toilet articles. My distraught mother brought the desired items and, after I had waited some more hours, a plain-clothes officer was assigned to take me to the Praesidium, the police headquarters with the adjoining central house of detention.

There, I went through the routine procedure for checking-in. I had to strip, empty all pockets, and place their contents on a table. An official compiled a list of all articles surrendered, and I had to sign the statement. The articles were placed in a paper bag, and the items of clothing were handed back to me except my belt, garters, and shoestrings. Holding up my pants, I was led down long corridors, through locked doors to a dark cell. The steel door closed behind me with a bang of finality. I stood in the cell for a long time in the belief that my eyes would get accustomed to the darkness. It was a vain hope. There was utter blackness around me. I had to depend on my sense of touch. The cell was about 6 feet wide. I located a small table, a stool, and a cot. I stretched out on the cot fully clothed, covering myself with my topcoat, and listened to the striking of a clock on a nearby church steeple. I persuaded myself to relax, but the thought of crawling bedbugs bothered me for some time. Eventually sleep descended upon me.

I awakened early; the hour was six by the chimes of the church's clock. Daylight came from a small, barred window 10 feet up. There was in the cell one more piece of furniture which I had not noticed in the dark: a commode, namely a covered seat hiding a bucket for one's bodily wastage. On the wall above the small table in a frame were the prison rules, which I read several times over. There was nothing else to do. Yet, the hours of my first day behind bars passed rather swiftly. The day started with a bang, followed by many more bangs of my fists and heels against the door of the prison cell in my attempt to summon a guard.

Upon his long-delayed arrival, I complained vociferously about my solitary confinement, declaring that I had done no wrong. The prison guard was impassive and stoic. The morning hours went by quickly with the emptying of the bucket, washing, breakfast, making the bed, and sweeping out the cell. Suddenly the guard ordered me to follow him. He took me to the prison office, where my personal belongings were returned to me, and I was handed over to the care of a policeman in civilian dress. He was instructed to take me to the internment camp for British civilian prisoners. When leaving police headquarters, the policeman turned to me and asked in a mellow voice whether I was planning to escape. Expressing my astonishment, I asked why he posed such a question. Equally calmly came his reply: "If you have any such intention I am going to clamp a pair of handcuffs on your wrists." I assured him that I did not like such an adornment.

4

RUHLEBEN INTERNMENT CAMP

12. British civilian prisoners and their quarters at Ruhleben.

A local, suburban train took us to Spandau and we negotiated the 2 miles to Ruhleben Camp on foot. Officials at the camp's office, however, refused to accept me as a new prisoner, because I had not passed through a Berlin prison regarded as a quarantine station. Thus, the policeman was compelled to take me to the Stadtvogtei prison in the center of Berlin, just one block from police headquarters.

After going through the now familiar procedure of checking into a prison, I was led through long corridors and locked doors to a screened-off section of the prison reserved for political prisoners and assigned to a large cell housing seven persons. In that group was a Boer from South Africa, 7 feet tall with long, flowing hair. He was a man from a circus sideshow, arrested because of his British citizenship, yet in the Boer War he had been a prisoner of the British. There was an Italian who had been sent to this prison because his German wife had complained to the German authorities about her husband's cursing the German Kaiser. To curse or criticize the German Kaiser or members of his family was a serious offence – lèse-majesté or contempt of His Majesty – was punishable by prison. There was also a Polish gentleman, characterized by refinement, fluent in several languages, who had been a director of a world-famous textile firm in Berlin. He alleged that the war conditions had given his German partners a convenient excuse to get him out of the way. A brooding British businessman from Namur, Belgium, attempted suicide in our cell's toilet by trying to pierce his heart with a pair of scissors. I found him bleeding profusely from the self-inflicted wounds, and only by shouting through the barred windows and banging against our cell door were we eventually able to attract the attention of the German prison guards. Eventually his mind broke completely, and he spent several years in a German asylum. He had been a successful drayman in Belgium, the owner of a fleet of carts and horses. However, the German Army had confiscated all his property, had arrested him and his teenaged son. German soldiers had told him time and again "jokingly" that: "Tomorrow is the day you'll be shot." The strain of these experiences had, undoubtedly, frayed his nerves, and his mind probably gave way when he observed the practical jokes and circus antics of our long-haired Boer.

In the prison yard I met at recreation time other political prisoners of many nationalities. I remember a German editor of a socialist anti-war publication, a British subject who was a correspondent of the London *Daily Mail*. There was a Belgian who, I learned months later, had subsequently been executed by the Germans as a spy, allegedly a Belgian officer caught in civilian attire behind the German lines. As can be seen, even in prison confinement one was not shut off from the ugly realities of war. Most political prisoners had private funds at their disposal. They often obtained their midday meals from nearby restaurants. I was not affluent enough to afford such luxuries, though I did receive a few parcels from my family. However, those without private resources or friends had a most difficult time, because the prison food was most unpalatable and insufficient. It seemed that the prison guards and their families lived off the food deliveries ostensibly consigned to the prison kitchen. I shall always remember with a certain shudder the unappetizing rice soup with prunes without any seasoning, a sickly-looking bluish-grey mixture.

These prison days came to an end after my three-week stay there, when a group of British subjects was taken with a police escort, via train and on foot, to Ruhleben (which name translates as "Life of Rest"). In pre-war days Ruhleben had been a popular race track for trotter racing. With the advent of war, the horses had been commandeered and the stables and hay-lofts were converted into barracks for prisoners. Ruhleben became an internment camp for British civilian prisoners of war. This time I was not refused entry but was "invited in" while the entrance gate was securely locked behind our group of six. There we stood at the gate, looking at the shabbily dressed creatures in mud-covered clogs, to be gazed at in return by the seasoned prisoners. A fellow prisoner gave a Shakespearean coating to the mingled feelings of the newly arrived when he wrote:

All the world's a cage,
and all the men within it weary players.
They have no exits, only entrances,
where each spends many months ere he departs.
At first the Newcomer,
with china bowl and palliasse of straw,
and apprehensive mien, as who should say
"What cruel lot has Fate for me in store?"

We were given our assignments, i.e. barrack, whether horse box or loft. I was given space in Barrack XI, loft. Then we had to get our German Government issues: a straw sack, actually a sack with wood-shavings; one towel, the size of a dish cloth; two cotton blankets and one Billy-can bowl for food. The bowl had to serve also as a wash basin. We got no knife, no spoon, no fork, no cup, no plate, no soap. The horse-stalls on the barracks' lower floor were 11 feet square and had beds of steel frame with wooden boards, six beds for the space designed for a horse. The central passage which separated the two rows of stables had two water faucets, originally intended for the watering of 27 horses, but then serving the needs of about 250 prisoners living in the barrack.

Latrines were located at the camp's two extremities. There, the social atmosphere was most democratic: rich men sat next to poor men, sailors next to landlubbers. The open pit was malodorous and attracted swarms of flies. There were no partitions of any kind. We held the truth to be self-evident that all men were created equal. The latrine at the camp's end near Spandau was called the Spandau Bogs, the name probably derived from the outhouses on Irish farms. The latrine at the other end, in the direction of Berlin, was termed the Berlin Bogs.

One year later, cold-water showers were installed adjacent to a modernized Spandau Bogs. The opening of the new latrines was memorialized in a ditty sung by one of our professional comedians to the tune of "It's a long way to Tipperary":

It's a long way to walk to Spandau
when the snow is lying thick.
It's a long way to walk to Spandau
when you've got to get there quick.
When you're dressed in thin pajamas,
overcoat and clogs,
it's a long, long way to walk to Spandau,
to the now Spandau Bogs.

Used to prison routine, I awakened early, before 7 a.m., sat up on my straw sack and took in the scene of my new environment. Most of my neighbors were seafaring men: captains, mates, deckhands, engineers, and stokers. Their ships, located in German ports at the declaration of war, had been seized and the crews interned. Some of my neighbors sat up, too, on their straw sacks in the early morning "reading their shirts." With their shirts outstretched before them like a newspaper, they inspected it closely for the evidence of any lice. Forewarned that there may be lice around, I bought myself some carbolic acid water which I put into the water of my wash-bowl. True, I smelled like a hospital, but I never found a louse on me. From time to time German soldiers used to take us to a fumigation station outside the camp. At such occasion they walked through the barracks shouting with doubtful humor: "*Haben Sie Läuse? Unten anstellen!*" (Do you have any lice? Line up downstairs!) Once a German-speaking prisoner inquired: "The lice, too?"

One soon became accustomed to the daily routine of the camp: 8 a.m. roll-call, when the two German soldiers assigned to each barrack checked the attendance to determine whether any prisoners had escaped. And we had a number of escapes. After the roll-call the prisoners would march in barrack formation to the kitchen to get *Ersatz Kaffee* (roasted acorns) and black bread. At noon the prisoners of each barrack had to line up for the march to the kitchen to fetch dinner in the Billy-can. The same march took place again between 5 and 6 p.m. to get substitute tea, a pinkish mixture. At 9 p.m. the German soldiers would remind the prisoners to retire by shouting "*Schlafen gehen*" (Go to sleep), and at 10 p.m. the lights were switched off.

It must be recalled that the Allied forces imposed a tight blockade on Germany during World War I. Food was strictly rationed throughout the country, and when the population had little to eat there was even less food for the prisoners. Thus the quality of food grew progressively worse: black bread was adulterated with sawdust, potato-peelings, and powdered bones. Horsemeat of

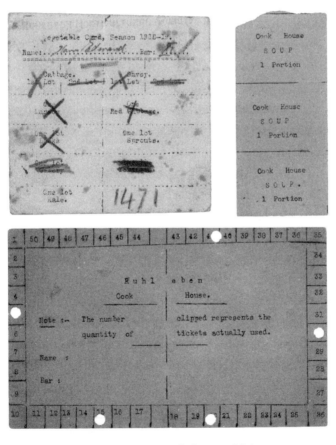

13. Harry's ration cards from Ruhleben.

animals killed at the front was pickled in brine and sent to prison camps in wooden barrels. Turnips were served as the only vegetable every day for four to five weeks. Whenever fresh meat was delivered to the camp, a big display was made as the half ox on a cart was taken to the kitchen. The arrival of fresh meat brought about the visit of many German officers to the kitchen, and after the judicious carving of the meat by the kitchen help for their own needs, there was little left for the mass of the prisoners. One comedian satirized the situation in a sketch in which he described the cook's "souping the soup," namely the stirring of the kettle with the big ladle and emptying its content into a Billy-can. The comedian said: "One piece of meat actually came to the surface and dolefully sang the first verse of 'Sole mio.'" One of our philosophers opined: "Sufficient unto the day is the soup thereof."

The prisoners expressed their complaints in the two letters and four postcards they were allowed to write each month. Many protests never reached their destinations because the German censors used to cut out any adverse comments. Nevertheless, many smuggled letters sent via neutral countries conveyed to the British public a picture of the worsening conditions prevalent in prisoner of war camps in Germany.

The cases of brutality occurred almost all during the first winter. One of the worst was the battering of a poor Maltese lad, a young sailor, who was badly beaten by a group of guards, without any provocation, and later died in the camp hospital. One guard was notorious for his cruelty and took pleasure in taking the belongings or the food of prisoners and pitching it into the latrine trenches.

On the subject of food, the weekly ration of a Ruhleben prisoner comprised 7 ounces of fresh meat, including bones and gristle, and 7 and a half ounces of fresh fish or 7 ounces of sausage or vegetables. The medical officer attached to the US Embassy certified in official reports that the POW rations in German camps were grossly inadequate. The then neutral USA were instrumental in facilitating better conditions and allowing foreign relief operations, which immediately swung into action and sent food parcels. The beneficiaries were especially the sailors, who had at times too much food, while many prisoners without any affiliations and contacts were starving. Eventually, in 1917 a rationing system was set up, under which everyone received one parcel of 5 kilograms, being 11 pounds per week, from the Danish Red Cross, paid for by British relief agencies. Parcels arrived irregularly because the rails were frequently blocked by German troop movements. Nevertheless, the new system was truly an answer to our persistent, fervent prayers: "Oh Lord give me a good digestion and give me something to digest." Followed usually by this meditation after the meal:

I thank the Lord for what I've had.
If it were more, I'd sure be glad!

Ruhleben Camp was administered by a group of retired German officers of the old Junker nobility: Count Schwerin, the Commandant, was a wealthy landed proprietor from Mecklenburg-Strelitz. Sporting a well-trimmed, white moustache, this septuagenarian was a handsome military figure, in spite of the cane which he sometimes needed for walking. He always displayed dignified manners, a friendly smile, and an amiable character. Although he had no administrative experience beyond the management of his estate, he revealed by word and action a philosophy that his function was not to bully but to protect the prisoners, whom he regarded as wards entrusted to him. Baron von Taube, the administrator, was a constant cigar smoker, who lived with his blonde and attractive young wife in the administration building in the camp. He was a former insurance executive inclined to quick emotional outbursts, but his anger soon subsided and he revealed a genuine humanistic trait. We were fortunate to have such military men at the helm of our camp. An order had come down from Berlin that there was to be no smoking allowed in Ruhleben Camp. Count Schwerin strongly objected to this edict, as he regarded smoking as a necessary element, promoting *Gemütlichkeit*, a friendly atmosphere in the camp. Baron von Taube, the inveterate cigar smoker, also viewed this order as unnecessary and cruel. Both urged the withdrawal of the order and offered their resignations if it were not done. The order was cancelled and the two officers were rewarded with a warm and lasting affection by the internees. When the camp learned the date of the count's birthday, the camp orchestra serenaded him in front of his office. I watched this impromptu performance and it was evidently a great surprise and deeply appreciated by "The Count," as far as I was able to judge by his gesticulations. It proved also to be a timely gesture on the prisoners' part, because Count Schwerin retired soon after from the position of Camp Commandant and died. The chief censor was Rittmeister von Mutzenbecher, an equally congenial person. He was assisted by his deputy, Prince von Thurn and Taxis, one of the wealthiest men in Germany, who had spent many years in a prestigious English school. They were officers who strained to be militarily and legally correct in all their actions.

The camp was surrounded by a barbed wire fence, beyond which was a well-lighted area at night, an area patrolled by reservists of the German Army. Within the camp each barrack had two German soldiers assigned to it, but internal government was truly home-rule, self-government. At the head of each barrack was a Captain, elected by the prisoners, assisted by an appointed deputy. They worked closely with the soldiers stationed there. Most frictions and problems were resolved by the Captain or jointly by all the captains, presided over by a Chief Captain, Mr. Joseph Powell, an excellent, hard-working film company executive. The latter's function was to establish and maintain good relationships with the German administrative officers and to gain as many improvements in living conditions as possible. He was allowed to go on occasion unaccompanied to Berlin to see the United States ambassador, under whose protection the British prisoners had been placed from 1914 to early 1917. After America's entry in the war, the Swiss delegation assumed those functions. To assist the captains in the maintenance of order among the 4,300 internees, there was a camp police consisting of prisoners who had volunteered for that service. The 50 policemen, distinguished by a blue and white armband, were supervised by an inspector and four sergeants. They were unpaid. The post officials were unpaid, so were the barrack cashiers, laundrymen, sub-captains, librarians and kitchen inspectors. The people working in the canteen obtained free dinners from the Casino, because they could not go for their meals at regular times. The same arrangement was made for the office staff and the attendants at the hot-water house, where one could buy hot water for tea, coffee, or soup. The camp carpenter, a volunteer who worked from morning to night, was allowed his dinner free at the Casino. Nobody could get paid over ten Marks per week, and the captains got nothing but grudging respect from both sides. Mention has been made of the Casino. This building had been converted into a restaurant, and access was only by passes issued by the Captain's office. All meals had to be paid for at restaurant prices. I was never rich enough to pay for a single restaurant meal, hence never saw the inside of the Casino.

Now, in this faceless, milling mass of prisoners an individual could easily be lost and become just one of many. It was my good fortune to find that a sports meeting had been scheduled to take place two months after my arrival. My successful participation in those track and field events enabled me to emerge as an athlete known to most of my fellow prisoners and become effectively inte-grated. I won the running events over the 75, 100, 220, and 440 yards and helped my barrack team to gain second place in the 1 mile relay. The running was on loose sand in rubber shoes, hence the times were very slow. For instance, 24 seconds was clocked for the 220 yards and hailed to be "excellent" for the conditions. There were races up to a mile, hurdles, walks and jumps, even a tug of war,

Ruhleben Camp Sports – August 1917
100 yds. Invitation Handicap. Final.

14. Sport played a pivotal role for Harry Edward in Ruhleben and for the morale of everyone in the camp. A few months after arriving, he won four events at the inaugural sports day. This picture shows him (third from right) winning the 100 yards handicap in the summer of 1917, run on loose sand and in rubber shoes.

which was won by the sailors of Barrack 4. In the field events, Oswald Groenings, of the London Polytechnic Harriers, who had fought in the Boer War and represented Great Britain at the 1908 Olympic Games, was the outstanding athlete. The track meeting was one of the morale-building and morale-sustaining events promoted by the camp's leadership. However, even before the plans could take shape, months of negotiation had taken place between the camp committee, the military authority, and the proprietors of the racecourse. The result of those talks was an agreement under which half of the racecourse was leased for sports purposes; the rent of £50 or 1,000 Marks per year was paid out of the camp fund. There were many professional sports practitioners among the prisoners, namely golfers, soccer players, racehorse trainers, and jockeys. The roster of soccer players included the names of many famous British football players, including former England internationals Steve Bloomer and Fred Pentland, who had been coaching in Germany at the outbreak of the war. The unfortunate Pentland had been preparing the German amateur football team for the 1916 Olympics in Berlin.

In the first summer of internment, sports activities literally burst forth and provided an incalculable lifting of the spirits. Sports served also in the building of a bridge of common interest and understanding to our German captors. Baron von Taube always kicked off the football season. The opening games were usually watched by him and his wife, the baroness. On the first Bank Holiday in Ruhleben, the first Monday in August, the prizes for the May track meeting were presented by the baroness to the winners. In response, Joseph Powell, Chief Captain of the camp, presented her with the ladies' prize, a dainty silver cup inscribed as follows:

To Frau Baronin von Taube
Souvenir of the Ruhleben Camp Sports, May 24, 1915

The baron thanked Mr. Powell for the kindness and said "I trust that peace may soon be restored and that you may all be able to return very shortly healthy and in good spirits to your homes and to the dear ones waiting for you."

The German administrators allowed us to run a "World's Fair," namely a number of sideshows with clowns, coconut shies, booths, stalls for the throwing of rings, and a roulette wheel. The German officers brought their wives and sweethearts to participate in the fun, nominal fees swelling the camp fund. Mr. Powell disclosed in a book published after the war that Baron von Taube confided in him that during that Bank Holiday his wife had cleaned out his pockets with the losses she had suffered at the roulette wheel. He had been obliged to go back to his quarters to get some extra money. This all took place against a background of regulations that forbade all gambling. Even the possession of playing cards was a punishable offence. But the event was a most pleasant diversion, and the baron's speech struck a responsive note and filled the minds of all of us often, very often. It also fathered this poem, "The Riddle Solved":

> Absolute certainty have I none,
> but my aunt's charwoman's son
> heard a policeman on his beat
> say to a housemaid in Downing Street,
> that he had a brother, who had a friend,
> who knew the date when the war will end.

The scientific and artistic world, too, was strongly represented in the camp's populace. It should be recalled that German universities in the period preceding World War I were highly rated for research and scholarship, hence attracted scholars from all over the world. German leadership in music was then unchallenged, and the group of professional musicians and graduate students among the internees added up to over two hundred. The presence of so many intellectuals stimulated the promotion of lectures and debates, which later grew into a camp school. Similarly, it was a relatively small step to expand small musical groups into a symphony orchestra.

One of the ideas for morale-building which emerged from the Debating Society was the promotion of a mock by-election in camp. It was thought that all prisoners could be involved in an election campaign, which would also provide a good catharsis for the expression of grievances. The idea gathered quick momentum and three candidates presented themselves for election to "procure, secure, obtain and retain the support and suffrages of the Burgesses of the ancient and honourable Borough of Ruhleben."

Alexander Boss, a wealthy gentleman of Surrey, England, with a waxed moustache, stout and pompous, was the Conservative candidate. Israel Cohen, a university professor, carried the Liberal label, and Reuben Castang, formerly elephant and monkey trainer of Hamburg's famous Circus Hagenbeck, became the protagonist of women's rights. Mr. Molyneaux, an artist, designed an elaborate Coat of Arms for the Borough of Ruhleben, embodying all the symbols and tokens of camp life: quartering, dinner bowl, black loaf, sausage, and clog; supporters: a rat and a mouse; motto: "Dum spiro spero" (Whilst I breathe I hope), all topped by the familiar British check cap.

The candidates organized their campaign workers, designed and posted signs extolling the numerous virtues of their platforms and their own. Mr. Boss claimed to have inherited a fortune of £2 million, an estate, and securities, the result of his ancestors' loan of 15 shillings to William the Conqueror in 1066. He believed that he could spend his fortune in no better way than in making Ruhleben a model borough. If elected he would call Parliament's attention to the excessive taxes on beers and spirits, tobacco, and tea, all necessary commodities for the working man. To compensate for the loss of revenue, he suggested a tax on sodas and mineral waters. Mr. Boss advocated, furthermore, the construction of an electric railway from one end of the camp to the other, promised "Truth, Justice and Honour," and, besides, champagne and upholstered armchairs for all those worthy sufferers.

Mr. Cohen claimed the support of Labour, i.e. the Clog Repairers Union, the Sock Darners Trade Union. He believed that four hours of daily work was sufficient to supply the world with all its needs. This would do away with unemployment. Old-age pension should start at the age of forty years, pension to be high enough to get married on. Beer, he regarded as the mainstay of British social life. As such, its manufacture should be municipalized and the precious liquid conveyed to every home by a tap, just like water.

The Women's Suffrage Candidate, Mr. Castang, said that he had ordered 4,000 tins of canned girls to be brought to the camp, to which the crowd responded: "We want real girls!" Amid vociferous cheers, Mr. Castang delivered the following oration: "Wouldn't you like to have girls, boys?" Cries of "Yes!" "Wouldn't you like to have fun, boys?" More cries of "Yes!"

Well then, boys, I'm going to give you girls and fun – hundreds of girls and buckets of fun! That's my ticket, boys – GIRLS, and plenty of them. Just you stick with me and you'll be all right. Three cheers for the girls, boys, and bless their little hearts. Hooray, hooray, hooray!

The hecklers had a field day. When they got tired of the candidates' tall stories and promises, they chanted their song of disbelief:

There was a cow,
climbed up a tree . . .
Oh, you bloody liar!

Or they sang to the melody of Big Ben's chimes:

Sit down, sit down.
Sit down, sit down!

The prisoners' participation became so enthusiastic and noisy that the military authorities advised the camp captains to dampen the crowd's spirits. Thus the beginning of the campaign was considerably more spirited than the later part.

The result of the by-election was:

Reuben Castang (and the girls)	1,220
Israel Cohen, Liberal-Labour	924
Alexander Boss, Conservative	471
Spoiled ballots	74
Total	**2,689**

Therefore ballots had been cast by about two-thirds of the camp's residents. Girls were the winning platform. However, fulfilment of that promise was years away. Yet, one sample of that species, a German girl, used to come into the camp once a week on a laundry wagon to deliver laundry packages. A crowd of leering prisoners usually came to ogle her. One of our artists recorded this event in a cartoon with the notation: "One touch of nature makes the whole world kin."

There is no doubt that the described events during the first summer of internment strengthened substantially the camp's morale and encouraged a spirit of kinship among the many social strata. In this period the Ruhleben Camp Song was born. It kept its popularity till the end of the camp. The song reflects the spirit of optimism which pervaded Ruhleben, that "bull-dog" determination to see things through. The lusty marching song went as follows:

So line up boys and sing this chorus,
shout this chorus all you can.
We want the people there
to hear in Leicester Square
that we're the boys that
never get downhearted.

Back, back, back again in England,
there we'll fill a flowing cup
and tell them clear and loud
of that Ruhleben crowd
that always kept its pecker up.

This was usually followed by a shouted query: "Are we downhearted?" which brought forth a thunderous and unanimous "NO!" To those not familiar with the British colloquial expression of the song's closing words, let me assure them that they are perfectly socially acceptable and mean "to keep one's courage up."

The first winter was a period of adjustment to a new, strange environment and strange neighbors, of a struggle to keep warm. In the summer the internees emerged into the open, circulating within the limited space enclosed by barbed wire. People sought and found people of like interest. Many exchanged living quarters to be with friends or in a more congenial environment. It was in this atmosphere that people asked themselves how best to utilize their time of imprisonment. Notices appeared on the bulletin board at the boiler house inviting people to join classes or lectures. The grandstands of the former racecourse became public forums.

The Arts and Science Union, self-appointed and loosely organized, believed the time opportune to organize the Ruhleben Camp School to meet the need of three classes of individuals: 1) Those whose internment had interrupted their preparations for such examinations as the London Matriculation, the various university degrees or the Board of Trade nautical examinations. 2) Those who had already entered upon a commercial or professional career. 3) Those who desired to pursue some form of learning for learning's sake. The Arts and Science Union had a wealth of talent available from which to select the board of directors for the school. There were a few doctors of philosophy, several masters of arts, many bachelors of arts from leading universities, several barristers at law and numerous specialists in the field of business, insurance, engineering, and nautical subjects. Ruhleben Camp School was no amateur affair from its very beginning. Space, money, books, achievement, and recognition of standards were the problems to be solved. Initial negotiations involved the German military authority and the American ambassador.

In the determining of subjects for studies, two possible courses were open to the Education Committee elected by the Arts and Science Union, namely: 1) to find out what the camp could teach, and offer a syllabus based on that inquiry, or 2) to find out what the camp wanted to learn and to satisfy that demand as well as possible.

The second course was adopted and a suggestive syllabus was drawn up and circulated, together with application forms. Over 1,100 of them were returned from among the 4,300 internees, ranging over a wide field of subjects, nearly all of which the committee had reasonable hope of being able to satisfy. Ruhleben Camp School started at the end of the first year, with 75 classes giving tuition to some 700 students on the third grandstand, sheltered but in the open; some classes were held in the loft of a barrack assigned by the military. The administration and teachers organized the school's activities into nine departments: 1) French, 2) German and English, 3) Spanish, Italian, Russian, and Dutch, 4) Science and Mathematics, 5) Engineering, 6) National Sciences, 7) Handicrafts, 8) Commercial, 9) Arts. Each department elected its own head.

One immediate problem to be tackled was the creation of a library. An interned educator wrote to his friend, a permanent secretary at the Education Board at Whitehall, who in turn apprised the Foreign Office. Then an appeal was launched to British universities and private individuals with approval of the president of the British Board of Education. The result of those efforts was the arrival of a reference library of 6,000 books twelve months later. They were first placed in rooms evacuated by German soldiers, causing an educator to remark: "Where Mars had retired, Minerva entered." Later those books were brought to shelf and better order in the then newly erected YMCA Hall.

The foundation of the Ruhleben Camp School was well laid. Efforts by all participants brought success and recognition in due time. The school was entrusted with the giving of examinations, which were evaluated in London. Thus, many passed the London Matriculation and other tests, while more internees received credit for undergraduate work done in prison camp. Many acquired language skills.

While the activities of the school were an index of the camp's spiritual courage and optimism, an even better measure was provided

15. The Ruhleben Dramatic Society in full dress rehearsal. Harry Edward is third from the left in the back row.

by the creative work in the theatre. Radio and television had not been invented then. A cinema with films came to the camp a little later, but even then could not successfully compete with live performances. The staging of shows with the designing of scenery, costumes, the setting of lights, the hand-sewing of costumes, the integration of music, and their total coordination was a highly creative process. It was also the free giving of people's energies and talents for the enjoyment of others. A healthy competitive spirit arose among the Ruhleben Dramatic Society, The Irish Players, the Société Dramatique Française, the German Language Theatrical Group – all vying for superiority in performance and favorable, critical comment. The list of their contributions adds up to a formidable record.

The Société Dramatique Française specialized in comedies with a distinct Gallic flavor, plays such as *La Petite Chocolatière*, *La Belle Aventure*, etc. The Irish Players attempted to mirror their native culture by presenting: *John Bull's Other Island*, *The Playboy of the Western World*, *The Night of the Wake*, *Mrs. McGinty's Lodger*, etc. The German Language Group focused its energies on comic operas, such as *Der fidele Bauer*, *Der Graf von Luxemburg* among others. However, the bulk of the production poured forth from among the members of the Ruhleben Dramatic Society. Among the approximately sixty English-language productions in the four years of internment, there were Shakespeare's *As You Like It*, *Othello*, and

50

Twelfth Night; several Gilbert and Sullivan operas; classics like *The School for Scandal, Eliza Comes to Stay, Lady Windermere's Fan, The Importance of Being Earnest*; comedies and mysteries. Popular were revues and the traditional Christmas pantomimes in which life in camp and its problems were lampooned.

A beauty chorus of *Ersatz* girls would charm the audience, singing in falsetto voice:

Come along you bad boys,
come along with me!
Never mind your cares and sorrows . . .

Then they would march onto the parading platform extending into the audience, singing to the tune of "Down the River We Would Row" the following parody:

For we're the girls, girls, girls,
and we would charm you
with our curls, curls, curls.
We wouldn't harm you but
we'd kiss you now and then,
kiss you now and then
and fool around
and fool around
and, then we'd kiss again . . .

Ending:

How the whole camp would buzz,
if they only had us,
for we're the girls, girls, girls.

Of course, writing and staging a revue or pantomime was the work of many hands and minds, and many imaginative ideas went into such creation. The scene in which the Ruhleben authors seemed to outdo themselves was, in my opinion, in a Christmas pantomime. As I remember it vividly, a huge Christmas package, gift-wrapped in gilded paper, was lowered onto a platform on the stage at the head of a huge stair. Out stepped our principal female impersonator, Mr. (Gertie) Underwood, dressed in a lacy, flimsy, transparent garment, singing in excellent falsetto while descending the stairs at the head of a beauty chorus:

> How'd you like, how'd you like
> me for a Christmas Box?
> I know the way to please you,
> I wrap you up and tease you.
> We'll have lots of . . .
> oh, come along and kiss me, honey!
> I can kiss, just like this.
> I'd often give you shocks.
> Oh yes, I put you through it,
> Oh yes, I guess we'd do it
> if you had me for a Christmas Box.

This brought down the house with clamors for encores.

As indicated, many arts and activities were associated with the production of plays. For instance, in costume designing the camp designer and dressmaker had not only to build the dress for the lady, but previous to this had to build the lady for the dress. Frocks, petticoats, capes were made from scarce raw materials of sateen, muslin, cotton, silk ribbons, gold braid. Hats and shoes were created from remnants. The armor of Roman soldiers was built from cardboard. Imagination plus free labor produced dresses for the beauty chorus costing 10 Marks or about $2.50 each.

The amateur designers and dressmakers could proudly point to great achievements, but might not the acquisition of such skills boomerang in their home environment? Imagine, if after the return home the proud artist or artisan should point out to his wife what dressmakers' bills really ought to be, may she not insist on some practical demonstration of his art?

Parallel to the unfolding of the theatrical "renaissance" was the dynamic growth of music making and music appreciation. Professionals and students were most eager to retain and improve their skills. Chamber music truly flowered among the professionals. There was much musical literature available. A real symphony orchestra came into being over the years, giving Promenade Concerts during the summer months. In the last year of internment, namely 1918, such summer Promenade Concerts were a bi-weekly event on the grandstand of the former racecourse. One of the last concerts on Tuesday, August 20, 1918 had the following program:

Ouverture	"Raymond"	by Thomas
Waltz	"Cagliostro"	Strauss
Selection	"Carmen"	Bizet
Orchestral Song	"Mattinata"	Leoncavallo
Mazurka		Glinka
Intermezzo	"Pas de Fleurs"	Delibes
Selection	"Shamrock"	Myddleton

Sports, such as soccer football, rugby, cricket, and track, were so much a part of British life and tradition that such activities grew almost spontaneously. The presence of professionals among the prisoners assured good organization and continuing interest. It is noteworthy to observe how much and how effectively the cultural background and the training in the democratic process influenced so many actions of the camp's internees. The home-rule management of the camp was originally patterned after the set-up of a British borough. The election of barrack captains and the appointment of their deputies have already been mentioned. They received no remuneration. Captains headed the following departments: Finance, Education, Recreation, Kitchens, Canteens, Sanitation, Watch, and Works. Committees strengthened by co-opted members of the camp assisted the departments. When the playing fields were opened, the Recreation Committee was subdivided into Sports Control and Entertainment Committees.

However, the groundswell of the expanding interest in the arts sought and even demanded representation, a share in the planning, and a share in the fruits of their efforts. Money was flowing into the box office of the theatre and there were varied opinions on the best manner of spending it for the benefit of the camp. Political pressure, even the threat of a strike by the arts groups, forced the reorganization of the Entertainment Committee and the inclusion of four representatives from the major groups. Here was democracy in action. However, what would happen when pliable democratic thinking and action should run headlong into inflexible Prussian military authoritarianism? It happened one day, and here is the story.

Baron von Taube, the original, cooperating, and understanding military commander had been transferred and replaced by a cavalry captain, Rittmeister von Glockel. The prisoners called him "Tin Guts." He had loose skin at his throat, like a turkey gobbler, always sported a monocle, assumed a strutting gait, usually snarled his military commands. He insisted on a "snap-to" compliance of his orders, which method just would not work with those non-military internees. In order to train that motley lot, he ordered special roll-calls in the middle of the day, breaking up football games and other schedules. This did not endear him to the prisoners, who would leisurely amble to their barrack's line-up. Tin Guts would stand at a strategic point in the center of the camp, visibly fuming.

As it happened one day, in the front line of Barrack 11 stood a prisoner, who, too, was in the habit of wearing a monocle. He was a well-to-do person, arrested on his honeymoon in Germany. He was always meticulously attired in silk shirts and on that day also in white flannel trousers. He stared sneeringly at the fuming Tin Guts, who glaringly approached him and stopped in front of him. Red-faced, monocled Tin Guts then shouted into the face of the monocled prisoner: "Stop laughing!" Thereupon the whole barrack of 250 men, all lined up for the roll-call, burst out into raucous guffaw. Tin Guts was offended. He ordered barrack confinement for the whole camp. According to his orders, no prisoner was to be allowed outside his barrack. That placed the two German soldiers assigned to each barrack in a quandary. How were they to handle the numerous requests to go to the latrine? The official instructions came down that prisoners having an urge should go to the latrine in barrack formation. Thus, the German soldiers asked the captains' assistance to get the prisoners lined up. Shouts went up and echoed through the hallways and lofts: "Barrack 11, line up for a shit!"

When a barrack in formation under the leadership of German soldiers marched and passed other barracks, lusty cheers went up, heartily reciprocated by the marching throng. This whole arrangement was gravely demeaning to the German soldiers. They requested and received the authority to issue passes, because the previous arrangement had them marching continuously to and from the bogs. By the end of that day, everybody had a pass and everybody was promenading in visible defiance. Democracy had triumphed over German militarism! Tin Guts was defeated.

He soon disappeared from the scene, whether he had resigned or had been transferred or dismissed we never found out, nor cared.

At occasions such as barrack confinement or inclement weather, all indoor sports like roulette, blackjack, and other games just thrived. Another popular indoor activity was the "attending of classes" which meant joining a group for the reading of smuggled British newspapers. This was, of course, before the birth of radio, and the printed word was relatively more important. Berlin newspapers with German censored news were available daily, but the great demand for Allied news and political interpretations caused entrepreneurs to smuggle in British and French papers and to organize "classes" at which a paper had to be read in one hour. The charge was usually 10 Pfennig per person attending.

Besides these examples of illicit, private enterprise there were undertakings of legal and approved nature. For example, the Horticultural Society stimulated the growing of flowers. Little gardens made their appearance in the drab spaces between barracks. The society's activities expanded later to the growing of vegetables, and a hot house was built on land leased from the owners of the racecourse. The profits derived from the sale of fresh and rationed vegetables and from the sale of hot water enabled the canteen management to sell necessary food and toilet items at prices below those of the German economy. With the passing of months and years, prisoners improved their living environment. The straw sacks and the wooden boards which raised them four inches above the concrete floors were discarded. Bedframes were built, camp beds and mattresses bought, and to overcome the hated 10 o'clock "lights out" electric storage batteries were purchased and bed lights hooked up. This made possible comfortable reading and studying in bed. A cartoonist sketched the delivery of freshly charged batteries and titled his vignette of camp life: "The Charge of the Light Brigade."

However, life in camp was not always peaceful routine. There were tragedies, sicknesses, deaths, suicides. The German military doctor diagnosed the many shades of the prisoners' mental disturbances as *Stacheldrahtkrankheit* (barbed wire disease). News from home about the sickness of kinfolk or other serious difficulties could prey on one's mind day and night, and one's incapacity to help could snowball into paranoic frustrations. Generally, we existed from day to day, making few plans for the weeks to come. On the first New Year's Eve we wished each other good luck and expressed the hope that the coming year would include the day of departure. However, on the third New Year's Day in camp we sang: "It may be four years; it may be forever!"

From time to time there were deeply disturbing events. The captain of a merchant ship was taken out of camp to answer the German Government's accusation of having rammed and sunk a German submarine. We learned later that he had been shot. There were numerous escapes, as a result of which privileges were withdrawn from the prisoners. For a time we became the pawns in international politics. An exchange of civilian prisoners was proposed. Great Britain suggested man for man, Germany insisted all for all. There were ten times as many German civilian prisoners kept in British camps, principally on the Isle of Man, than there were British civilian prisoners in Germany. News of these negotiations kept nerves on edge for a while and wild rumors circulated. Agitation increased when a small group of men over forty-five years of age, medically certified as militarily unfit, left the camp for Holland. A poster announcing an issue of our magazine had to be withdrawn in the agitated atmosphere. It read: "IN RUHLEBEN CAMP, OUT TOMORROW." *In Ruhleben Camp* was the name of our magazine which ran for seventeen issues and provided a valuable record of life in our internment camp.

We had a hospital barrack in the camp and a daily clinic visited by a German military physician. The professional standards and the services rendered by those military doctors varied considerably. Dr. Lachmann was humane and considerate, but he died of appendicitis after a few weeks of duty. Dr. Reiche, a surgeon, was regarded as brutal and was transferred. Dr. Geiger expressed at various occasions his hatred of Englishmen and refused to visit sick patients in lofts or boxes.

I was most fortunate in maintaining relatively good health; yet, on three occasions I felt obliged to go to the clinic to overcome stomach ache and gastric difficulties brought on by eating German bread adulterated by sawdust. We also had many cases of food poisoning and of dysentery. In fact, in the summer of 1917, 300 cases of dysentery were recorded, though happily no fatal ones.

One could hear in the camp not only the Celtic brogues, but also the broad accents of the Cockneys and the Australians, the

Canadian-American twang, the distinctive Lancashire and Yorkshire dialects, and, of course, the class-conscious Oxford drawl. There were about 300 colored British subjects hailing from West Africa, the West Indies, Zanzibar, and the South Asian continent, the last mentioned called Lascars. Most of them had been stokers on the British coal-fired freighters, sequestrated by the Germans when anchored in German ports. We had several barracks sheltering almost exclusively maritime engineers and deck personnel, while in Barrack 21 were congregated a large number of teenaged sailor apprentices. In 1916, at the height of the starvation period, the camp administration made a special plea for extra food rations "for growing youths." This appeal was successful and the youths – and I was among them – became the beneficiaries of a fresh milk allotment of a pint per day and one egg per week for about two months.

The German military found other ways of grouping and classifying internees. They regarded the large group of Englishmen, Scots, Irish, Welsh, Canadians, Australians, South Africans, New Zealanders, Indians, and Jamaicans as "Stock Englander." There was a French group of Britishers from Quebec, Belgium, and Northern France; and also a large German-speaking group. Some of the long-term British residents in Germany caused initially some complications, with German sympathizers – called PGs or Pro-Germans – segregated in their own barracks.

BEST WISHES from RUHLEBEN
CHRISTMAS 1916.

16. Hope on the horizon?

By arrangement with the German military, rebellious Irish nationalists were invited to a meeting, where they were addressed by an Irish leader – it was believed it was Sir Roger Casement – and invited to join an Irish regiment in the German Army. About thirty left the camp. A year later the Germans proposed to move the colored population out of Ruhleben. This suggestion was vigorously rejected by the captains. It was obvious that this was a clumsy move to divide the camp.

Fortunately, the future was hidden from our eyes. If we had known that we had been "condemned" to about four years of incarceration, the suicide rate would have been substantially higher. As it was, we lived from day to day, solving problems as they occurred and in the best manner we knew, and carried on within the framework of our prisoner of war society.

Late in 1917, a group of British subjects arrived from Poland. They had been resident in that country for some time as managers of British textile mills and other enterprises. They brought us the latest information and impressions of the Russian Revolution in October and November 1917. Repercussions of the Russian Revolution were felt also in Germany throughout 1918, when war-weary German armies began to crack and crumble. The Bolshevik Party of Russia found a parallel in the German Spartacists, who demanded the establishment of a dictatorship of the proletariat by armed force. They provided the framework for the first revolutionary wave, namely the establishing of Sailors' and Soldiers' Councils, which replaced the Imperial German officers corps.

The revolt began in the German navy on November 9, 1918. Two days later the first columns of sailors reached the camp, opened the gates, while a soldiers' council replaced the camp's officers, taking from them their swords, epaulettes, and other insignia of rank. On Sunday, November 10, the first news of the armistice was received in camp. During those exciting days the camp's captains held a number of meetings and counseled calm and a posture of non-involvement. Our volunteer police took over the guard duties of the German soldiers during their frequent gatherings and consultations. The prisoners' morale remained high and their discipline exemplary. The captains announced the granting of passes to anyone wishing to go to Berlin, thereby keeping some control over the prisoners' movements, counseling all to keep in constant touch with the camp or with the Swiss Legation.

A few hundred prisoners risked brief vacations to the German capital. There was an element of risk, because the revolution was still simmering and erupted into violence sporadically in unexpected places. I spent four days with my mother and sister in Berlin, took a stroll along the Unter den Linden, where I exchanged experiences with French soldiers. I made two more short trips, taking with me scores of cans of miscellaneous foodstuffs for my family.

In Berlin and throughout Germany a power struggle was taking place between the Spartacus Party and the Social Democrats, in which the latter emerged victoriously. Socialist members of the Reichstag came to the camp and made a plea to "leave without any ill feeling or hatred . . . not to hold the German people responsible for the deeds committed by its former autocratic leaders." Applying good psychology, an official statement handed to us read in part:

> The four years spent in this camp have left their marks on some of you, some regret the loss of a friend, some have been losing their health not to speak of financial losses. You are leaving the camp with your heads high, bound for freedom and home. History will record the years you have spent in the camp, and how you have bravely borne your captivity. Freedom and all it means follow four years of privations and sorrows. We congratulate you on your bearing, that nothing ever broke your spirit, or made you lose faith.

We accepted the compliment and proudly sang our camp song:

> So line up boys and sing this chorus,
> shout this chorus all you can.
> We want the people there
> to hear in Leicester Square
> that we're the boys that
> never get downhearted.
> Back, back, back again in England,
> there we'll fill a flowing cup
> and tell them clear and loud
> of that Ruhleben crowd
> that always kept its pecker up.

As usual, this was followed by the shouted question: "Are we down-hearted?" followed by the thunderous response: "NO!"

5

OPENING THE GATES TO FREEDOM

The day of deliverance was near. In fact, it was very near, because the prisoners of Ruhleben were to be the first batch to be repatriated, having been incarcerated the longest. November 22, 1918 – the day of departure – seemed dream-like and unreal. Loading was on schedule, well planned. Slowly two long passenger trains puffed northward, traveling through the night and arriving in the morning, via a ferry to the port of Sassnitz on the Baltic. A German steamer took us to Copenhagen through minefields screening Danish territorial waters. At the Danish port we transferred to two larger ships flying the Danish flag and "manned" by six Danish hostesses in Red Cross uniforms – a delightful sight. After passing through the rough waters of the Kattegat and the Skagerrak we steamed through the North Sea, the two ships always in sight of one another as they carried no radio, reaching the Firth of Forth on the fourth day. There we saw ships of the surrendered German fleet and many, many ships of the British fleet. The British bluejackets [naval ratings] gave us loud cheers as we steamed slowly by, and we reciprocated equally cheerfully in the damp weather. However, after passing about two score of ships, our vocal organs became strained and finally gave out.

The reception at Leith, Scotland, was a gala affair with an admiral and a naval band on the docks. Lady volunteers brought us food placed on long tables set up in the dock's warehouses. We were now ex-prisoners, which was hard to believe. Groups were organized for the various destinations, and ambulances and small trucks conveyed such groups to the station at specified times. A bunch of excited, teenaged, Scotch lassies jumped into the ambulance taking us to the railroad station and insisted on kissing all of us. We were embarrassed with this unaccustomed outpouring of affection, but we put up no resistance, yielding without protestations. From the station at Leith some of us began the long journey to London via Edinburgh and Newcastle. At London's King's Cross Station two buses awaited us and took us to small, private hotels, where we stayed until we had made arrangements with relatives or friends regarding domicile and found a job.

My first endeavor was to ascertain the result of the matriculation examinations I had taken in camp. To my pleasant surprise I learned that I had not only passed, but that I had won in addition a Special Language Prize of £2 to be applied to the purchase of books. I selected a number of law books, such as Company Law, Mercantile Law, etc., subjects I planned to study in the furtherance of my career. I then filed for some public examinations organized by the Royal Society of Arts, London, in Advanced French and German, desirous of strengthening my credentials. After a few weeks of unsettling job search, I procured a job as a teacher of German and French in a branch of Pitman's School for Commercial and Civil Service Training.

The adjustment from a prisoner of war to a free man involved far more than just a transfer from one locale to another. For many weeks I found it uncomfortably strange to be up after 10 o'clock in the evening. Friends had to tell and convince me that I could stay up and move about town after that hour. For weeks I also spoke in whispers, at least so it appeared to the people around me. This, too, was a hangover from life in prison camp. There, we had to lower our voices so that they may be audible to the person spoken to, but not disturb our neighbors separated from us by thin cardboard walls. It had become part of our nature to speak softly without our being aware of it. Time and again I was urged to speak up. However, this habit was soon lost when I stood before the classes of students and explained to them the importance of accidence, orthography, syntax, and pronunciation.

With the daily challenges of a new life before me, the memory of the nearly four years of imprisonment slowly slipped into the distance, swallowed up by the subconscious. In American educational terms, those days had been my high school and junior college years. Fortunately, I had acquired a British matriculation diploma as the result of some book learning which I had undertaken, but there was no diploma for the lessons of life learned in living relatively harmoniously in close proximity with all strata of British society. The adjustments to the various culture values had not always been easy.

For instance, in the small group around my bed in prison camp there had been a bi-lingual Englishman, a former clerk in a commercial concern, very quiet and retiring by nature. Another Englishman, born in the Jewish faith, had become a fervent Seventh Day Adventist. Besides, there had been a former third hand of a fishing trawler from Hull, boisterous, always swearing and blasphemous. Another member of our group had been Ali Baba from Zanzibar, dark, with large rolling eyes, Mohammedan. He had been hired by the German Socialist leader, Philipp Scheidemann, as a houseboy and had thus come to Germany.

One evening a discussion unfolded on the subject of angels. Ali Baba, Mohammedan, asked the Seventh Day Adventist whether angels were white or black. The latter replied that they were white and cited as evidence some paintings which he had seen. Ali Baba was saying with strong insistence that they were black "just like me," quoting the Koran. The fisherman had been listening attentively to the heated discussion when he suddenly broke in, saying with his customary swearwords interspersed: "If there were any black angels around, the devil would have rounded them up a long time ago and used them as stokers." Thus each one had approached the subject from his own culture background.

With some awareness of the diversity of human beings and their backgrounds, I viewed with curiosity and astonishment my London environment. London was host to Allied troops from all over the world, and I witnessed the elite of the armed forces on parade in the great Victory March.

There were representative units of all services from Australia, New Zealand, Algeria, Morocco, the United States, France, most of them on their way home. World War I had come to an end without a single, truly decisive battle having been fought. German resources had become exhausted, and German morale had collapsed. At the end of the war, German troops were still occupying territory from France to the Crimea. Throughout Europe there was not only a war weariness, but a general revulsion to any kind of war had spread from that continent to the rest of the world. World War I had claimed over 10 million dead and 20 million wounded, while starvation and epidemics were threatening Europe in the post-war years.

In this atmosphere President Woodrow Wilson's Fourteen Points were like a life-raft tossed to survivors struggling in a stormy sea. Mankind reached out for it as the hope for a permanent peace. The first five points were general in nature and may be summarized as follows:

1) open covenants openly arrived at,
2) freedom of the seas in peace and war,
3) removal of economic barriers between nations as far as possible,
4) reduction of armaments to needs for domestic safety,

5) adjustment of colonial claims with concern for the wishes and interests of the inhabitants, as well as for the titles of rival claimants.

There were eight points referring to the adjustment of problems in specific geographic areas, and the last point proposed "a general association of nations." I was deeply influenced by the hope held out by President Wilson's declaration, and when I came upon an assembly session of a secondary school on Empire Day I was surprised and depressed by the discordant, jingoist outpourings of the speaker, a brigadier general, glorifying and defending empire-building.

6

ATHLETICS AND THE OLYMPICS

A Vehicle for Self-Expression

In this post-war period, it was sports again which provided me with an opportunity to emerge as an individual and to express my philosophy of international sportsmanship and brotherhood. I joined the Polytechnic Harriers of London, whose athletic goodwill ambassadors I had met in competition in pre-war days.

Life in and around the Poly Institute, on Regent Street, with its school and clubs, became a very important factor in my growth into manhood and in the making of life-long friendships. In my first track race, namely in the then famous Stamford Bridge sports arena, I

17. Harry in full Polytechnic Harriers colours in 1920.

18. Harry Edward with some admirers at a Polytechnic Harriers garden party in Chiswick, west London.

won two prizes presented to me by His Royal Highness Prince Albert, who later became King George VI. In the following Open Championships of the Amateur Athletic Association of 1919, I was beaten into second place in the 220 yards, while in the 100 yards final I failed to finish among the first three. On the preceding evening I had stayed for a long period of time in a warm tub-bath. This made me very sluggish on the day of competition. I learned the lesson of that experience and never made that mistake again. In spite of my relatively poor showing, I was invited to a number of athletic meetings in London, Liverpool, and Glasgow, where I met the British sprint champion W.A. Hill, who had defeated me in the championships. I was able to win several races from him, and our rivalry stimulated speculations among sports writers, who discussed our strengths and weaknesses in the sports columns of the British press.

Late in 1919, the decision of the British Olympic Council was announced to send a team to the Olympic Games to be held in Antwerp, Belgium, in the fall of 1920. Thus, throughout the early part of the year a feverish anticipation gripped the sports world, and the results of every athletic event were analyzed and evaluated in terms of the approaching Olympic Games. I took my preparation and training quite seriously. Almost every evening after working

Aberfoyle, Aug 10th 1919

19. This blurred photo is all that remains of Harry Edward's first track expedition to Scotland. It was taken in the village of Aberfoyle the day after the Celtic FC Sports. The man on Harry's right is the reigning AAAs 100 yards champion, Surrey AC's Billy Hill. Harry won the 220 yards handicap and the mile medley relay for Poly Harriers, in front of a 45,000 crowd. The *Sunday Post* declared him to be 'the best coloured sprinter we have seen since the days of J.B. Taylor'. The *Star Green 'Un* asked, 'has England found a new sprinter, or has Germany found him for us?'.

hours I used to do calisthenic exercises in the garden behind the house, while on Saturdays and on at least one evening per week I would spend two hours on the cinder track at the Paddington Recreation Grounds in London.

In my first encounter [of the year] with W.A. Hill, the AAA champion, I was victorious, winning the 100 yards race by a few inches, having an easier time in the 220 yards. I repeated these results in the Olympic Trials, but the real test for a berth on the Olympic team came with the AAA Championships with their international entries. From the United States had come a team of Princeton University athletes, among whom Randolph E. Brown, the intercollegiate champion, was my antagonist in the furlong. South Africa had sent their champions: Bevil Rudd in the middle distance, Jack Ayres Oosterlaak in the sprints, Cecil McMaster in the walk. There were several athletes from France and Australia, and, of course, England, Scotland, Ireland, and Wales were strongly represented. I tackled the races with great determination, winning my heats and semi-finals, and in the final of the 100 yards I came through in first place, closely followed by W.A. Hill, the previous AAA champion, Oosterlaak, the South African champion, and Harold Abrahams, who would win the Olympic gold medal in the 100 meters four years later. In the 220 yards final I was pushed hard at the beginning by the American Brown; however, I pulled away to a comfortable margin in the last 50 yards.

A group of us, British athletes, made a hurried trip to Glasgow, Scotland, at the invitation of the Rangers Football Club. Over 40,000 fans came to see the prospective candidates for the imminent Olympic Games. The weather was beautiful, and a fine day of sports was enjoyed by the throng. I failed to win from the scratch mark the 100 yards handicap on grass, but overtook my competitors in the 220 yards handicap race in my last strides to the thunderous applause of the crowd.

The Olympic Games seemed suddenly upon us. The excitement mounted with its approach. The strengths of the various national teams and the merits of the leading competitors were being discussed in the sports columns of many newspapers. Articles appeared in magazines recalling the history of the original Olympics, which had run continuously every four years for at least 1,200 years in ancient Greece. The first recorded Games were in 776 BC and the last of that cycle in AD 394, at which time Roman Emperor Theodosius I suspended the Olympic Games. The ancient home of the Olympics was Olympia, which site belongs to mythical times and legend as recorded by poets, historians, and archaeologists. Greek mythology claims that the Olympics began as religious celebrations and games in commemoration of Zeus's having defeated Cronus in a mighty wrestling match of the gods for possession of the earth.

However, most stories appearing in magazines dealt with the rebirth of the Olympics and the Olympic spirit in the twentieth

20. All smiles after the race – new champion Harry Edward with the 1919 champion Billy Hill.

21. On 17 July 1920, Harry Edward had his first big win in England. After placing second in the 1919 AAAs 220 yards, he takes the Kinnaird Trophy 100 yards at Stamford Bridge in 10 seconds flat, from (obscured behind Harry) Harold Abrahams in second; Vic D'Arcy (far right) Harry Edward's Poly teammate in third; and Guy Butler (no. 9) in fourth. South Africa's Bevil Rudd (second left) finished fifth. All five finishers would become Olympic medallists.

22. The Great Britain sprint squad. There was a great debate within the Amateur Athletic Association about whether to send a team to the 1920 Olympics at Antwerp. Back row, left to right, are Billy Hill, Guy Butler (reserve), Harold Abrahams and Denis Black (reserve). Front row, fellow Poly Harriers Victor D'Arcy and Harry Edward.

23. Harry Edward in his Great Britain Olympic uniform before the grand parade of athletes, 1920.

century. World War I was barely two years in the past, hence the appeal of Baron Pierre de Coubertin, the originator of the modern cycle, fell upon a most fertile soil. It was recalled that as a student of political science, education, and sociology he had written:

> Olympia and the Olympics symbolize an entire civilization, superior to countries, cities, military heroes or even the ancient religions.
> The entire planet is its domain, all sports, all nations.

Yet in the year 1920, so close to the war, the universality of the Olympics was amended and restricted. Germany and its allies were excluded from participation in the Games. However, remembered was Baron de Coubertin's fervent plea made prior to the first Olympics in 1896, when he presented his plan to the Athletic Sports Union in Paris:

> Let us export oarsmen, runners, fencers; there is the free trade of the future – and on the day when it shall take its place among the customs of Europe, the cause of peace will have received a new and powerful support.

Many small countries which emerged after the Versailles Treaty of 1919, like Finland, Estonia, Poland, Czechoslovakia heeded that appeal and sent young men and women as their ambassadors to the Olympic Games. Finnish athletes made a particularly strong impact on international sports. The names of Hannes Kolehmainen and Paavo Nurmi were emblazoned on the record books over two decades, but this is jumping ahead of the story.

On the basis of my performances at the Olympic Trials and at the AAA Championships, I was selected as a member of the British Olympic team and my name was entered for the 100, 200, and 400 meters races, as well as a member of the relay teams. I realized that I might not be able to participate in all events, but I was determined to do my best while remembering Baron de Coubertin's admonition:

> The important point in the Olympic Games is not to win but to take part, just as in life the most essential thing is not so much to conquer as to have fought well.

I took a two-week vacation from my clerical position in a small import house, a job which I had accepted after completing a term as a teacher. A busy and exciting period preceded the departure for Belgium. Work and training had to be kept up, a uniform was made to measure and had to be tried on, a passport and a visa had to be obtained, travel instructions digested and followed. The trip was by steamer up the long and winding Scheldt River to the port of Antwerp. We were quartered in a high school, where cots had been set up in classrooms. Meals were taken in the school and buses took us from the school to training grounds adjoining the Olympic Stadium. Our arrangements, although not ideal, were, nevertheless, considerably better than the accommodations provided for a large part of the US Olympic team, which was quartered on board the United States naval cruiser SS *Frederick* and the army transport *Princess Matoika*, docked in the harbor of Antwerp.

There was little time for training. We had to go through rehearsals for the grand march into the stadium. The opening ceremony on Saturday, August 14 was a colorful event. The national teams entered the arena in alphabetical order, according to the spelling of their country's name in French, hence the large team of the United States of America, over 300 strong, was near the head of the procession under "États-Unis d'Amérique." The host country, Belgium, was the last to enter. A salute was given to their Majesties, King Albert and Queen Elizabeth of Belgium. His Eminence Cardinal Mercier, a very popular prelate, Baron de Coubertin, and to many other noted dignitaries as the teams marched past the Royal Box.

The chairman of the Organizing Committee delivered a short address and requested the president of the Games to invite the King to open the Games. The president thereupon made the request to the King. King Albert of the Belgians then declared the opening of the Games with these words: "I proclaim open the Olympic Games celebrating the VIIth Olympiad of the modern era." The Olympic flag of five interlocking rings, representing the five continents, was raised. A fanfare of trumpets was sounded and was followed by a ceremonial release of pigeons, symbolizing peace. Thereupon massed bands played and massed choirs sang. The Olympic oath was taken on behalf of all competitors:

> We swear that we will take part in the Olympic Games in loyal competition, respecting the regulations which govern them and desirous of participating in them in the true spirit of sportsmanship for the honor of our country and for the glory of sport.

Recessional was rendered by the bands and choir, and the national teams departed from the stadium. At Antwerp we did not have the ceremony of lighting the Olympic Flame by a torch carried from Olympia.

On the following day the competitions started in earnest. In the shorter distances the elimination heats were followed by a second round, then by semi-finals, and the crucial, important final. Along the road to the final were many disappointed hearts suffering the agony of defeat. It was my good fortune to qualify in all tests of the 100 meters, only to be left behind at the starting gun of the final by an incident vigorously protested by the French Committee.

I had drawn the outside lane near the grandstand. I loosened up especially my shoulder and arm actions and dribbled a short distance. Some of my opponents had a few bursts out of the starting

24. Heat 8 of the first round of the 1920 Olympic 100 metre competition and Harry Edward cruises in beside American multiple world record holder and favourite Charley Paddock.

holes dug into the cinder track, others bent and stretched, loosening up in their own fashion. The band stopped playing and a hush settled over the stadium. Then came the starter's voice: "À vos marques!" and we responded by digging the balls of our feet into the pre-dug holes, placing our fingers behind the white starting line. "Préparez-vous!" shouted the starter, and we got set, awaiting the crack of the pistol and the release of the concentrated tension of mind and muscles. While in the momentary, nervous suspense the starter's aide and linesman at my right said in English: "Paddock, take your hands back, behind the line!" This broke my tension just as a false start would have done. Then the pistol went off. I jumped out of the holes more vertically than in the proper forward direction. I put tremendous effort into my strides, found myself about 4 feet behind the leaders at half distance, regained an improved forward-leaning position, and ended with a tremendous burst, passing everybody at the end. Alas, I passed them about 3 feet behind the finishing line. The judges gave me third place behind Charley Paddock and Morris Kirksey of the United States. There was a great delay before the results were announced. Every participant sensed or knew that the start had been a doubtful one. Jackson Scholz, a US finalist, said to me at the end of the race that it had been a false start. He had been left on his knee at the start. Ali-Khan, the Algerian, wearing the colors of France, was equally positive that

25 & 26. The 'California Cannonball' Charley Paddock leaps through the tape to win the 1920 Olympic 100 metre final, while his compatriot Morris Kirksey (on the inside lane) slows as he infamously turns to see where Paddock is. The fast-finishing Harry Edward, in the outside lane, pips American Jackson Scholz on the line for the bronze medal, and within a second was past the whole field – albeit 3 yards beyond the tape.

the start had been unfair. I, too, was puzzled and unhappy, and spoke to Harry I. Barkley, Honorary Secretary of the AAA, who was on the track as a representative of the International Olympic Committee. I filled out a written protest in the hope of getting the final re-run.

One of our active athletes was Philip Noel-Baker, winner of the Olympic silver medal in the 1,500 meters, a young man trained in matters diplomatic. He examined the rules, learned that the starter's word was final in all things relating to the start. He made discreet inquiries into the views and attitude of the starter, only to ascertain that he would not reverse his action. I was counseled to withdraw the unfiled protest and did so. The French Committee pressed, however, for a reversal of the decision in the 100 meters final. Their protest was rejected by the committee having jurisdiction 4:0 on the following day.

Although disappointed about the result in the 100 meters, I had the hope of proving my worth in the 200 meters. I won the first and second rounds of the elimination heats, recording the fastest time. Then came the semi-final at 9.30 on a cold and windy morning. This time I had drawn the inside lane for the staggered start in the curve, a position not suited for my long strides. Jumping out of the starting holes, I felt the sharp, piercing pain of a "Charley horse," a pulled tendon. I strode through the race, putting the minimum of pressure onto the injured leg, finished in second place, qualifying for the final to be run in the afternoon.

27. Harry Edward writes his protest after the starting debacle of the 100 metre final cost him any chance of a win. But British 'etiquette' dictated that the protest would never make it to the Olympic officials.

28. Semi-final of the 1920 Olympic 200 metres and, after clocking the fastest time in the competition in the quarter-finals – 22 seconds flat – Harry Edward finishes second to American Loren Murchison to qualify for the final, despite pulling a tendon.

In the intervening time I received the visits of concerned coaches from many lands. The Australian coach sent his trainer-masseur, who warmed and massaged my leg muscles and, prior to the race, strapped the injured leg with adhesive tape. When walking to the starting point for the 200 meters I was the recipient of numerous good wishes. It was a race run in a grimace of suppressed and conquered pain. I strode as far as the pain would permit me with the maximum allowable pressure in each stride, finishing in third place.

Allen Woodring from the USA was the winner. Immediately after the race he turned to me. After I had expressed my congratulations, he replied: "Edward, that should have been your race!" Thank you, Allen Woodring. I had competed against him in the second round, a race which I had won comfortably in the fastest time. Thus ended my participation in the Olympic Games. The European press was most sympathetic to my predicament, saying in many columns that I had been the unluckiest athlete at the Games. However, looking back I blame myself for the strained tendon in the 200 meters. I should have spent a little more time and effort in thoroughly warming up for the race on that cold, blustery morning.

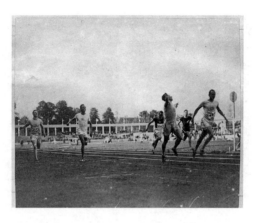

29. Harry Edward's 200 metre final was ruined by his pulled tendon. But he ran through the pain barrier to take a brave bronze medal behind Woodring and Paddock, who both came home in 22 seconds flat, the same time Harry had clocked in his quarter-final.

The Olympics of that year yielded a very important by-product, namely the development of the social side of the Games. The time and the atmosphere were propitious. A world war had ended barely two years before, a war-weary world looked forward to peace and international understanding. Baron de Coubertin was among us and had contributed his enthusiasm and energies toward the revival of the Olympic Games. The dream of a League of Nations was becoming a reality. Youth sought an outlet for concrete expressions of its idealism.

The British team had as its administrative head a military man, Brigadier General R.J. Kentish, CMG, DSO. This caused initially some apprehension among us athletes. On the boat trip to Antwerp we organized a committee of athletes to function as liaison with General Kentish and his deputy, Col. Ronald Campbell. I was elected to that committee of which Philip Noel-Baker was the chairman. Phil Baker had been active in promoting international contests as an athlete at Cambridge University. He had been instrumental in bringing to Great Britain a combined Cornell–Princeton team to compete against Oxford and Cambridge. He was secretary to Lord

Robert Cecil, Britain's representative at the League of Nations, hence was working in the diplomatic field, but most importantly he was fluent in French, Spanish, Italian, with a working knowledge of Greek.

In the first speech by General Kentish to the assembled athletes, he made it clear that he was a military man who was acquainted with war, hated its cost, and would do his "damnedest" to prevent another holocaust. He was in sympathy with the philosophy of utilizing the gathering of athletes from many lands for the promotion of international understanding. He made a hurried trip to England and persuaded British military authorities to release and assign to Antwerp the regimental band of the kilted Black Watch. We arranged and organized visits by athletes to our schoolyard on evenings known as "Spanish and Latin American Night," "French and Italian Night," "American Night," and "Scandinavian Night." The band would play for dances, and the bagpipers and drummers would give a display of their skills.

At the first occasion we discovered that there were not enough girls to go around. Brigadier General Kentish said that he would contact some lycées for a supply, and urged the athletes to assist him in making up the shortage. Never was a problem in the field of international understanding solved with greater alacrity. There were also many return visits to the quarters of other national teams. At those social occasions exuberant youth found expression for esteem and admiration of some Olympic athletes and their contributions. I have the happy memory of being carried on the shoulders of Scandinavian athletes to the rhythm and melody of a song, at the end of which I was tossed into the air and caught by strong arms three times in succession. These social events and their potentialities left a strong impression with me and influenced the course of my life. Later I had occasion to captain many teams in international competitions and serve the United Nations for over five years. Philip Noel-Baker devoted his life to diplomacy and work in the international field, becoming Britain's ambassador to the United

Nations, Britain's minister of colonies, and the recipient of the Nobel Prize for Peace.

Reverting to the Olympic year of 1920, I did not compete again that summer, and in the following season was less active than previously. However, I did defend my championship titles successfully against international competition. The AAA Championships of 1921 saw a very strong team from Sweden, which scored heavily in the field events, while the hurdles title went to France. In that year the Harvey Memorial Gold Cup for the best champion of the year was awarded to me.

30. Harry wins the final of the 1921 AAA Championships 100 yards in 10.2 seconds, in front of more than 20,000 fans at Stamford Bridge stadium, just half a yard in front of Harold Abrahams (no. 22), with former champion Billy Hill (no. 14) chasing hard in third.

31. Man about town. Harry Edward's studio picture from 1921, sent out to fans who requested photos and autographs. Harry was now happily based in a flat at 70 Huntley Street, in fashionable Bloomsbury.

7

THE ROYAL AAA CHAMPIONSHIPS

However, 1922 proved to be a banner year and the zenith was the Amateur Athletic [Association] Championships honored by the visit of HM King George V. My club had entered my name in the 100, 220, and 440 yards. In the preceding year I had helped our Polytechnic Harriers relay team to victory by a fast quarter-mile as anchor man, hence the entry for that championship event.

I was doubtful whether I should compete in all three events and asked a friend whose judgment I respected for advice. He replied in an oracular manner: "You can do it if you are head and shoulders above your competitors." The challenge of the contests appealed to me. I felt fit and recovered from a strain suffered five weeks before. I felt confident. I joined a group of athletes for a week's vacation at Brighton before the championships. Some heats were scheduled to take place on Friday evening and the remaining elimination contests and finals on Saturday afternoon.

A proverb says: "There's many a slip t'wixt the cup and the lip." It happened that on the Wednesday before the races I twisted my ankle when I fell while descending a circular stair. "To be or not to be fit" that was the question, which bothered my friends and me. On Friday I ran gingerly through the heats with strapped ankle and

32. Harry Edward wins the 1922 AAA 100 yards final at Stamford Bridge in 10 seconds flat – the first of his extraordinary triple inside one hour – with army sprint champion Lancelot Royle (no. 27) second and South Africa's Christiaan Steyn (fourth from the left) in third. July's edition of the *Polytechnic Magazine* revealed that Harry's amazing feat almost didn't happen at all. Earlier in the week he fell down a flight of stairs and badly twisted his ankle. He made it to the stadium the day before the events began and only intense treatment got him to the start line.

33. Harry Edward wins the 1922 AAA 220 yards in 22 seconds flat – essentially a solo race against the clock, because only two athletes made it to the start line and Harry stormed to victory by some 15 yards in front of Switzerland's Josef Imbach.

thighs. I held together. On Saturday I sailed victoriously through the semi-finals and qualified in all three races. The competition was, as usual, quite international. Athletes had come from Italy, Norway, Sweden, Finland, France, and Switzerland seeking the coveted AAA Championship titles. The scheduled appearance of Olympic athletes and foreign champions attracted a crowd estimated at 20,000, whose excitement was increased when it was learned that HM King George V was expected. When this popular monarch made his appearance on the grandstand a tremendous cheer went up, providing a special, royal setting to these championships. The King did not remain long in the stand, but descended onto the track, where he mingled with officials and athletes.

My mind was, of course, on the finals for which I had qualified. The start for the 100 yards was fair, the race strenuous, and the margin of victory comfortable. The honorary secretary of the AAA came to me immediately after the finish of the race and said: "His Majesty wishes to speak to you." Within seconds I stood before the King, who by his gracious and relaxed manner tried to make me feel comfortable. I was still somewhat tense and out of breath after the race. His Majesty inquired into my studies and activities while photographers snapped pictures and film cameras whirred.

It was thirty-five minutes later when I went to the starting mark of the 220 yards, in which my most serious opponent was the Swiss champion Josef Imbach, an Olympic semi-finalist two years before. His opposition did not prove as dangerous as anticipated, and I felt not hard pressed in the last yards of the race. I learned later that there was tremendous speculation among the press and the thousands of onlookers whether I would be able to win all three events for which I had entered. Such triple victory had never been recorded before in the long history of those amateur championships.

Twenty-five minutes after the finish of the furlong, I stood at the starting line of the 440 yards final, in which Guy Butler of Cambridge University, runner-up in the Olympic quarter-mile, was my most serious antagonist. This thought was in my mind when I looked at Butler before the starting command. For many years friends told me repeatedly that I had intentionally "psyched" him on that occasion. There was no such intent, but my thoughts might have been that intense as to convey that impression. We did not have separate lanes in that race. Thus, I took the lead immediately after the starting gun had sounded. Using more a rapid striding than a powerful sprint action I widened the lead at the back-straight and felt that I had much reserve as I rounded the last curve. In the final stretch my lead was not challenged and I coasted to a safe victory. The time was a disappointingly slow 50.4 seconds, much slower than the 48.8 seconds quarter-mile I had been clocked in the relay race the preceding year. My times of 10 seconds for the century, 22 seconds for the curved furlong may seem very slow these days: yet the international and Olympic competition had been there.

34. Harry Edward completes his historic triple – all inside one hour – at the 1922 AAA Championships by winning the 440 yards, in a time of 50.4 seconds, with the 1920 Olympic silver medallist Guy Butler (left) 3 yards back and one of Harry's Poly Harrier teammates, Tom Cushing, in third.

35. The Lord Mayor's Show, London, November 1922, and
some of the Polytechnic athletes, dressed in their Olympic finery, pose
for a picture. They include 1920 Olympic heavyweight boxing champion
Ron Rawson (second left), 800 and 1,500 metres champion Albert Hill
(front row, third left) and Harry Edward (second right).

It must be acknowledged that over the last five decades we have learned to build better tracks with improved layers and drainage, starting blocks have been introduced, training methods refined, food intake corrected. All have contributed to produce a better crop of athletes, improved performances, and new records.

In reporting the AAA Championships the sports press throughout the world was most generous with praise. My name was again entered on the Harvey Gold Cup, the challenge trophy awarded annually to the best champion of the year. I received invitations from Finland, Sweden, Denmark, and France. As I had to consider my obligations toward my employer, I declined the invitations from the Baltic countries among others, but accepted appearances at the Sunday meetings of the Stade Français and the Racing Club de France of Paris. Involved were only overnight boat trips to France. However, in one case I used the airplane. I ran in a race at Croydon at 3 p.m. on a Saturday and caught the plane for Paris from the adjoining airfield at 4.30 p.m. In those days of 1922 there was only one daily service from London to Amsterdam, Brussels, and Paris in single-motored bi-planes with a sole pilot in an open cockpit. The passenger cabins had wooden benches and accommodated from five to nine persons. The cruising speed of those planes was 90 miles per hour. On the day of that flight it had been raining and the wind was gusting up to 40 miles per hour. I was the only passenger on the plane, the other passengers had cancelled their bookings. I learned later that all flights had been suspended after our departure. Croydon Airport was just a meadow then; there was no landing strip, hence the lift-off from the field was rough and bumpy. Bumpy, too, was the low flight over the dunes of southern England. It became calm over the English Channel and bumpy again over France. My stomach was unaccustomed to the up and down motions of the plane, with the interspersed sideway sway-ings, and my nostrils found the oil and gasoline smells most objec-tionable; therefore, I was glad that I was the lone passenger. I could give vent unrestrainedly to my strong physical emotions.

We, Pilot Palin and I, reached the Le Bourget airport, Paris, after a flight of about three hours. My French host asked me to thank the pilot for the safe flight. I did so by reaching up to the cockpit, grasping his outstretched hand. It seems that this was the custom of those early days of commercial flying. A reception committee of representatives of the International Olympic Committee and of the sponsoring club was awaiting me, and the hospitality of my hosts was warm and genuine. Equally sincere were the receptions I received on my visits to Liverpool and Glasgow during that year.

In the post-Olympic years I had been able to establish myself economically as a French-German correspondent in import and export houses, and as a cost accountant in a manufacturing concern. I had taken a number of courses at the Polytechnic Institute in commercial law and business administration and had passed the Intermediate Examinations of the Chartered Institute of Secretaries of Joint Stock Companies, a British professional society with branches in the dominions and colonies. Those societies and their examinations were akin in nature and acceptance to those of the Certified Public Accountants in America.

The year 1922 was important to me not only because of exploits in sports, but also in a private and sentimental way. I took an important step in life. I married Mrs. Antoinette Kohler Regner, whom I had known for nearly four years, a neighbor of friends of twelve years' standing. I extended my August visit to the Glasgow sports meeting into a honeymoon in the Scottish Loch Country. With new responsibilities as head of a household, with work and studies, I spent a full and busy winter.

8

THE NEW WORLD

Early the following year I received an invitation from the promoters of the Wilco Games at New York, scheduled to take place at the Yankee Stadium in September. I discussed the matter with my family, my coach, and friends at the Polytechnic Harriers, both the aspects of my participation in competitions in America and my possible emigration. America was then quite a long way from Europe; the fastest ship took five days, most passenger steamers about seven days. This meant that my taking part in only one sports meeting would require a vacation of at least three weeks. An economic recession then engulfed Great Britain, and I hesitated to make a request for such a long vacation period, a request which would surely have been refused me by my employer. Yet, the possibility of migrating to the New World intrigued me. Having worked for over two years in import houses, I was acquainted with the obstacles thrown into the path of the free exchange of goods by the tariff walls which were being raised by European nations. Part of my work was to calculate the sales price of certain lots of steel products in British pounds sterling, shillings, and pence per long ton, when it was quoted by Belgian, French, and German mills in kilograms and in their currencies. These computations were complicated by fluctuating exchange rates and the imposition of import and export taxes. It seemed that all nations were trying to get rich at the expense of their neighbors, strangling thereby their trading possibilities. In the United States a similar trend existed, culminating in the Hawley–Smoot Tariff Act of 1930. However, in America there was a huge trading area free from any hindrances. There was also the memory of Wilson's Fourteen Points, as against the picture of European statesmen fighting inflation, depressions, and fearful of the resurrection of a revengeful Germany.

Eventually I arrived at the decision to migrate to the United States. I set in motion the necessary steps for the obtaining of a visa and the permission from the Amateur Athletic Association to take part in sports meetings approved by the Amateur Athletic Union of the United States. Then came a psychological setback. I was defeated in the championships I had held for three years. I ran in the AAA 100 yards, felt that I was not up to championship level and decided not to contest my other titles. The sprint championships of that year were won by the Scottish champion Eric H. Liddell, who, a year later, captured the Olympic gold medal for the quarter-mile.

All my thoughts in the summer of 1923 were focused on my trip to the United States. The hopes of my wife and mine were rosy that I would find an adequate, economic base which would enable my wife and stepson to join me soon in the New World. When I bade them a tearful goodbye at London's Euston Station for my journey to the Liverpool dock of the Cunard Line, we felt we would and could overcome obstacles. We counted on the many lessons of life learned in World War I, on our physical, educational, and spiritual resources, and on a "little bit of luck."

I got that "little bit of luck" when I met Paul J. Furnas, Treasurer of Sandura Company Inc., who invited me to join the staff of that corporation when the Paulsboro, NJ, factory started manufacturing felt-base rugs. There was, as it may be remembered, a threatening sword of Damocles dangling by a hair over our heads. The

British Flash

H. F. V. EDWARDS, England's
great colored sprinter, who is
here to match his speed with
America's best at the Wilco
games next Saturday.

FAILED!

H. F. V. EDWARDS,
Crack colored sprinter of England,
who failed to qualify in the dashes
at the Wilco A. C. games in New
York on Saturday. This meet
marked Edwards' first competitive
appearance in this country.

36. These two cuttings illustrate the American reaction to Harry Edward's
track debut stateside at the Wilco Games, at the Yankee Stadium. One pre-
event, one post-event. The second is a rather blunt, but accurate summary of
his lacklustre sporting performances in the States. After these self-styled
pre-Olympics, where Edward failed to make the 100 yards or 220 yards final,
he ran in Boston and again in New York, but saw no improvement. He hung up
his spikes for good soon after. It was suggested in athletic circles that he had
followed the advice of a coach to refrain from heavy winter training and rely
on massages. The result was that Harry emerged in the 1923 season over-
weight and lacking stamina, and never found his form again.

six-month visa granted my wife and son was about to expire. This
meant that they would be forced to return to London to await there
their immigration number. All my personal inquiries at the old
immigration office at Gloucester, New Jersey, brought nothing but
negative and disappointing results. It seemed that only a higher
level of authority in Washington, DC could possibly give favorable
consideration in a review of this case. My director and friend made

careful inquiries among directors of nationally known, large corpo-
rations located in Camden, New Jersey. He obtained from them
guidance how to proceed and to whom to appeal. Armed with such
information, he traveled to the nation's capital. In the labyrinth of
the Federal Service he was referred from one department to
another, but was able to get favorable action on a permanent immigration visa before the end of a strenuous day.

Many years later it occurred to me that I would never have
succeeded, had I relied on my own personal efforts, even using the
same arguments and proofs. Washington, DC, was, it must be
remembered, a Jim Crow town and the Federal Service reflected
that pattern. There were no Negroes in professional or clerical
positions. My personal appearance would have undoubtedly created
unsurmountable prejudices in my appeal.

Even in the Quaker-managed, liberal, humanistic, and paternal-
istic Sandura Company traces of racial bias were noticeable. In the
plant there was in one department a Negro crew, in another a
predominantly Italian crew, in another a crew of Scottish and Irish
descent. The average wages of each department gave also a measure
of existing prejudices. No doubt, management would have defended
discrepancies, claiming that its judgment was based on the varying
skills required. However, the least skilled jobs were invariably
assigned to blacks. After working six months as a laborer in the
paint shop, I was transferred to the office, where I quickly applied
my experience in accounting. I lived with my family in a building
adjoining the plant, a former dormitory for workers of a munition
factory whose physical plant Sandura Company had purchased and
converted. Next to our living quarters was the former recreation
room with a service counter. By arrangement with the management of Sandura, my wife and I rented that space and set up a
factory commissary and restaurant, which my wife managed at first
alone and later with a helper. The income derived from the restaurant broadened the economic base of our family. My stepson, too,

joined the staff of the company and learned the skill of a block cutter.

Our working hours were long, extending from 7 o'clock in the morning, when we opened the commissary, to the evening hour of 8 o'clock, when we finished supper and cleaned up the restaurant. Saturdays were taken up with trips to Philadelphia for the purchasing of items for sale, such as cigarettes, cigars, tobacco, soaps, gloves, socks, handkerchiefs, as well as food items like boiled ham, bolognas [baloney sausage], cheeses, etc. Work behind the counter of the commissary proved to be a good vehicle for my wife's making contact with most of the company's staff. My paymaster's job, which was combined with work as a cost accountant, offered me similar opportunities.

Again sports became a bridge, this time to the Paulsboro community. At the invitation of a volunteer-leader of a YMCA group, I gave a talk about the Olympic Games which was enthusiastically received by the high school boys. The following year I was asked by the same group to be their leader.

In the year which had elapsed since my coming to Paulsboro, I had learned a lot about the racial biases of South Jersey. The only cinema in that town followed the custom prevalent throughout that area, including Philadelphia, namely to seat blacks in balconies only, denying them access to orchestra seats. A diner, located in the town's main thoroughfare, had a large sign displayed behind the counter: "We do not solicit colored trade!" In the first months in Paulsboro I had gone to the only barbershop I had noticed. The first time I got my hair cut by the owner who asked a number of questions about me and my work. On my second visit, I was asked to sit in the rear of the shop, where I got my haircut but without much conversation. However, this time the barber gave me a handful of Klan literature with its virulent outpourings against Catholics and the Pope and told me quite politely to seek another barber. I related this incident to some of my Quaker co-workers, who remained silent, looked serious and perplexed, sighed, and shrugged their shoulders. My director was enraged when reading the unfamiliar hate literature of the Ku Klux Klan. He asked for a few copies and expressed the intention of discussing the matter with "concerned" members of the Philadelphia Quaker leadership.

Having become aware of the various strata of this small community and their prejudices, I moved with caution and circumspection when considering the proffered "leadership" of the YMCA group of white boys. I sent them back to discuss their wish with their parents and the YMCA Committee of local community leaders. The professional full-time Y secretary of Gloucester County came to see me and expressed the desire to publish an article about me in the monthly magazine of the county YMCA. After receiving all around agreement and acceptance on the proposed volunteer leadership position and after the publication of the article, I was swamped with invitations to speak at many white Y-groups throughout the county. There were no Negro YMCAs in Gloucester County at that time, nor was the door to the then existing facilities open to the needs of black youth. The realization of those facts gave a certain challenge to my volunteer endeavors.

After discussing with the Y-boys a possible program for the season, it was clear that sports, namely baseball and basketball, were their prime interests. When planning our list of speakers we also agreed to reach beyond the limits of the community by "bringing the world to Paulsboro." After discovering some musical talent among us we started a small musical group. The pursuit of all those interests consumed much time in meetings, planning, practicing, and, of course, games against other groups. Many members of our Y were also members of the baseball team of the high school, which had an excellent pitcher, a Negro. The desire to strengthen our Y team led to the invitation of the Negro youth to join us. The same young man was also an excellent basketball player who earned the esteem of the group as "a good sport."

One day I learned that there was a young, talented Negro youth in the local high school who was quite proficient on a trumpet. At an opportune moment I discussed with him his plans and his life's ambitions. I found him reserved, poised, and quite mature in his attitude. I inquired whether he would be willing to join our Y's musical group if invited by the members and found him ready to do so. After some reflections I proposed the young man's candidacy to the Y-group at a weekly meeting. Desirous of having the youths discuss the pros and cons of this application freely and uninhibited, I absented myself from this meeting. The president of the Y-group apprised me of the group's decision, namely to admit the candidate "but not everybody." There was evidently some fear reflected not to have many Negro members in the club. At rehearsals the new member proved himself to be a good musician, regular in attendance, thus he gave strength to our band, which consisted of three violins, two trumpets, one drummer, and piano. I played the piano. We played at the local Methodist Church (white), at a meeting of the Knights of the Golden Eagle (white by the provisions of its charter) and at other local functions.

In our yearly report I expounded the virtues of music by quoting Molière:

> Without music a state cannot exist. All the disorders, all the wars which we see in the world, only occur because of the neglect to learn music. Does not war result from a lack of union among men? And were all men to learn music, would this not be the means of agreeing together, and of seeing universal peace reign throughout the world?

We felt proud of the accomplishments of our musical group of seven, created out of a total membership of seventeen. The fruitful efforts of our baseball and basketball teams were equally praiseworthy. In fifteen games played during the season against other

Y-groups, boy scouts, church groups, and local teams, not a single contest was lost. It is amazing, however, how quickly the atmosphere can change.

At the yearly meeting of the county committee, held at the country club at the county seat, attended by committee members of many local groups with their wives, our little band played at their invitation. I was called upon to say a few words and I reported on our program "to bring the world to our community." I cited programs which we already had: a Chinese student from the University of Pennsylvania, the vice president of a local bank, the superintendent of the Vacuum Oil Company, and I said that "we hope to have a representative of Labor in the near future."

The following week I was approached by the superintendent of Sandura Company's plant, who inquired about "the red talk" I had given at the meeting of the County YMCA. It seemed that suddenly I had become persona non grata in that non-union town in which the Vacuum Oil Company and Du Pont had plants. Social pressures upon our YMCA group and our work began to be felt.

The recreational facilities of the local high school were denied us henceforth. Another Y-group was formed based in the high school, given access to the gymnasium and the baseball diamond there. The local YMCA Committee asked me to attend their meeting in which the chairman, who was also the clerk of the school board, questioned me about the religious practices of our group. "Do you open your meetings with a prayer?" was the question posed me. I replied honestly that all meetings were in the hands of the group itself and that I was at the sideline as an advisor. There were times when we had meditation and at other times we had none. This gave rise to a bombastic sermonizing on the need for prayers and on the true and proper procedures for YMCA groups to conduct their meetings. I got the message without "losing my cool." I accepted the verdict and learned the following lessons: that any discussions on the place of organized labor in our economic structure were deemed dangerous, that having a Negro as a volunteer Y-leader provided a disturbing image, that white and black youth should not mingle in musical harmony nor in imitation of the Olympic spirit. The insidious method employed for the dissolution of our Y-group must have been highly disturbing to our youthful members. The white boys were directed to the newly formed High-Y-Group at the school, the Negro boys were dropped.

My casual remark "to bring the outer world to our community," to have the boys listen to the problems of capital and labor had brought on a local revolution. It was at a time when Émile Coué, a popular French lecturer and psychotherapist, preached salvation by optimistic autosuggestion: "Day by day, in every way, I am getting better and better!" Huge billboards proclaimed: "Business is good, keep it good!" and *Systems* magazine listed monthly as business's greatest asset: "Herbert Hoover in the White House." Profiting from the perspective of history, we know today how tragic the blindness to realities proved to be. Business was not good and the country was plunged into a deep depression. In less than ten years after the described incident, all labor became organized in Paulsboro, New Jersey.

Then, in 1927, the happenings did not disturb my economic base – not yet. Work was still plentiful, the company prospered, my services as office manager and cost accountant were appreciated.

However, there were circumstances far beyond my control which ignited the explosives of the ever-present racial prejudices. I shall cite one instance. I was the bonded paymaster of the factory. The headquarters of Sandura Company had moved to Philadelphia, PA. Our chief accountant there, who lived in Paulsboro, was scheduled to bring the payroll check to me after business hours. However, it had to be signed by two officers of the company, hence the chief accountant had to take the check to the home of a director to obtain the second signature. There, he and his wife who was accompanying him, were invited to dinner by the director's wife. The former declined, stating that they had an engagement with me. To have a director's dinner invitation refused in preference to an engagement with a Negro was a sin and an affront, which the lady never forgot nor forgave. The esteem paid to a Negro by fellow workers or by her husband was to her intolerable. Her attitude influenced measurably the disposition of her husband who, as Director of Production, was my supervisor. Thus, indirectly she vitiated the very working atmosphere. There was nothing I could do about it.

The working relationship with my staff of six clerks and accountants, all white, was cordial and it seemed that they were anxious to stimulate the pervading atmosphere of harmony. They initiated a number of theatre parties for Philadelphia shows, at which occasions my wife and I sat with the group in orchestra seats. There were only two occasions which mar the memory of agreeable staff relationships. Once a local, white, female clerk refused to take instructions from me, preferring to resign rather than to comply. At another time, a Christmas party sponsored by the company and held in a Philadelphia restaurant extended invitations to every member of the office staff except me. The staff working under me felt greatly embarrassed; I felt greatly hurt and expressed my disappointment to the employee charged with the organization of the party. It was obvious that racial prejudice, always present under the surface, proved greater than the spirit of Christmas.

As nearly all social channels were closed to Negroes in a small South Jersey community, I attempted to open contacts with the business community along professional lines. Thus, the superintendent of the Vacuum Oil Company, who had spoken to our Y-group, showed me around his company's plant and explained their costing system. The manager of the Del-Bay Farms conducted me through his processing plant and elaborated on the costing procedures used there. My friend, the chief accountant of Sandura, had joined the Philadelphia Chapter of Cost Accountants. He inquired about the possibility of my joining that professional association, only to be told that colored people were not admitted to membership.

After a year's residence in Paulsboro, NJ, my wife and I had acquired a second-hand Studebaker. An automobile is a highly appreciated investment for a black person. It saves and prevents so many mental hurts and bruises which white society knowingly and unknowingly inflicts so often upon its darker fellow humans. With a car one is not forced into contact with all kinds of white persons in trains, buses, or other means of public conveyance. One can be selective in the choice of one's companions and in the choice of areas and places to be visited. My family and I enjoyed the Jersey beaches and the accessible Pocono Mountains. However, access to pools was denied me. There were restaurants which refused service, some charged exorbitant prices or gave bad service in the quality of food or in attendance at table. We circumvented the degrading rudeness of white society by carrying adequate provisions in the car, and we learned also to be independent of hotel accommodation by having a tent, rubber air mattresses, and cooking utensils stowed away. Our vacation trips were pointed northward, never below the Mason–Dixon line. At a Quaker school I had met Dr. John Hope, President of Morehouse College, Atlanta, GA. He enlightened me cautiously, almost apologetically, about the racial conditions in the South. He pleaded not to take my wife to the Southland unless she was prepared to claim that "she was of the race," meaning Negro. The claim of any fraction, even one sixty-fourth part, of Negro blood would make her eligible for a Negro label. He pointed out that far too many white Southern gentlemen would feel "justifiably enraged" at the sight of a white woman married to a Negro, enough to take the law into their own hands and murder one or the other or both of us. For the safety of my wife, I decided not to proceed with naturalization, but to keep valid my British passport, with the protection it gave her. In time I also learned the peculiar twists of reasoning often found in the white American's mind.

When I played on occasion the enraged and offended foreign visitor to these shores, the astonished American would often become apologetic and admit that his rudeness was prompted by the thought that I was an American Negro. Oh, yes! There is the story that a black American who donned a turban and affected a foreign accent received profuse salaams and deference from the staffs of the South's best hotels. A State Department official told me the following: as part of the reception of a French-speaking African graduate student, this official took him to a Washington, DC restaurant for lunch, where they received excellent service. The following day the student returned to the same restaurant alone and, wishing to demonstrate his knowledge of languages, he spoke in English. The restaurant refused to serve him. Such stories could be duplicated a hundredfold and, alas, the many expressions of such prejudices have borne much bitter fruit in international relations.

After the demise of our YMCA group, I took an active part in the inter-racial committee of the Society of Friends, Philadelphia. In this group I met many sincere and kind persons who were as baffled as I was in the face of the many racial barriers around us. We failed to develop any plans of attack or any joint, constructive action. However, I received a number of speaking engagements with white church groups, high school assemblies, and classes, also with Quaker Meetings. In this manner I made contact with representatives of many strata in the City of Brotherly Love. I also wrote a number of articles and reports for the *Philadelphia Tribune*, the weekly Negro paper of that city, and on one or two occasions I accompanied a reporter of the *Philadelphia Record* on his assignments. This activity gave me an insight into some of the perplexing social problems of a city. Research into the growth of the black community of Philadelphia uncovered the fact that blacks had formed a very influential segment of Philadelphia's economic structure during the early part of the nineteenth century. They had been ship chandlers, clock makers, harness makers, caterers, building contractors, and were strongly represented among the artisans. However, with the growth of industry, both the owners and organized labor had squeezed the blacks out of skilled jobs.

The father of a Negro friend of mine was light of skin color and an excellent auto-mechanic. He had risen to the position of foreman in the shops of the fashionably elegant Pierce-Arrow Auto Company, where he was regarded as white. My friend related to me how his family had to peep through the curtains before admitting anybody to the house. After years of practicing such caution it did happen. A fellow worker of his father had found his way to their house and had discovered the Negro composition of their family. "Dad was out of a job the next week," my friend told me. My speaking at teas to kindly disposed ladies seemed an empty and ineffectual way to combat the sinister operation of racial bigotry.

Whatever feeble efforts I had put forth had been observed by some Quaker friends, because they offered me a half scholarship in 1929 to the first International Institute held at Haverford College, PA. The two weeks' period spent there proved to be very stimulating and challenging. True, the focus was on non-violence and peace in the Quaker tradition, yet the approaches were varied, from many angles, and the historical reviews most thought-provoking. Among the many university professors and lecturers, the most famous names were Bruno Tannenbaum on Latin America and Norman Thomas on economics and socialism.

The same summer, four months before the stock market crash, which nobody expected or dreamed about, I invited my mother to visit us. When she arrived from Germany she was suffering from severe asthma attacks, which illness had plagued her for many years. I obtained for her the best medical attention available, namely the care under the chief of Jefferson Hospital's Asthma Service and Clinic. In spite of the attention given her under the supervision of one of America's outstanding specialists, she died after six weeks of hospitalization.

An undertaker telephoned me from Philadelphia, and I agreed to let him handle the necessary details for her cremation. When he came to my home to discuss particulars and to obtain my signature, the gentleman was truly aghast and crestfallen. He stammered that he could not handle a black body for cremation, because the only crematory in Philadelphia would not accept Negro dead. Here was a form of discrimination of which I had not been aware. When I explained to him that my mother was – or rather had been – white a smile of satisfaction wreathed the undertaker's face. The business trip had not been in vain. Those, too, were times that tried men's souls, my faith in the decency of white men's institutions. If my mother had been black, she could not have received the requested services in the City of Brotherly Love.

In my continued attempts to maintain natural, cordial relationships with my fellow workers, and to keep up physical fitness, I had joined Sandura office workers in forming a basketball team, to which we invited some young high school teachers. This led to another activity, namely a debate with the local high school debating team.

9

FIGHTING SCHOOL SEGREGATION

In the spring of 1930 some of the young, white teachers (there were no black teachers in the integrated high school) came to me and related that the school board was planning to segregate the black children from the white in the up-coming school term of September 1930. At that time the Paulsboro schools had been the only integrated system in South Jersey. Some grade schools north of Trenton had been mixed, but most Jersey schools had segregated grade schools and integrated high schools, the latter for economic reasons. When I heard this news I inquired whether there had been any incidents which could have prompted the proposed action. Neither the teachers nor any members of the community could think of any reason why such segregation should take place.

I contacted the clerk of the school board, whom I had met as the chairman of the local YMCA board. He confirmed that such plans had been under discussion, and invited me and a committee of Negro residents to appear at the school board's next meeting. At a hastily called meeting of representatives of the Negro community, I apprised the group of the plans for segregating the Negro children from the white ones at the next school term and asked them whether this was their wish. It seemed that nobody had heard anything about such proposed action, nor was there any desire for a change. I asked the group to elect a committee and extended to all the invitation to attend the meeting. I became a member of the committee of three to act as spokesman for the Negro community.

Having learned from my YMCA experience the insidious methods of the local "power group" I deemed it necessary to organize well the presentation and representation. I visited the chairman of the Philadelphia branch of the National Association of Colored People, who was a practicing attorney. I urged Attorney Herbert Millen to be present as an individual. He suggested that Orrin C. Evans, City Editor of the *Philadelphia Tribune*, accompany him. I also telephoned Paul J. Furnas, Treasurer of Sandura Company Inc., my employer, then on a business trip in New York, and he assured me that he would be present at the school board's meeting. I deemed his possible testimony important, because he was the chairman of Woolman School, a Quaker institution near Westchester, PA. Dr. Don Young, Professor of Race Relations, University of Pennsylvania and Assistant Editor of the *Annals*, was unable to come, but attended a later meeting of the board.

At the school board's meeting held at the high school, there were about a dozen Negro families from the community, besides the invited guests facing the eight stern and uncomfortable-looking members of the board. There was also the nervous-appearing superintendent of the school system. The heavy-set clerk opened the session with a frank admission that the school board had decided to segregate the grade school along racial lines with the advent of the new term. The board had felt, he explained, that "the colored children would feel more at home in their own school with their own teachers." He divulged that the board had already interviewed a number of Negro applicants for the teaching positions and that they had selected candidates with outstanding qualifications.

Attorney Herbert Millen then pointed out that racial segregation would be clearly against the law, and he cited the judgment of a New Jersey Court in a similar case at Toms River. He also gave expression to the belief that the proposed action was unwelcome by the residents of the community. The suggested change would confine Negro children to the oldest and antiquated school building in town which he estimated to be about fifty years old. The clerk of the board interrupted here to say that the school building was seventy-five years old and "as good as on the day it was built." Orrin C. Evans spoke eloquently about the experiences of his family. His wife was a teacher and his mother and his sister were in the same profession. He stressed that all of them were unhappy about conditions in the segregated Philadelphia school system and about the philosophy engendered by segregation. My director, Paul J. Furnas, described the international atmosphere of Woolman School, with its students and faculty of many races and from many lands. In my brief remarks I emphasized the importance of building a community jointly without separation or divisions.

The clerk acting as the chairman then invited members of the board to speak. A young member, wishing to be kind and flattering, said that he had never heard thoughts expressed so clearly and in such excellent English. Attorney Millen turned to me and whispered: "What does he think we are going to law school for?" The contributions made by other board members were equally innocuous.

The clerk turned to the assembled, black residents of Paulsboro and asked for their comments. The elected spokesmen were brief and to the point. A stout, middle-aged Negro woman was nudged by the visitors to speak. She got up slowly and hesitatingly and made, in a homespun fashion, a psychologically sound and persuasive appeal to the stony-faced board members. First she identified herself with the community and her place in it. Addressing herself to the young board member who had spoken, she reminded him of the many years she had worked for his parents and how harmonious their relationships had been. Then she mentioned a resident of the town and said: "She is white and she comes from way down south, Alabama." "However," she explained in her eloquent testimony, "when she comes to visit me, she does not stop outside the front door, but comes right up the backsteps to the kitchen where we enjoy a wonderful visit over a cup of coffee." "You know," she explained to a rapt audience, "too many of us, when we meet, stop at the look of the skin instead of getting to know one another from the inside out."

When we walked through the schoolyard at the conclusion of the meeting, somewhat occupied with our thoughts, I was asked to return to the board's meeting room. I was told by the clerk that the board had decided not to proceed with their plans. I thanked the board members for their consideration and relayed the news to the members of the community still waiting in the yard. There were smiles of satisfaction, but no jubilation.

About a week later the superintendent of Sandura Company said to me: "Harry, how come you are getting mixed up with those n-----s in town? You know, I have always treated you like a white man." I disregarded the last remark and the use of the term "n-----." It was the first time that I had heard him use it. However, I addressed myself to the subject matter discussed at the board meeting, concluding with the comment that I was glad that agreement and a happy solution had been found by the school board. His rejoinder was: "Agreement? Hell! If it were not for the mixed schools we would have a better class of people living in this town." The revelation of his attitude and the inference that the school board's decision had not been in good faith were ominous.

Yet, it seemed to me that I had acted with honesty and caution, followed the suggestion of the clerk, truthfully expressed the wishes of a concerned segment of the community, and had brought to the board the knowledge of experts. The apparent result had been that we had won the opposition over to our point of view in an open debate, in as democratic a manner as it was possible. However, the facts are not always as they seem, especially in a situation charged with emotions in which cool reasoning is often brushed aside.

Three months later I was out of a job, a job which I had held for six years and three months. There was no reflection on my work, competence, or integrity. I was just notified that my services would no longer be needed. The date set for the severance of my connection with the company was August 4, 1930, at the onset of the worst depression the United States had ever experienced.

Reconstructing the events which had destroyed the basis of my livelihood, I pieced together the following: the plan to impose racial segregation upon the school system of Paulsboro was the brainchild of the superintendent of schools and some young aspiring politicians, for whom service on the school board was the first step on the political ladder. In their eyes they had suffered a political defeat. The Republican Party ran the town. Their organization always counted upon the Negro votes to be delivered as a bloc by one of their white members. My appearance on the scene seemed to threaten this comfortable arrangement. In their view, my prior activities in the YMCA and my subsequent involvement in the school affair stamped me as a person who did not know his subordinate place in the community. I was a new factor which disturbed the equilibrium of that local society. The town's influential people, "the power structure," used to meet once a week at the local Kiwanis Club's luncheon. It was there that the young, budding politicians of the school board "worked on" my director, whose wife had previously felt offended by my friend's declining her dinner invitation. My director's mind had seemingly been "softened" by the irritating arguments of his wife, who had always maintained that the position of an office manager and cost accountant was never meant to be occupied by a Negro. The biases aroused by past incidents thus seemed to converge in the school crisis. Conscious of the effort that I had poured into the many expressions of interracial goodwill, I had to accept and learn with great reluctance that

Halt Proposed Jim Crowing Of N. J. School Children

Plans to Inaugurate Separate School System in Paulsboro Are Nipped in the Bud

EDUCATION BOARD CHANGES PLANS

(By a Staff Correspondent)

Paulsboro, N. J., June—Plans for the segregation of Negro school children in the public school system here were nipped in the bud Tuesday night when a delegation led by Harry F. V. Edwards, one-time British Olympic sprint champion, filed protests against the contemplated dual school system which would consign Negro children from the first to sixth grades to an old separate building under the tutelage of two teachers, both of whom were to have been colored.

This delegation met the local Board of Education and pointed out to this body that school segregation is the keystone of more general, specific and dangerous segregation and discrimination.

"I, as a Negro who was born and raised in Europe," said Edwards, "cannot understand the peculiar prejudices based upon race and the color of a man's skin in this country. Oversea all are bending their efforts towards better international and interracial understanding and sympathy."

APPEALS TO FAIRNESS

Assurances of his belief in the fairness of the men constituting the Board of Education were given by Edwards as he appealed to them to reconsider their plans.

So impressive were the protests made by Attorney Herbert Millen, president of the Philadelphia branch of the National Association for the Advancement of Colored People, Walter Furniss, white, treasurer of a large linoleum concern, who had come here from New York to attend the meeting, and Orrin C. Evans, City Editor of the Philadelphia TRIBUNE, that the Board of Education reconsidered the proposition and informed the delegation that the school system would remain mixed.

"We felt that we were merely giving the colored people of Paulsboro what they wanted, and we were bettering their condition by placing them under colored teachers and to themselves so they could develop better," a member of the Board of Education stated during the conference.

The poorer educational facilities generally accorded the Negro school in a dual school system were emphasized by Attorney Millen. He also called attention to the illegality of the proposed denying entrance to colored children in public schools of New Jersey.

Over a dozen colored parents attended the meeting to state their position in the matter. All vehemently went on record as opposed to a separate school system.

———oOo———

Dies In Bathroom

Frank W. Cranshaw, 1625 Christian street, died yesterday (Wednesday) at nine o'clock, A. M. from the effects of a fall in the bathroom of his home.

Mr. Cranshaw was born January 1st, 1876 at Wake Forest, N. C., and had been a resident of Philadelphia for forty-five years. He was a member of the First African Presbyterian Church and of the Light House Lodge of Elks.

He is survived by his widow, Mrs. Minnie Cranshaw, one son, Theodore, and one daughter, Mrs. Mabel Patterson.

———oOo———

Philly Girl Honored

Hazel Virginia Clarke, young North Philadelphia student at Bluefield Institute, Bluefield, W. Va., was elected valedictorian of the 1930 class. The magna cum laudae student is a graduate of the Abington High School, Willow Grove, and is twenty-one years old.

June 5ᵗʰ 1930 — Phila Tribune

37. June 1930, Paulsboro, Pennsylvania. The *Philadelphia Tribune* reported on Harry Edward's successful campaign to halt public school segregation – a success that would ultimately cost him his job.

38. Harry and friends at a church training retreat in the Pennsylvania
countryside in the summer of 1930.

although the outward attitude of most whites may be friendly, it is
too often a charitable stance dripping with consciousness of a gulf
between. Crushed was my concept of the American society as a
fluid in which every individual might rise depending on his buoyant
capacities and services to society. I became very much aware of the
weights which a bigoted America had clamped upon the blacks,
thus preventing them from rising in the economic scale.

10

MARGINALLY EMPLOYED IN THE DEPRESSION

I was forced into the growing army of unemployed to seek and struggle for scarce jobs when a lot of Americans with jobs considered themselves examples of survival of the fittest. For several months I spent much time and effort in the organizing of a Morris Plan Bank. There was an obvious need for a small-loan bank in Philadelphia at a time when financial institutions disregarded the small wage earner and completely overlooked the black component. I had many conferences with the financially secure and even prosperous Negro doctors, lawyers, and undertakers, but failed to enroll their interest and participation. However, this was really a blessing, because the depression grew to truly titanic proportions, and unemployment cut particularly deeply into the black working class. My search in the labor market of Philadelphia uncovered no job openings in which a Negro, trained in office work, might find employment. I recalled that even when my employing company was moving its headquarters to Philadelphia, two years previously, I had been told that the position of manager of the factory office would be the highest obtainable job for me. I was informed then that I should not count on joining the headquarters' staff. A seemingly sympathetic member of that staff said to me at that time:

"Harry, you should be by now a vice president of the company. It's a pity you are colored!" Really, I could do nothing about that.

My dismissal from Sandura Company meant also the surrender of my lease of the commissary and the end of my wife's earnings derived from her management and work. We had to give up also the apartment on the company's property, which we had occupied for those many years. For a time we moved into the rented house of my stepson, married by then, a very crowded arrangement as we stored our furniture there, pending the finding of a new job and location for living.

I went to New York City in search of work. The signs of a creeping depression were as evident there as in the rest of the country plagued by bank failures, farmers' revolts, marches by veterans. However, there was a significant difference in the political climate of New York, as compared to that in Pennsylvania and New Jersey. New York State, under the leadership of Governor Franklin D. Roosevelt and his Commissioner Harry L. Hopkins supervising social services, created a number of temporary projects for the alleviation of hardships and possible solution of pressing social problems. In New York City, industrial and banking groups raised 10 million dollars for the relief of New York City's unemployed. There was an awareness of the serious social conditions and a determination among socially conscious groups to do something about it.

Friends directed me to the recruiting officer of one of the State's projects, where I was hired at the salary of $15 per week for the packing of food parcels. Soon, however, I was transferred to a project attached to the New York State Employment Service to interview and register the unemployed and to seek job openings for their skills. The director, Fritz Kaufmann, gave his personal attention to the training of about forty of us, special project employees. His enthusiasm and energy imbued the staff with a missionary spirit to go out and to serve the people in need. Although the project was of relatively short duration, I derived, nevertheless, great satisfaction from the spirit that animated the operation under the leadership of Frances Perkins as Industrial Commissioner of New York State.

My next job was with *The Crisis* magazine, the independent monthly under the editorship of Dr. W.E.B. Du Bois, affiliated with the National Association for the Advancement of Colored People, the NAACP. My functions were those of a bookkeeper and advertising manager. Those were days of struggle for survival for *The Crisis*, the NAACP and their employees. The association was then a relatively tender reed attempting to sink its roots deeper into the American soil. Its staff was toiling on legal and political fronts, attempting to bring social wrongs to public attention, while the association's management was struggling to meet monthly payrolls. Its executive secretary was at that time James Weldon Johnson, a brilliant writer, poet, and composer. Walter White, then assistant secretary, focused his strength and imagination on political strategies, after having increased his prestige enormously by his energetic actions leading to the defeat of Justice William Parker of North Carolina, President Hoover's nominee to the Supreme Court.

There was ferment in the air. Young poets, writers, and artists were emerging. Names like Langston Hughes, Countee Cullen, Dr. Bud Fisher joined those of the older generation of Dr. W.E.B. Du Bois, James Weldon Johnson, etc. On the labor front, the voices of Philip Randolph and Frank Crosswaith were heard. I, too, felt the urge of recording my brief, depressing experiences in the New York State Employment Service and wrote a one-act sketch called "Job Hunters." To my great surprise, Dr. Du Bois published it in *The Crisis*. Later it was produced in Chicago by a theatrical group, and the royalty of $10 was shared by *The Crisis* and me. Suddenly I was a playwright!

In this period of depression, human beings were concerned with the basic needs of food, shelter, and clothing. Reading and the pursuit of the arts were postponed until the concern for the basic needs was no longer paramount. *The Crisis* magazine, together with many other periodicals, had a difficult time in those days. There came the day when staff had to be cut, and a letter from Dr. Du Bois announced also my separation among others. The depression had taken on great dimensions by that time. The unemployment rate was about 27 percent; one out of every four employable was out of work. The parks on New York's Riverside Drive were then shanty towns, with makeshift shelters constructed from packing cases, tin cans, and cardboard. Unemployed men were selling apples at street corners to those lucky enough to have a job.

In such a social setting, my ten-year marriage went to pieces. My wife had come to New York City. The obtaining of an apartment was beset with difficulties. After she had selected some and I appeared upon the scene to finalize the contract, landlords claimed that there must have been some mistake, some misunderstanding. We found some accommodation in the peripheral areas of Harlem, with its overlapping ethnic composition. However, it was not the racial factor as such which accounted for our drifting apart, but the different rates of our growth and the loss of our prior relatively sheltered economic security. In periods of unemployment, the strains and stresses upon the affected individuals are very great indeed, but during the great depression they were enormous, especially when the evidence of dozens of evictions was before one's eyes daily in the streets of New York. The courts interpreted leases and rental contracts strictly by the written clauses. Human considerations and concepts of equity had not deeply penetrated the halls of justice. Such views and legal constructions were introduced later with the advent of the social legislation of the New Deal. The threat of having one's furniture put on the sidewalk in the case of delayed or non-payment of the monthly rent was real and nerve-shattering. My wife was courageous and practical in those hard times. She obtained a job as a maid to a famous designer of fashions, where she could make also a contribution drawn from her experiences in dressmaking. I sought contacts among new groups of acquaintances to find job possibilities and leads. Economic problems, disappointments, fatigue, and raw nerves contributed to the deterioration of our relationship. There is no doubt that I did not clearly perceive and understand her concealed loneliness, sensing only her jealousy of new acquaintances, new interests, and even of the time I devoted to books and studies.

In evaluating the early cruel days of the depression one must bear in mind that there existed no unemployment insurance, no system of social welfare, no relief supplies for the needy. I remember that the only place in Harlem to which hungry and needy persons could turn to obtain food and clothing was the Salvation Army. At a public meeting called by social-minded businessmen and philanthropists at Town Hall under the chairmanship of Lee de Forest, the leaders of the Whitney and Prosser Committees, who had raised private funds for the alleviation of hardships, declared that relief was beyond private effort. They called upon the Federal Government to take over the burden. By and large the Hoover Government resisted such appeals, repeating to the end that relief of social conditions was a local responsibility.

In the face of the desperate situation around me, I reasoned that people have to eat to sustain life, hence deduced that the food industry should be the most stable one offering some employment. Therefore, I canvassed the chain stores of food distributors. The Atlantic and Pacific Tea Company and the James Butler Stores listened, but were not interested in my services. Their staff consisted almost entirely of native Irishmen. The personnel officers of Daniel Reeves and Sheffield Farms took my application under consideration, and eventually Sheffield Farms Company offered me the job of a store manager, provided I could successfully pass the training period.

For seven weeks I worked as a clerk and trainee in a Sheffield Farms Company store in New York's Hell's Kitchen. The Irish manager had me clean up the basement and the storage space, made me deliver bags of sugar to apartments hiding hootch-distilleries. I weighed hundreds of one-pound bags of rice, beans, sugar, etc., served customers and was thus "trained" to be a manager. I was assigned to a store on Harlem's Eighth Avenue, a money-losing store about to be closed. I became the second Negro manager of chain stores in New York City; the first one was Mr. Roach of Sheffield Farms Company in the Dunbar Cooperative Apartments, Harlem. I worked very hard from 7 a.m. to 7 p.m. daily and Saturdays to 11 p.m. I spoke at parent–teacher associations and church clubs in the evenings, urging the ladies to buy their groceries at my store. Sales climbed, red-ink losses turned into black-ink profits. I was transferred to a larger branch store on Eighth Avenue, a store which had declined in sales. During the next twelve hard-working months I was unable to increase substantially the store's turnover. Suddenly I was checked out from that store and asked to take over another money-losing branch store, on Lenox Avenue, scheduled to be closed. The company's use of my strength and efforts to pull their stores out of the red was galling to me. Under that policy I was deprived from enjoying the benefits of my efforts in building goodwill and sales, with a percentage calculated on the weekly turnover. However, what embittered me most was their referring back to the store which I had to leave the previous Jewish manager, who had failed to make a go of a new Broadway store, where he had incurred a serious stock shortage. It was said that he had been sent back because he knew how to make up shortages from Negro customers. I began to loathe the ruthlessness and impersonality of the chain store system.

The year before, I had been asked to join the company union, but I declined, being told, besides, that it was not obligatory. When the period of summer vacations came around, I was informed by the supervisor that I was not entitled to a vacation, because such time off was the result of a contractual arrangement between the company and the company union; hence I was not included. Politely I asked the supervisor's permission to check with the offices of the National Recovery Administration. Within three days the

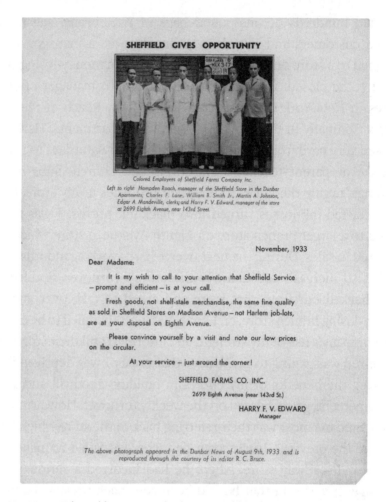

SHEFFIELD GIVES OPPORTUNITY

Colored Employees of Sheffield Farms Company Inc.
Left to right: Hampden Roach, manager of the Sheffield Store in the Dunbar
Apartments; Charles F. Lane, William B. Smith Jr., Martin A. Johnson,
Edgar A. Mandeville, clerks; and Harry F. V. Edward, manager of the store
at 2699 Eighth Avenue, near 143rd Street.

November, 1933

Dear Madame:

It is my wish to call to your attention that Sheffield Service
– prompt and efficient – is at your call.

Fresh goods, not shelf-stale merchandise, the same fine quality
as sold in Sheffield Stores on Madison Avenue – not Harlem job-lots,
are at your disposal on Eighth Avenue.

Please convince yourself by a visit and note our low prices
on the circular.

At your service – just around the corner!

SHEFFIELD FARMS CO. INC.

2699 Eighth Avenue (near 143rd St.)

HARRY F. V. EDWARD
Manager

The above photograph appeared in the Dunbar News of August 9th, 1933 and is
reproduced through the courtesy of its editor R. C. Bruce.

39. Harry Edward became only the second black chain-store manager in New York when he took over the Eighth Avenue Sheffield Farms store in Harlem. Twelve-hour days and strong customer service turned the store from loss making into profit making – a success that got Harry repeatedly transferred to other loss-making stores to try and repeat the trick.

supervisor told me that my proposed action was not necessary, because vacation time had been granted me by the company and that I could select the period. In a labor market in which thousands of unemployed were clamoring for jobs, the squeeze on the employed by unscrupulous management was enormous. In this climate the

Roosevelt Administration's National Industrial Recovery Act introduced and established the working man's civil right to organize in unions of his own choosing. President Franklin D. Roosevelt was thus able to establish a political counterweight to the previously unbridled political power of "business," the organized, political expressions of industry and commerce.

As indicated, I was thoroughly disillusioned with the chain store's disregard of the human factor in its operation. Their administrative frame provided no hope for advancement and seemingly no reward for imaginative effort, especially by black workers, who were viewed as marginal and expendable. I declined the proffered management of the Lenox Avenue store and resigned, as no other work opportunity was offered me in the organization. After two years of often exhausting work in the food retail trade, I was again unemployed. However, I was known in a small geographic area of Harlem as a hard-working store manager. I tried to build an organization on this frail foundation. In cooperation with the Dunbar Apartments Housewives' League I organized a consumers' cooperative, Harlem's Own Cooperative Inc., for the distribution of milk, a milk route concentrated in the cooperative Dunbar Apartments and the adjacent Harlem River Houses, a federally financed public housing project.

For the next four years I felt committed to get up daily at about 4 a.m. to supervise and assist in the distribution of milk to cooperators and customers, summer and winter, rain, snow or shine, seven days a week. My compensation for the three to four hours of work each morning was $5 per week on an average. At dozens of meetings I preached consumers' cooperation and its advantages. I had visited the cooperative store owned and operated by the Amalgamated Clothing Workers and had dreamed that Harlem consumers might do likewise. I was well acquainted with the history and growth of the cooperative movement in Europe and especially in the Scandinavian countries. However, I also realized the difference in the cultural background. In the class-conscious stratification of Europe, people did not often aspire to levels beyond their class and were more patient and disciplined to effect small savings as consumers. In contrast, the average Harlem consumer was impatient and eternally optimistic to "hit the numbers" some day, or by some miracle or good luck get rich and drive a Cadillac.

In organizing the cooperative and conducting its prosaic, routine business, I had the encouragement and valued, moral support of the Reverend Dr. William Lloyd Imes, a courageous and inspiring churchman and Harlem leader in the days of the depression. He was the president of our small cooperative. On occasions he could be found on picket lines, protesting the non-hiring of blacks as store clerks, bus drivers, streetcar conductors. In the movement registering objection to Fascist Italy's invasion of Ethiopia and the veritable slaughter of defenseless tribesmen, Dr. Imes led New York City's protest march as Grand Marshal. Let not the youth of the 1970s think that older generations of American blacks lacked courage, persistence, and love of liberty. Thorn-bestrewn was the Negro's rocky road in the post-Reconstruction era. Generations of today's parents and grandparents were involved in two world wars, faced a devastating economic depression, and racial discrimination and violence far more vicious than in the seventh and eighth decades of the twentieth century. The statistics of lynchings of a twenty-year period at the turn of the century, compared with a more recent, similar period, give a cold, grisly reflection and measure.

Lynchings of Negroes by five-year period

1889–1893	579 men and women
1894–1898	544
1899–1903	455
1904–1908	354
Twenty-year total:	**1,932**

1939–1943	23
1944–1948	14
1949–1953	2
1954–1958	1
Twenty-year total:	**40**

Out of the depth of the great depression of the 1930s there arose a patchwork of federally sponsored work projects that salvaged the souls of men and women, black and white, as well as their health and bodies. The Works Progress Administration (WPA) gave hope to people, it gave a chance to thousands to preserve their skills; above all, it preserved some measure of human dignity. WPA projects were required to meet some public demand without competing with existing private industry. Their main object was to reduce unemployment. Today we have in New York, as monuments to the imaginative leadership of those days, thousands of play-grounds, thousands of miles of parkways, thousands of acres in public parklands and beaches, La Guardia airport, Triborough Bridge, Jones Beach, and other public improvements too numerous to mention.

11

THE NEGRO THEATRE

Road to Self-Respect

I was asked to submit my application to the WPA Theatre Project then being set up. Hiring of personnel was an urgent problem at that time, and with my administrative background I became at first personnel director and later administrative director of the Negro Theatre. These activities opened up a little-paying but most exciting chapter of my life.

When Uncle Sam undertook to cure the depression by putting people to work, it was assumed by many that the jobs must be of that penitential nature usually considered suitable for persons in economic distress. Let them saw wood, dig ditches, or shovel snow! Yet, New York had no wood to saw nor were there many people accustomed to that task. We had, however, a great number of actors, musicians, writers, artists, stagehands, and other skilled workers without employment. Many theatre houses were dark and deteriorating. Most people hated to think about the unemployed. They wanted to forget them. They disliked even more to think of the black unemployed and any social responsibility toward them. Later the opponents of the New Deal whipped up these prejudices into a political frenzy with charges of "boon-doggling" and WPA waste.

40. John Houseman (right) with Orson Welles during a rehearsal for the Federal Theatre Project in 1936.

In this milieu and atmosphere we had to prove ourselves. We had to try to involve the mass of unemployed theatrical people in meaningful and creditable productions. The Negro Theatre was, from its beginning, an integrated venture, having on its roster John Houseman, producer and director; Orson Welles, director and actor; Virgil Thompson, composer; Abe Feder, lighting designer; Nat Karson, stage designer; Augustus Smith, playwright and director; Hubie Blake, musician. There were many Negro actors and actresses with impressive backgrounds. Out of the large staff there emerged a choral group under the direction of Leonard De Paur, an orchestra affiliated with the WPA Music Project under Joe Jordan, and actors working under various directors with their stage managers.

On February 4, 1936, there appeared the first play *Walk Together, Chillun* by Frank Wilson, followed four weeks later by *The Conjure-Man Dies*, a mystery play written by a Harlem physician, Dr. Rudolph Bud Fisher. On April 14, 1936, there opened with much fanfare Shakespeare's *Macbeth* with a Negro cast and the scene laid in Haiti, directed by Orson Welles. This was followed by *Turpentine* by Augustus Smith; *Noah* by André Obey; *Bassa Moona*, an African dance pantomime by Norman Coker and Momodu Johnson; *Sweet Land*, a drama by Conrad Seiler; *The Show Off*, a revived comedy by George Kelly; *Haiti*, a historical play by William Du Bois. There

41, 42 & 43. A show dubbed 'Voodoo Macbeth': a twenty-year-old Orson Welles switched the action of the Shakespeare play from Scotland to Haiti and recruited an all-Black cast. The production became a box-office sensation when it opened on 14 April 1936 at Harlem's Lafayette Theatre, and sold out for ten weeks. On opening night the show stopped traffic for five blocks in every direction.

were many more plays produced for performance on the movable stage designed for public parks.

While most of my energies were focused on the work in the Negro Theatre, I was also aware of the work of my co-workers in productions exhibited at other New York theatres. The Living Newspaper [a dramatic interpretation of current events] produced the exciting and controversial *Triple-A Plowed Under*, 1935, *Injunction Granted*, *Power*. There were the successful *Murder in the Cathedral*, *Class of '29*, *It Can't Happen Here*, *Chalk Dust*, *Dr. Faustus*, among others. It was an exciting and creative period.

The depression had drawn many professionals, black and white, closer together. There were organizations, called unions, of the rank and file, and organizations, called councils, of the supervisors. In that period, Communist penetration of unions and of all kinds of groups and associations was widespread. The arts projects, too, had among their workers many who followed the Communist line. I observed this specially after being elected to the committee of the Theatre Supervisors' Council. I became the council's secretary, in which capacity I wrote the minutes and handled the correspondence. This work gave me contact with the supervisors' councils of the Arts, Music, and Writers' Projects with whom we affiliated into a Federation of Supervisors' Councils, which in turn became the nucleus of an enlarged federation joined in by organized lawyers, dentists, etc. Somehow, I was chosen secretary of New York's Federation of Supervisors' Councils. In this manner I became involved in many political activities of those days. We organized trips to Washington, where we lobbied for and against legislation under consideration. We were interested in the continuation of the WPA with increased funds and expanded activities, as well as in all aspects of social legislation assuring greater economic security for the nation's citizens. There were also valid grievances about racial and religious discrimination.

In my position as secretary of the Federation of Supervisors' Councils I was called upon to document and register a particularly overt case of racial discrimination. The WPA of New York City was under the directorship of Colonel Brehon B. Somervell, a career officer and administrative expert. He had sent his field worker and protege Captain Grower to inspect the administration of the Federal Theatre Project. When reviewing administrative charts and meeting some of the incumbents he frowned upon a Negro's holding a supervisory position and said: "I don't want a Negro as supervisor. I don't take orders from a Negro and don't expect any white man to take orders from a Negro!" This was undoubtedly the spirit in the segregated army of the United States at that time, but did not reflect the cooperative spirit of the Federal Arts Projects of New York City. It fell upon me to obtain sworn statements from the witnesses, to prepare a summary setting forth the facts, and to submit the matter to Colonel Somervell. The colonel refused to see our committee and we were obliged to leave the written statement with an assistant. We learned later that the colonel declined to censure Captain Grower, in whom he expressed "complete confidence."

At a meeting of supervisors' councils it was decided to convey our grievance directly to the President of the United States. Legal minds and members of the Writers' Project drafted the document, which I handed to Western Union for transmittal to the White House. The response was not long in coming. The witnesses and I were approached by telephone or in person by representatives of the Federal Bureau of Investigation and questioned on the facts of the incident. Some of the witnesses felt annoyed and embarrassed by the pressure brought upon them and by the frequent quizzing by FBI agents. Those witnesses declared later that they would never again give testimony. However, the facts stood up unshaken. Suddenly a meeting was called by the Arts, Music, Writers', and Theatre Projects and the announcement was made that those projects were to be administered as a separate group. They were severed from projects under the supervision of Colonel Somervell, seemingly a mild rebuke from the White House. Captain Grower was quietly transferred to active army duty.

The Federal Theatre Project scored impressive, artistic successes during the three years since its birth. Leaders in the theatrical profession believed the time opportune to launch a national theatre sponsored by the Federal Government or theatrical units under-written by state or municipal governments. Such a system had been in existence in European countries for more than a century. It was the belief that the proven, successful features of the Federal Theatre might be absorbed into a new structure and become the nucleus of such a project. Delegates from supervisors' councils and from established unions, such as Actors' Equity, met under the chair-manship of Burgess Meredith, the actor and director, to explore possibilities, while approaches were being made in Congress. The response there was cool and unenthusiastic; noted was a certain condescension toward the WPA projects and their workers. The President had compared war on depression to war on the battle front. Yet, war on depression was not stylish. WPA workers were not heroes going to die for us, or even to kill for us. This was a war to keep people alive, and as such it was unpopular. Congressional disinterest and apathy permitted the arts projects to wither away. Yet, looking back over the last three decades we see that many of today's well-known American painters were working artists on WPA rolls during the depression. The birth and growth of musical groups and organizations throughout the country also dates from that period, while the Writers' Project was instrumental in uncov-ering a wealth of American folklore and documenting the many peculiarities of American speech and customs.

The Federal Theatre Project can claim to its credit the revival of road shows to places where theatres had previously been closed. The study of drama took on new life in schools and colleges. Above all, the Theatre Project laid a solid foundation for the subsequent healthy growth of the American dance and ballet. In pre-depression days famous producers and directors like Earl Carroll, Florenz Ziegfeld and the Shubert brothers gave glamor to their shows by having statuesque beauties prance up and down glittering stages. Today no musical on the stage, screen or television is considered complete without skillfully choreographed dance numbers. It can be seen that the depression had caused America to look inwardly to discover its hidden strength.

With the upturn of the country's economic activities following the government's pump-priming, some courage and faith had entered the spirit of theatrical people. The white members of the Negro Theatre's integrated staff found or created opportunities in New York's theatrical life. Houseman and Welles started the Mercury Theatre, Virgil Thompson became music critic on the *New York Herald Tribune*, Nat Karson was signed up by Radio City Music Hall as stage designer, Abe Feder was engaged by theatrical producers and department stores to design electrical lighting for shows and exhibits.

The black staff found fewer opportunities for their talents. Integrated casts were barred and ostracized south of the Mason–Dixon line. Washington's only legitimate stage, the National Theatre, yielded to integration only after a long boycott by Actors' Equity. Mixed choral or other musical groups, although unseen on the radio, were not contracted for transmission over Southern stations. The South regarded blacks only as performers of menial tasks or as the king's jester with the white man as the king. For the Negroes' theatrical talents, black vaudeville shows provided the only outlet.

In confirmation and elaboration I will relate the heart of a speech given by DuBose Heyward, author of the stage play *Porgy*, to a Quaker group in Philadelphia at the end of the show's run. DuBose Heyward, as a reporter, had written the newspaper story of crippled Porgy's brush with the Charleston, SC, police. The expanded story formed the basis for the stage play he created in collaboration with his wife Dorothy. After completing the play they canvassed for a producer. They found no interest on Broadway for a drama about life on Catfish Row at Charleston, a play to be acted mostly by Negroes. "We insisted," he said, "that all Negro parts were to be played by Negroes." This was somewhat revolutionary, even for Broadway at a time when Otis Skinner was playing the title role in *Uncle Tom's Cabin* in black-face. It happened that the Theatre Guild, the highly regarded producing group, had a rule to sponsor one original American play after promoting three or four revivals or established money makers. DuBose and Dorothy Heyward submitted their script and the directors of the Theatre Guild accepted it with doubting hearts. Before the authors was the enormous task of finding a sympathetic and skilled director and of gathering together a cast of actors with a reasonable amount of experience. "We had to look abroad for a director untouched by the racial bigotry of America," DuBose Heyward said in substance. "We found him in Rouben Mamoulian, a Russian-born Armenian, of Israeli [sic] parents." "Together we began to look for actors in vaudeville houses, cabarets, and 'honkytonkies.' When we told them the story of Porgy on Catfish Row their puckered brows reflected the doubts they entertained about this white man's story and his plans." The author confessed that it took months of travel and untiring effort to convince candidates of their sincerity and to assemble a cast courageous enough to share the risks of an uncertain length of employment on Broadway.

Eventually the cast was completed and rehearsals began. Something interesting evolved during the rehearsal periods, namely an enthusiastic participation by the actors in the shaping of the script, as they recalled incidents from Charleston. "Do you remember the strawberry man?" somebody asked. There followed the imitation of the chant of the strawberry man selling his wares, which was promptly included in the scene, together with other vignettes. According to DuBose Heyward, the dress rehearsal was coldly received by the directors of the Theatre Guild, who suggested some script changes. Opening night brought condescending reviews by New York's critics, and the playwrights decided to labor on the proposed changes. When they returned to the theatre on a Saturday afternoon to arrange for a rehearsal schedule for the changes, they saw a crowd gathered in front of the theatre. DuBose inquired and Dorothy explained that it was a waiting line. The play had captured the interest, curiosity, and imagination of New York's theatre-going public. The enthusiasm of the cast had extended across the footlights to the audience, and the larger the attendance the warmer became the response. This condition was absent in the empty theatre at the dress rehearsal. On that Saturday, DuBose and Dorothy Heyward enjoyed the show together with the audience, went home, and tore up the script changes.

This story, as it was told by the author, reflects the struggles and efforts of pioneers, who believed that the stage should mirror also the life of the darker segment of America's population. *Porgy* and its musical version *Porgy and Bess*, by George and Ira Gershwin, became milestones in the liberation of the American stage. In the period between these plays, the WPA Negro Theatre performed a useful function not only in revealing the wealth of talent, but also in building and preserving for a time a reservoir of theatrical expertise. Some black actors of the Negro Theatre went forth to make a name for themselves: Rex Ingram, Canada Lee, Alvin Childress, Dooley Wilson, Edna Thomas, "Butterfly" McQueen. Perry Watkins continued on Broadway and on television in his chosen profession of stage designer. Carlton Moss pursued his writing in Hollywood. The stagehands were herded into segregated locals of the American Federation of Labor and restricted to work in circumscribed areas. The story of racial barriers erected and maintained by the craft unions of American Labor has been and remains a sad and depressing tale of violations of basic human rights.

In my work in the Federal Theatre I saw much talent unused and frustrated, causing me to speculate where and how outlets might be developed. At that time a friend of my fiancée and wife-to-be

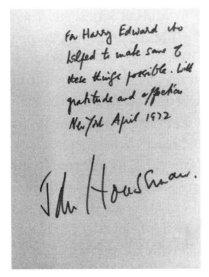

44. More than thirty-five years after the landmark production of *Macbeth* in Harlem, and despite the rather grudging praise in his autobiography, producer John Houseman sent Harry Edward a copy of his book and inscribed this personal tribute to Harry's role in the Negro Theatre Project.
The inscription reads: For Harry Edward who helped to make some of these things possible. With gratitude and affection, New York April 1972

came to me and proposed our handling the management of the American tour of a famous Netherland pianist, his teacher. Our friend had been instrumental in obtaining a number of engagements for the artist and believed that a concentrated effort in promotion on our part might bring good results. As activities in the Federal Theatre began to decline, my New Orleans-born wife and I, having become married, pinned great hopes on the development of a concert agency, registered under the name of Musical Artists' Bureau, nominally managed by my wife Gladys Hirst Edward. In this kind of business a tremendous in-out of time, effort, and money is required without any return for almost a year. Contracts for the services of artists are usually procured and signed between October and April. Services will be rendered and paid for in the concert season beginning the following September. Therefore, while still working in the theatre I hoped to build a business the following year.

We were successful in obtaining contracts with renowned orchestras and concert series for our European artist [Dutch pianist Egon Petri], namely with the Chicago Symphony, the Cleveland

Orchestra, New Friends of Music, the Town Hall Series, etc. Then suddenly the war clouds of World War II burst, drenching Europe in blood while our artist was still in Poland. There was an exchange of cables, one stating that he was awaiting passage with his wife in Rotterdam. There was the question whether he would succeed in reaching New York in time for the contracted engagements. It happened that he obtained passage and reached these shores with a narrow margin of time to fulfill his contracts. As war conditions prevented his return to Europe, the responsibility devolved upon us, as managers, to obtain additional engagements so late in the season. However, we were quite successful, helped by the highly favorable comments by critics everywhere on the performances of this pianist. Olin Downes, first-line critic of *The New York Times*, referred other artists to us and a number of Negro artists signed up. Yet, it proved to be a most difficult task to sell Negro talent to concert promoters and, furthermore, I found it impossible to break into the monopolies of NBC's Civic Series and CBS's Community Series of concerts, the focuses of a later anti-trust action. Racial prejudice again raised its ugly head and destroyed in part this venture in concert management. The head of a university's music department persuaded our Netherland artist to sever his relations with us, stating that his image was adversely affected by Negro management and that the agency of Chicago's ultra-conservative Colonel Patterson could do more for him. This prediction was not fulfilled. I felt very badly about the reason given for his leaving at a time when we were fighting Nazism with its racial master-race theories.

12

ENFORCING EQUALITY

Rationing and Price Control

World War II, in which we became totally involved, caused our government to take stern measures in rationing and price control on the home front. The shift from a peace-time to a war-time economy caused a rearrangement of priorities, an emphasis on war-related activities. I applied to the Office of Price Administration, the OPA, and was selected to head the uptown office of the War Price and Rationing Boards, having jurisdiction over one-third of Manhattan, namely from 110th Street, at Central Park, to Spuyten Duyvil, some 7 miles north in The Bronx. This appointment opened up an exciting, hardworking chapter of my life's activities, involving hundreds of hours of unpaid overtime in support of the war effort. It was an organizing effort of large proportions, comprising the selection and training of a staff, studying the many rationing rules and regulations in depth, and advising volunteer board members and Red Cross volunteers on their assignments. The work kept me in daily contact with the public, especially the irately objecting section of it.

Looking back, I must acknowledge that New York's rationing organization was admirably conceived and, I believe, well administered. Rationing is a painful process, in which the government limits or disallows the consumption of certain goods by its citizens.

An applicant for a rationing document was courteously received by Red Cross volunteers upon entering the OPA office. These uniformed, poised ladies, drawn mostly from the upper middle class, gave a certain dignity and decorum to the offices, and by their friendly assistance calmed tense nerves. After filling in the required forms, the applying citizen was conducted to the three-man rationing board, who were volunteers giving ten hours per week to the war effort – a jury of his peers. They would listen to and evaluate any hardship cases in rationing. The civil service "bureaucrats" were in the back office handling the paper work, or were called upon occasionally in the solving of perplexing and difficult cases.

Gasoline rationing, particularly in its early phases, was a most difficult matter, especially when forceful salesmen objected vociferously to the alleged curtailment of their work because the reduced ration would limit visits to their territories. Physicians and clergymen felt offended that anybody could possibly question their right to unlimited rations. The subsequent establishing of a board of retired, blue-ribboned surgeons and physicians proved to be an excellent method of rationing equitably the varying needs of the medical profession. Resident doctors of hospitals were directed by their peers to use the subways, while family physicians and gynecologists were generously treated in their rationing allowances.

Later I was transferred to the Midtown Office in the General Motors Building, regarded as OPA's Central Office of New York County. The task assigned to me was the organization and supervision of Fuel Oil Rationing, an exciting project whose national program was described in later years as the best and most successful of all rationing systems. The elements which made it a success were, according to my observations, firstly the composition of its policy-setting and directing personnel drawn from many areas, i.e. the oil industry, university faculties, the civil service; secondly the free flow of information up and down the line; thirdly visits by the Washington staff to field offices to inspect operations and innovative procedures; fourthly an open and flexible mind in top-level management which was quick in formulating amendments to the regulations for the avoidance of hardships. It was hard work; it was fun.

I acquired a high regard for the basic honesty of the oil and kerosene consuming public of New York County. There was practically no chiseling or fraud. Subsequently I gave six months' service to the inauguration of federal rent control under the inspiring direction of Louis H. Pink, administrator. Here again we stressed compliance and not prosecution. Let it be recorded that in the temporary war-time structure of the Office of Price Administration I found little racial bias among the staff or in dealings with the public.

In the year 1945 the war was visibly coming to an end. In 1943, President Franklin D. Roosevelt, in collaboration with forty-three other nations, had set up an international organization, the United Nations Relief and Rehabilitation Administration, UNRRA, to grapple with anticipated post-war problems, namely missing and displaced persons, shortages of food and medicine, rehabilitation of agriculture, shelters, industries, means of transportation, etc., a tremendous task hopefully to be accomplished under the auspices of the United Nations, then in the process of formulation. Word had gone out to all governments which had opposed the Nazi-Fascist axis and its allies to meet in San Francisco for the drafting of a charter for the United Nations. Hope for the building of a better world was in the air, and I felt a strong urge to have a share in that task. I reasoned that I knew what it meant to be a prisoner of war, hence had an empathy with the millions enslaved by the Nazis. I believed that I understood some of the manifold fears and actions of those embracing the master-race ideology. I was able to converse in French and German. I had administrative experience, especially in the field of rationing; thus I submitted my application to UNRRA, the United Nations Relief and Rehabilitation Administration, under the leadership of the highly esteemed ex-governor of New York

State, Herbert H. Lehman. This step was taken after some discussion with my wife, with much consideration given to the growth and future of our son, then seven years old. There was also the thought that I might be sent to Germany, where I might be able to trace my sister with her husband and son, with whom I had lost all contact during the war years. However, overshadowing all was the hope that I might work in an international atmosphere of freedom, without the encroachment of racial prejudices resulting in discriminatory working conditions.

13

JOINING THE UNITED NATIONS
AND REVISITING ENGLAND

In May 1945 I had to report in Washington DC for interviews and physical check-up, then followed security clearance and a battery of injections and outfitting in army uniforms with special UNRRA insignias. We were housed in dormitories of the University of Maryland at College Park, just outside of Washington, DC. It came to me as a shock that my first contact with UNRRA in Washington should reveal an example of racial prejudice. In the assigning of rooms by an American lady, a former clerk on a senator's staff, keys were handed out in quick succession on the basis of first come, first served. However, I was asked to return my key and requested to step aside. After some file search I was handed another key. In the evening my room-mate showed up, a graduate of Howard University, an assistant professor at Shaw University, the Negro institution at Raleigh, NC. The next morning I discussed my impression and suspicions with members of the office staff and received sufficient confirmation to cause my taking it up with a member of the faculty, a Swedish diplomat and former delegate to the League of Nations. He told me the following day not to take the matter any farther nor to discuss it with any other faculty or staff member or with students, assuring me that he had adjusted the rules and penalties around the violation of ethical standards. My observations confirmed the truth of his assertions.

Induction into UNRRA service and the introduction into its training schedule was a routine affair by June 1945, when I was a member of Class 51. Classes were set up from Mondays through Saturdays from 8.45 a.m. to 5 p.m., three sessions in the forenoon and three in the afternoon. On several evenings there were special classes, lectures, or films from 6.30 to 8 p.m. Most foreign-language classes began at 8 in the morning. The topics covered a broad spectrum: review of UNRRA organization, liaison functions with inter-Allied occupation authorities and military security, capsuled history of the League of Nations, Germany, Greek relief, and relief work of MERA, the Middle East Relief Administration. There were lectures and discussions on work in assembly centers [for displaced persons], on the composition of their people and their needs, self-management, mass-feeding, housing problems, sanitation and hygiene, medical care, welfare, child care, use of and liaison with voluntary agencies in Germany.

Some faculty members had been with the League of Nations, others had come from American colleges or from the staff of the US Department of State; a few came from the Mediterranean area where they had supervised large assembly centers. The student body hailed from all parts of the United States, Canada, Central and South America. Many citizens of the United States and Canada had been born in Europe, several were bi- and tri-lingual, some had prior experience in international work. Washington was UNRRA's recruiting and training center for the western hemisphere.

One day, eighteen Cuban physicians arrived in a group at College Park. They were all dashing, vibrant Latins in the Valentino tradition, carrying with them guitars and bongo drums. The place "jumped" and our girl students were fascinated and attracted. The next day a sign appeared on the bulletin board: "Another group of Latin doctors is expected. Will all interested girls please record their names underneath."

There were a few evenings of lighthearted fun, but the prevailing mood throughout among the student body was of great eagerness to digest the study material and to get on the way at the end of the three weeks' training period. This UNRRA song to the tune of "Old Black Joe" reflects their impatience:

Gone are the days when we came to College Park.
Gone are the days when we thought this all a lark.
Gone are our friends – they've been leaving one by one.
We hear the gentle voices calling "Come, come, come."
We're coming! We're coming!
If they only let us go.
We hear the State Department saying:
"No, no, no!"

There came, of course, the day when "yes" was the answer to "the gentle voices calling" and UNRRA workers proceeded to Europe by ship and plane.

I was assigned passage to England on a British flying boat, on one of the last transatlantic crossings of such amphibious craft having a cruising speed of about 150 miles per hour, accommodating eighteen passengers and a crew of six. We had Pullman berths for the two nights spent aboard. Leaving the waters off Sparrows Point, Baltimore, Maryland, at midnight, we flew with all curtains drawn through the night, to descend in the morning on an inland lake at Botwood, Newfoundland. After refueling, we took off at about noon and twenty-four hours later came down on the surface of sheltered waters at Poole, England.

The passengers on the plane were almost exclusively top-level civil service personnel of Great Britain's Foreign Office, Admiralty, War Department, and Board of Trade who had assisted the political appointees in the drafting of the United Nations Charter and its many clauses at San Francisco. I was curious to learn what had transpired in the various committees of experts or at the plenary sessions there, and posed what I thought were intelligent, well-phrased questions. "Well," I was told, "you should ask this gentleman, over there," only to be told by that person that another was the expert. I realized soon that I was being bounced around like a toy ball in a game enjoyed by those tight-lipped, aloof Englishmen. During the three daily meals set up in those confined quarters on the plane, I seemed to fail completely to penetrate the armor-plated British reserve.

After disembarkation at Poole, all passengers had to pass through British Security. The supervising officer of that service looked at my American passport then bestowed a long look upon me, ending in the query: "Aren't you Harry Edward of the Poly Harriers, the former British Champion?" "Yes," I admitted, adding, "you certainly merit the supervisory position in the Intelligence Service. Do you realize that twenty-two years have gone by since my active days on the track?" I could almost hear the wiggling of my fellow passengers' ears. Those gentlemen plied me with questions on the short bus ride to Southampton. By the time we boarded the train to London, the conversation was warm and uninhibited. I had made the grade. I had been accepted.

Not having seen England for more than two decades, my eyes roamed over the small compartment of the British train, over the signs posted there, as well as over billboards in the station. It seemed that I saw everywhere in large letters "Spiller's Shapes," nothing else added. I pondered what it might mean. Eventually I asked one of my fellow passengers of the transatlantic trip: "Those Spiller's Shapes, are those foundation garments?" A ripple of laughter greeted that question. I was informed that Spiller's Shapes was a dog biscuit. "Spiller" was the manufacturer and "Shapes" denoted the bone-shaped product. How was I to know?

After checking in at the London headquarters of UNRRA in compliance with my travel orders and getting a referral to a small hotel, I betook myself to the Polytechnic Institute where I had spent so many hours in studies and many more in the gymnasium and in the Poly Harriers club room. After a lapse of twenty-two years the place still looked the same. There was my name on the roster of club champions, on the list of life members, and also inscribed in granite at the entrance of the school, a silent welcome creating a feeling of belonging. I identified myself to new members present, who sent out the news of my visit to the older group, my contemporaries. Many of them attended the next committee meeting, to which I was invited and where I gave a brief, informal speech with a few reminiscences and a description of my United Nations assignment. On the following day I visited an old club member who was indisposed. After greeting me, he called his wife and said: "Mary, listen to 'arry, 'e talks like a bloody Yank."

Differences in speech were even more pronounced at UNRRA's London headquarters, where the UNRRA staff of the Americas met the British staff and some recruited in Western European countries. There were undoubtedly many instances when the forthright and deliberate manner and twangy speech of the American western plains grated the nerves of Englishmen and women trained and accustomed to regard the slurred Oxford accent as the universal standard of the English language. However, the real integration of the many nationalities into smooth-functioning international teams was to come a few weeks later in UNRRA's staging camp and training center at Granville-Jullouville, in Normandy, France. In the meantime there was much to be done and seen by newly arrived UNRRA workers in London. War-time emergency laws required prompt registration and the obtaining of temporary ration-books. I reasoned that my daily money allowance for a hotel room might well be spent in the more congenial atmosphere of a Poly member's home, hence I inquired regarding such accommodation. I found room and board with a former athlete, who also appreciated the addition of my ration allowances. In conversations around the dinner table I learned to understand in some degree some chapter of the Battle of Britain as seen through the eyes of my friends. One German buzz-bomb, a specimen of those early rockets launched by the Nazis from the coast of France, had landed in the adjoining garden behind their house, shaking their home, causing furniture to move from one side of the room to the other. The stoic determination to endure the bombing and to resist the threatened German invasion was reflected in their calm recital of war-time events. Great Britain then had stood alone, facing the Nazi legions triumphant on the European continent.

To many UNRRA people in uniform, this visit to London was their first one. I felt like an expert among them and thus it happened that I proposed a sightseeing tour of historic landmarks. I remembered having visited some twenty-five years before an old Norman church near Smithfield Market and having inspected a church register recording the parish's loss of members during the Black Death or Great Plague of London in 1665. Vivid in my mind was also the visit to a Roman wall. Those tours I had made as a member of the Polytechnic Ramblers' Club. The mental picture I retained was quite clear and my sense of direction perfect. However, when reaching Ludgate Circus at the head of our group of five, we faced nothing but ruins. Those ancient relics and landmarks had been completely obliterated by the bombing of World War II. The nearby Holborn Station had also been wrecked by bombs, but some rails had been repaired and trains were running. I apologized to the Australian, Canadian, and American members of our group about my inability to produce the promised historic sites, but hoped to take them to the Roman wall, which they were eager to see.

I recalled the entrance to the Roman wall located in the yard of London's General Post Office, found it, but the door was locked. I was directed to the supervisor of the loading platforms and found him among hundreds of mailbags stamped in bold letters "OHMS," On His Majesty's Service. Yes, in Great Britain all power and public service flows constitutionally from and through the Crown. When I told the supervisor that a group of visitors wanted to see the Roman wall on Post Office grounds he said that he had never heard of a Roman wall. Politely he referred me to the administrative offices, a block away. There I inquired again about the procedure to view the Roman wall. "A Roman wall?" was the astonished comment to my question, echoing everywhere with a typically English, rising inflection. "A Roman wall??" "Don't know of a Roman wall on our grounds but I inquire, please wait." I must have heard that a dozen times, as officials referred me from one office to another. Well, those officials did inquire and I did wait almost one hour when a broadly smiling civil servant brought the key.

I found my friends still waiting and I was glad to have been able to reward their patience with the sight of a hand-built structure erected 1,900 years ago. A concrete stair led from the courtyard of the General Post Office down to the foot of the wall and rampart some 25 feet below. The wall itself, consisting of hewn stones, was about 18 feet high. The path on top of the wall seemed to be about 8 feet wide. We were able to inspect this preserved historic land-mark leisurely in the light of hastily installed electric bulbs. It appeared that we were the first visitors since the beginning of World War II. It seemed somewhat ironic that I – a visitor to the British shores – was able to "lecture" to my friends and to many English post office employees who had followed us the lesson I had absorbed a quarter-century before, namely that "Old Bailey," the criminal court building, as well as St. Bartholomew's Hospital were erected on the continuation of this Roman wall. It is always impressive to note how new civilizations build upon the ruins and dust of prior ones. Before our eyes was the evidence that the foot of the 1,900-year-old Roman wall was from 25 to 30 feet below street level. The Roman wall encircled approximately the present, ancient City of London on the north bank of the Thames. This area of about 1 square mile has never been occupied by a foreign foe nor conquered by kings or queens of England. Should the Queen wish to visit the City of London, she will request the City's permission to enter. She will be met at or near any of the former gates by the Lord Mayor and conducted into and around the ancient City.

However, neither the study of English history nor sightseeing or archaeology were uppermost in the minds of UNRRA workers. We were anxious, even impatient to proceed to the places where our services might be needed. After a stay of almost two weeks in London, we were ordered to travel by cross-Channel steamer to Le Havre, thence to Paris, and without delay to Granville. At the station of Granville, Normandy, we were received by a British brigadier general, who gave us an outline of events to come, namely a few days' stay at a Granville hotel, then transfer to nearby Jullouville, where UNRRA had a training school and where teams would be made up. We were sent to Jullouville as soon as sleeping accommodation and class-room space was available. The more comfortable sleeping facilities were given to the women. I accepted a litter bed in a Quonset (prefabricated) hut. Washing and shaving had to be done under an open tent, and those mornings were cool under the grey skies of Normandy. My companions in the hut were nearly all Frenchmen, former members of the left-wing Maquis underground resistance forces. Their nightly recital of past adventures opened up to me another previously unseen and little-reported chapter of the war.

The teaching at Jullouville, a former lycée for girls, was pointed to practical ends. Most of the classes were led by people who had just returned from the field. Great emphasis was placed on leader-ship abilities, resourcefulness, and flexible attitudes to enable people to work with one another as a team. The UNRRA workers gathered here came from the Scandinavian countries, Great Britain, Holland, Belgium, and France. We also had many Poles who had fled their native land. There was, besides, the large contingent from the western hemisphere, graduates from College Park, MD. English and French were the official languages and most classes were given in both tongues. Topics dealt with the registration of refugees, mass feeding including the building of outdoor kitchens, aspects of sanitation and welfare, liaison with German local authorities, and with military occupation forces. The technique of role-playing was extensively used. While classes were in progress frequent explosions shook the school's window panes. German prisoners of war under Allied supervision demolished the many minefields in the school's vicinity.

The faculty watched carefully the students' behavior at studies and play for the purpose of giving as equitable an evaluation as possible of their potentials as field workers. One European faculty member was heard to say to another: "Watching the Americans at play you would never think that there is a racial problem in the United States."

The making-up of teams to handle displaced persons operations was in the hands of a very conscientious French Army captain still in uniform, who confided to a group of us the difficulties of his task. A standard team for the operation of an assembly center for displaced persons consisted of

1 director,
1 assistant director,
1 welfare officer,
1 medical officer,
1 nurse,
1 messing officer or nutritionist,
2 administrative officers, supply and stores,
1 administrative assistant,
1 secretary,
2 truck drivers.

It was the policy to have as international a composition of the staff as possible. The blending in of the varying abilities of candidates presented a problem, according to the captain, especially as some candidates had been referred to the training school not on the basis of their background and training, but because of their political connections. He had in mind particularly countries which had suffered a severe drain on their manpower during the war. However, in spite of many difficulties, teams were made up and rolled out of Jullouville in trucks to their various destinations in Germany, prepared to assist in the relief or solution of the displaced persons problems. At that time it was estimated that there were approximately 4 million displaced persons and refugees, mostly Nazi-conscripted labor, in Germany.

14

ASSIGNMENT TO GREECE

At the end of the two weeks' training period I was expecting to see my name on one of the departure schedules for Germany which were posted daily on bulletin boards. Fate determined differently. There arrived in the center the head of displaced persons operations in Greece, Evert Barger, anxious to recruit for his team sixteen persons. He submitted his needs to the director of the school and requested the latter's recommendations. Thus it happened that some of us were interviewed and selected by Mr. Barger for service in Greece. The departure of the "Greek" team was something novel, and fellow members of UNRRA decorated us with crowns and garlands fashioned from branches and leaves. My French friends of the Quonset hut insisted on carrying my musette and duffle bags to the truck, a friendly gesture gratefully appreciated. The send-off was cheerful and boisterous. Our two trucks reached Paris in the evening and UNRRA's central registration office directed us to the Hôtel du Rhône, where we found lodging. Food was taken at the centrally located US Officers' Club during our brief stay in Paris.

We sought air transportation from Paris to Athens, Greece, but learned that we could reach our destination only by flights from

London. We were, therefore, obliged to struggle for scarce, priority-restricted transportation to the British capital. After three days, we secured space on planes of the Royal Air Force, but we had to split our team into two groups. Commodore Rayner, formerly of the Australian Navy, led the group of ten women in the first transport, while five men including myself followed in a plane five hours later. The trip in the RAF-marked DC-3 plane was smooth and uneventful.

At our arrival in London we met Rayner, who was eager to tell us in his broad "Australian" dialect his adventure on his flight to London. "Give me 200 sailors or marines, but no more women," he shouted. In response to our curious inquiry, he related:

> First there was Miss X, who forgot her luggage and delayed our departure from the hotel. Then on the trip to the airport Miss Y missed her passport and we had to return to the hotel to pick it up. Eventually I got them all safely into the plane and seated. When we were up in the air I heard a terrific roar and the plane began to shudder and shake. There, I saw Miss Z with the door of the emergency hatch in her hand. I called for a member of the crew (there was only a pilot and a navigator) and rushed over to close the hatch. Then I asked Miss Z what had happened and she said honestly and naïvely that she had read: "To open, turn handle!" Then she explained: "I turned it and it did open." And Miss Z is a lawyer!

Then he returned to his opening statement and theme: "Give me 200 sailors or marines, but no more women. No more bloody women!"

Two days later, Commodore Rayner was called to Australia House, where the Commissioner and London representative of the Dominion decorated Tom Rayner with the Distinguished Service Cross. It was not for the events he had so colorfully described, but for having sunk during the war five German submarines within four days.

Our one week's stay in London included the Bank Holiday, the first Monday in August, celebrated as a national holiday. A big athletic event was scheduled at White City Stadium at Shepherd's Bush. The stadium was filled to capacity and about 20,000 persons were turned away. I struggled against the crowds to reach the gates of the arena, found an official who recognized me and who obtained for me a starter's badge, enabling me to enter. I saw Gunder Hägg of Sweden win the 2 miles race and his countryman Arne Andersen beat England's Sydney Wooderson in the 1 mile. I also watched my successor to the quarter-mile AAA Championship and club member, the Jamaican Arthur Wint, capture his race. It was a pleasure to shake the hands of so many acquaintances, although the fast-moving program on the track gave no time for leisurely conversation.

The seven days in London were busy ones. I visited many fellow members of the Poly Harriers, also the former Olympic athlete Philip Noel-Baker, Member of Parliament, who had just been appointed minister of state, namely ambassador to the United Nations. He introduced me to his son who, at the age of twenty-five years, had become the youngest member of the House of Commons. Together with Mrs. Baker, of Greek descent, we discussed aspects of Greece's rehabilitation, to which task I had been assigned.

All our team's problems were concentrated at Western House, UNRRA's headquarters in London. During our long waiting hours there, we could observe how badly snarled many administrative lines were. I took the initiative in attempting to solve some of our group's problems, i.e. obtaining travel advances, getting air accommodation confirmed, procuring comfortable hotel rooms for members of our team. Happily I found the channels of communication open to UNRRA's hard-working chief executives, Colonel Katzin and Mr. Levison. I wrote a news release on the award bestowed on our team member Tom Rayner and placed it with UNRRA's Publicity Department, and induced the British Film

Institute to supply visual education films to UNRRA's training school in Jullouville.

On the morning of August 15, 1945, we left British soil in a sturdy DC-3 plane piloted and navigated by two Royal Air Force sergeants. Our destination was Rome, with a refueling and luncheon stop at Marseilles. The plane was not air-pressurized and heated, and we found it quite cold 10,000 feet up in the air. Canvas seats on steel frames had been installed, but everything else seemed to have been left unchanged from the plane's service as a transport for parachute jumpers. Notices with directions and instructions for jumps were left intact on the sides of the plane.

At Marseilles airport we found the hangars and bunkers of ferro-concrete construction twisted and smashed, no doubt the result of many air raids by both belligerent forces. A similar sight of destruction greeted us at Rome's airport, whose pockmarked surface had been covered by steel grids for safe landings on its small field. As we had touched ground in the afternoon at 4 o'clock and were due to leave Rome at 4.30 the following morning, little time remained for sightseeing. We did manage, however, to view the Colosseum and the Forum before darkness closed in on us. Awakened at 3.30 a.m. we were all in an RAF truck at 4.30 a.m., had a fast ride through dark, narrow streets and roads to the airport, and were airborne at 6.40 a.m. We gazed upon the unfolding scenery below like tourists: Taranto, the Adriatic, the Greek island of Leukas, the Gulf of Corinth, then descending we saw Corinth, Piraeus, and after circling Athens we landed at the large Hassani Airport, Athens. Noticing all British military personnel in shorts and shirts with open collars, we became aware that the temperature was 85 °F, and it was only 10.30 a.m.

During the two hours' wait for a truck, we looked at the hundreds, yes hundreds of wrecked planes, jeeps, trucks at the borders of the airfield, casualties of war. A swift trip to the city brought us to UNRRA's Athens headquarters, where assignment to accommodations was quick and efficient. We were anxious to be put to work, only to learn that on an ordinary working day this time of the day would be the siesta. However, that particular day was a holiday, namely the Feast of the Assumption of the Virgin Mary, and we learned that the following day had been declared a Greek national holiday, meaning that all offices would be closed. There was nothing else to do but to fall into the rhythm of the new environment. Thus I attended on the second day the ceremony at the Tomb of the Unknown Soldier at Constitution Square, where I witnessed the Regent Damaskinos and Premier Admiral Voulgaris lay wreaths in front of the bas-relief representation of a Hellenic soldier lying prone over the tomb. Military bands played anthems of allied nations.

The following days were taken up with orientation: the administrative regions of UNRRA's Mission to Greece, channels of contact with agencies of the Greek Government, the many special services contracted for, UNRRA's internal administrative structure, special forms and reports, etc. Those of us assigned to displaced persons work were directed to inspect reception facilities in and around Athens. We first visited the Outbound Clearing Station of Hadjikyriakion at Piraeus, run by six British ladies of the Guide International Service, which visit introduced us to the problems of legal and emotional entanglements left in the aftermath of war. There were Yugoslav and Italian nationals of Greek birth, Greek women married to foreign nationals, etc. Then we visited the Larissa Center in Athens, the Greek Government's Reception Station for returning Greeks, consisting of three large buildings, barbed wire barriers set up around them, with soldiers guarding the gates. We were also shown a modern school building which the government thought of converting into a reception center. We found toilets filthy and inoperative, and the water supply inadequate. Those visits introduced us to the different sanitary standards prevailing in this geographic region.

We traveled to Eleusis Airport outside Athens, operated by the US Air Force, where eight trucks were waiting in vain for the arrival

151

of a previously announced transfer of displaced persons from Italy. Radio and cable communications over military facilities were extremely poor in those days, making the efficient assignment of scarce trucks very difficult. The departure points for the transport of displaced persons by air from Germany were Brussels and Munich. The American Air Force directed all movements out of Munich, while the British Royal Air Force supervised flights out of Brussels. One day our group went to Hassani Airport and saw the landing of fourteen black-painted Halifax bombers, disgorging about 140 displaced persons and their belongings from their bomb holds. On that day the returnees were personally greeted by the Greek minister of resettlement and repatriation, who also supervised their registration.

With the end of the war in Europe, tens of thousands of Greeks were returning to their homeland. Those who had been conscripted or had volunteered for work in Nazi factories returned by the described means, because rails had been ripped to pieces over long distances and rolling stock largely destroyed. Many came by sea from Italy, Turkey, Egypt, and other North African countries. However, the greatest migration homeward was an internal population movement from Western and Central Macedonia to Eastern Macedonia and Thrace. About 40,000 Greeks had fled when the Bulgarians moved into Eastern Macedonia after the "Blitz" and steam-roller entry of the German Goering Division into Western and Central Macedonia. Those Greeks preferred the harsh German occupation to that of the hated Bulgarians, allies of the Nazis. The regulating of the homeward movement to Eastern Macedonia and Thrace and the coordinating of the necessary services for the returnees' settlement and rehabilitation became my prime concern over the next eighteen months. After nine days in Athens, I received my assignment to the northeastern area of Greece bordering on Bulgaria and Turkey. My office and station was to be Kavala, the administrative center of Eastern Macedonia. I was able to obtain a priority-laden plane reservation for a flight to Salonica scheduled six days later. The time in between was taken up mostly with careful reading and study of numerous reports. In that period I met by chance two former fellow prisoners of war from Ruhleben Camp, Germany. They were in the service of the British Red Cross. Such coincidence made, of course, for most interesting conversation about the days spent in our internment camp twenty-seven to thirty years ago and on happenings since then.

Upon arrival at Salonica, I followed the usual now-familiar procedures of handing in my travel orders, also some instructions and reports from headquarters, passing on to certain individuals oral messages and greetings, obtaining referrals to sleeping accommodations, direction to our UNRRA mess, and information on hours of meals. I also checked in at the US Consulate at Salonica, apprising the consul of my presence in his area of jurisdiction. I was to proceed to Kavala on the third day following my arrival in this ancient capital of Macedonia. I had, therefore, two days at my disposal to acquaint myself with the facilities developed by that area for the handling of refugees. I learned that thousands of internal migrants had settled in Salonica, swelling its population far beyond the availability of adequate shelter, causing serious social and political problems. Foreign nationals, refugees from beyond the borders of Greece, were housed at Pavlos Melas on the outskirts of the city. At the time of our visit we found one part of the former army barracks used by the Greek Army for military prisoners of war, another part by the Indian Division of the British Army as their quarters, and still another by UNRRA for displaced persons. I found the refugees' sleeping quarters, in general, fairly clean. Family units had their sections partitioned off by blankets hanging over ropes; people sat and slept on cement floors. There were no glass windows. Latrinc facilities in the yard were inadequate and filthy. In the kitchen were three German Army kettles in excellent condition; the hospital, too, was adequately well equipped and cleanly kept. A section of the camp was screened off, housing about 200 persons in quarantine because of the occurrence of four cases of typhus.

In the courtyard I watched the loading of displaced persons into trucks destined for Athens, a two-day trip because rails, tunnels, and bridges had been destroyed by the German Army in their retreat. They were Greeks returning to their homes farther south after a three years' stay in Czechoslovakia. Many had married Czech women. I conversed with some of them in German, the lingua franca among the displaced persons forced to work in German factories. When leaving the Pavlos Melas camp I became aware that the road at the main entrance was paved with marble slabs. They were tombstones from the nearby Jewish cemetery, a silent reminder that the Nazis had been here. It set my mind to dreaming how many legions had marched over this strategic road since the founding of Salonica about 315 BC: the Romans, the Crusaders, the Venetians, the Turks, and in the present century: the French and the Germans. Even the United States of America became involved in this area with the declaration of the Truman Doctrine, when the security of this region sheltering the historic East–West highway, the important road from the Vardar Gap to the Bosporus, was threatened by the designs of a hostile force. From Pavlos Melas our small group went to the old, international fairgrounds, of which a part had been converted to a transient camp for refugees coming from Western and Central Macedonia, proceeding to their former homes in Eastern Macedonia. This camp was called Mrs. Joly's Camp after its energetic director, Mrs. Joly, a Smyrna-born, multi-lingual Brit. We observed the arrival of two families in an open truck: laden with its human component, plus pigs, goats, and personal belongings. By the control of trucks UNRRA attempted to regulate the movement of returning refugees to those rural areas where adequate shelter was available and security established. Mrs. Joly's Camp was, therefore, a holding camp until clearance to eastern administrative centers was received.

On the second day I was taken by jeep to a reception center a few miles south of the Kula Pass at the Bulgarian border. That assembly center at Sidirokastro was operated by the Palestine Jewish Council for Relief Abroad, usually referred to as the Palestine Relief Team, under the direction of Colonel Sheppard of the Australian Army. This team, as well as other groups of volunteer workers, was attached to and worked in conjunction with the UN Relief and Rehabilitation Administration. There were only 120 displaced persons living in the camp, consisting of former Greek Army barracks, which had a capacity of 1,500, but in emergency could accommodate many hundreds more. The camp with its hospital, food stores and supplies, sanitary facilities was in fine shape and spotlessly clean. When we reached the Bulgarian border, sixty-six Greeks and their wives had just arrived by train from Sofia and were turned over to us. Through an interpreter I exchanged a few courtesies with the Russian officer in charge of this border station, while behind me an emotional scene was enacted. The Salonica-born messing officer of the Palestine Relief Team, Miss Buena Sarfatty had recognized two former fellow prisoners of the Salonica Nazi-run concentration camp from which she had escaped in a laundry barrel. After making her way to Euboea, Turkey, Syria, and Palestine, she had joined the relief team, hoping in her work to gather some scraps of news about her brothers and sister who had been swallowed up by the Nazi concentration camp before her arrest. The men she questioned had been conscripted as slave labor and had been sent to Germany. We returned to Salonica late in the evening, after having spent about six hours of that day in a bouncing jeep over rough and dusty roads.

Early the following morning an LST (Landing Ship Tank) was due to leave Salonica for Piraeus with a full load of refugees. I was up early to witness the loading and to acquaint myself with the necessary documentation. However, I learned that a jeep had been booked for me for the trip to Kavala, a little over 100 miles to the east, hence I had to prepare myself for that journey. We, the regional administrative officer and I, followed the road skirting the Strimon Bay. The road was in fair condition; however, all bridges had been blown up, forcing us to ford many small streams. However, the fast-flowing, broad Strimon we crossed on a wooden platform kept afloat by a number of barrels lashed together and held by loops to a suspended steel cable. The whole platform with the jeep and passengers was pulled across by human power, namely by a man turning a pulley, a drum around which the cable pulling the "ferry" would coil. After a change of tire due to a puncture, we reached our destination in the early afternoon. The administrative officer introduced me to the director of that region, with whom I had later an extended talk, in the course of which it developed that we were both residents of Princeton, New Jersey, where he had married a local girl. As my wife had served four years there as secretary of the Young Women's Christian Association (colored) I knew many members of the community by name. It's a small world at times. There in Eastern Macedonia, two residents of Princeton met by the twist of fate.

On the following day the regional director introduced me to the heads of departments, and all the files relating to displaced persons were handed over to me. He presented me also to the governor general of Eastern Macedonia and Thrace, as well as to the mayor of Kavala. Both assured me of their wholehearted cooperation in our humanitarian work. The next two days were taken up with the digesting of reports, conferring with persons who had worked on problems of migration, relief, resettlement, and the organization of an inspection trip of the region. I learned that rail services existed from Salonica to Serres, the administrative center of the prefecture of the same name, situated on the Strimon river about 20 miles south of the previously mentioned Kula Pass. The problem was to transport the returning refugees from there to the prefectures of their home districts, thence to their villages, providing them with food rations for the first month, and referring them to the Greek Agricultural Services, an agency strongly assisted by UNRRA. On the third day I was on my way in a jeep to take an inventory of the situation, accompanied by a member of the British Save the Children Fund who had previously handled some of the [displaced persons] DP work. It was clear after a quick trip through Eastern Macedonia that the repatriation of displaced persons was impeded by the lack of shelter, particularly in the Drama and Serres prefectures. About 4,000 persons were forced to remain in the town of Drama alone, and several hundred more families in smaller towns because of the destruction of their homes in the border villages. With a constantly pressing flow of refugees homeward, amounting to a weekly average of 1,500 persons for the region, with their baggage, livestock, seeds, and farm equipment, the situation called for prompt and vigorous action.

The initial report rendered ten days after my arrival was discussed in depth with the regional director and with the member of the British volunteer organization who had made ad hoc efforts in DP work during the preceding three months. I suggested that the latter present the report in person to our Athens headquarters and supplement the data by his own observations and experiences. This was done. A few months later we noted with a measure of satisfaction that the suggestions advanced in the initial report had been incorporated in the law governing shelter rehabilitation. I was then asked to take over shelter rehabilitation for Western, Central and Eastern Macedonia, and Thrace in addition to the duties of displaced persons officer. All invasion routes into Greece led through Macedonia, hence Northern Greece suffered considerably from war damage, particularly the prefectures of Drama and Serres bordering on Bulgaria, and the prefectures of Kastoria and Kozani, the invader's route from Yugoslavia and Albania. In order to command an overall view of the problem, I compiled the following table from Greek Government sources:

Degree of destruction in war-damaged villages	Shelters destroyed in North Greece	Percentage of total Greek destruction
80% to 100%	16,356	13
51 to 79	7,031	5.8
41 to 50	1,922	1.6
31 to 40	1,773	1.5
21 to 30	3,411	2.8
1 to 20	7,600	6.3
	38,093	**31%**

Hence Northern Greece suffered about one-third of the shelter destruction of Greece. This serious destruction with the socio-political implications arising from the confinement of farmers to cities and the vulnerability of the sparsely settled border areas to Communist infiltration, all were matters of concern to the various Greek governments which followed one another in Athens. Each appointed a new set of governors and prefects as their representatives in the provinces and prefectures. This unsettling situation offered at the same time a challenge to UNRRA workers by providing continuity to rehabilitation. The government of Admiral Voulgaris was followed by governments headed by Kanellopoulos, Sofoulis, and Tsaldaris, four governments in the two years of our work there. Severely disturbing were the changing concepts and emphases, i.e. building of temporary shelters, permanent dwellings, general rehabilitation, building by farm cooperatives, and the promulgation of laws changing jurisdictions and administrative procedures. There were six such laws changing supervision in shelter rehabilitation from the Agricultural Banks to the Ministry of Agriculture to the Ministry of Public Works to an Under Ministry of Reconstruction to an independent Reconstruction Agency. Behind these changes were not only technical justifications, but also many political ambitions. Our United Nations agency, as guest of the country, had to adapt its organization to the changes of the government in power.

Priorities in the use of UNRRA shelter material had been established by agreement:

In the relief period priority in the rehabilitation of essential shelter or accommodation in the liberated areas should be given to: hospitals and schools, habitations for homeless persons, especially for workers engaged in essential public services and in industries having high priority in relief, as well as for farmers and agricultural workers.

Preference was also to be accorded to villages with a high percentage of destruction.

Adherence to these guidelines was most difficult and complex in actual operations in the field. Lumber, nails, glass, roofing paper, working tools, etc. arrived by ship and were stored at the docks. Scarcity of trucks made difficult the transportation of supplies to the interior, where they were needed. Skilled labor was also available in or near cities; therefore, rehabilitation work proceeded there much quicker. I was faced with these situations: the governor of a province had directed the Greek engineers to rebuild his partly destroyed home village, also a village near the Bulgarian border to redeem a political commitment. Both villages had less than 50 percent destruction, hence a low priority. Should I have disturbed a good relationship with the governor? Kindly note, houses were being built. In another province, 100 cubic meters of lumber disappeared, stolen. It had been used by the Greek Army for the repair of their barracks to protect them from the cold of winter. What could one do but to make the incidents a matter of record and leave to Athens the discretion whether to take corrective action.

Complete supervision in the distribution of relief supplies was impossible. Therefore, we set up committees of representative citizens in the administrative centers to handle the equitable allocation of scarce supplies and to formulate guidelines. One international representative would attend their monthly meetings and receive a copy of their minutes. He would also hold himself available to receive complaints from the public. Supervision was especially difficult when we had to work under pressure and limitation of time. When the winter was approaching at the end of 1945, we knew that communication with many mountain villages would be completely cut off by snowdrifts: hence all members of the international staff assisted in the distribution of medical supplies to First Aid Committees in the villages. The transportation of rationed wheat flour to villages was rushed, as was also the handing out of clothing. The distribution of used clothing which had been collected in the United States was the cause of much dissatisfaction and complaints from the populace, which had had no clothing for five years. The bales of clothing were handed to the prefectures for sorting. Heavyweight clothing was to go to the mountain villages, lighter clothing to the people in the valleys. The sorting of clothing became a highly sought, political job of prestige. It was said that workers looked thin and frail when going to work and stoutish when leaving. The handing out of those scarce items in the villages was also a fought-over affair. The Greeks – with a sense of humor – made up a parody to the then popular tune of "She'll be coming o'er the mountain, when she comes." The words described the clothing distribution: one person getting a sleeve, another a trouser-leg, etc. At one occasion I was greeted with smiles and smirks when the following story of clothing distribution was unfolded. First a preface.

As indicated, the international staff assisted one another as we visited various places. Thus we inquired always about public health, water supply, medical items, wheat and clothing distribution, road and bridge maintenance, shelter rehabilitation, availability of farm tools, seeds, water buffaloes, mules, etc. Information was then passed on to the respective rehabilitation officer at the mealtime of our UNRRA mess. This institution helped considerably in the diffusion of information and in the creation of effective teamwork. Now the story.

In the spring of 1946, I arranged for a trip to the peninsula of Athos, the Holy Mount, the prefecture which never allowed women in its domain and which forbade, and still forbids, the importation of all female animals. There are in Athos over one hundred monasteries of the Orthodox Church, some large and some small. We, a Greek engineer and I, visited among others the large one of Lavra, founded in the year AD 963. As was my custom, I inquired about conditions and supplies. With some hesitation or trepidation, the black-robed, bearded Fathers introduced the subject of clothing distribution, inferring that the gift proved "not particularly suitable" for the prefecture's citizens. In the rush to conclude all clothing distribution before the onset of the 1945 winter, we had shipped bales to all administrative centers of prefectures, including Athos, for sorting and handing out, as explained. When the Fathers opened the bales, they beheld tantalizing-looking, sinful female garments mixed in with male clothing. This sight must have been startling to the residents of this peaceful land, where people had lived without women for over 1,000 years. However, the impact of the shock appeared to have worn off at the time of my visit, because the Fathers seemed to smirk and smile behind their bearded camouflage.

One of our nurses, a first lieutenant of the US Public Health Service, a tall, serious, and dedicated officer, encountered the following situation: when inspecting a prison, she checked on the stock of supplies for hygiene, in particular on the delivery of a case of soap she had ordered. Through our female interpreter, she asked the prison officials to produce the case of soap, which she learned had been delivered. There was great consternation and much whispering. In a plain and forceful manner she said: "I want to see that case of soap. I am not going to move until I see it." The interpreter again translated, and a long conversation in Greek ensued.

Straightening herself to her imposing height of 5' 7", the nurse repeated her order sternly. Thereupon her interpreter took a deep breath and, drawing upon her studies of English literature taken at the American Antioch College at Salonica, she said: "I am told that the case of soap has been taken to a house of ill repute." Our nurse, the first lieutenant, reflected for a moment and said to her interpreter: "Let's go, maybe the soap is doing more good to Greek hygiene there than here." Yes, there were instances of misappropriation and theft. Some we could curb, some we reported. However, we had to push on and not lose the momentum of our efforts.

Changes of governments and appointed officials, of laws and regulations, and of the historic tendency to keep power in Athens, all tended to snarl work in endless red tape. These circumstances caused UNRRA and Greek provincial administrators to encourage us, international field workers, to go to Athens once every three or four months, to cut through the red tape, solve problems, and get action. In this manner I learned in Athens that four jeeps which I had requested for the use of shelter construction engineers serving the mountainous regions of Macedonia had been granted and handed over to the Greek Government but had never reached Northern Greece. I followed through and had a conference with the vice president of the bank to which the jeeps had been assigned. He argued that the vehicles had been handed to the bank for use at his discretion. He frankly admitted that he had kept one for his own use, because his work as vice president was important for the overall reconstruction, and he, therefore, required that transportation. I replied that I would look further into the pertinent resolution which had been passed at a higher level. Thereafter two jeeps turned up in Macedonia. Other pressing matters and the impossibility to stay in Athens any length of time prevented my following up the disappearance of the other jeep.

Once a five-ton truck disappeared from the motor pool of the British Army in Salonica. I listened to the story of the theft's discovery by the distressed young lieutenant in charge of the place over a cup of tea in the officers' mess. An Australian colonel in our group spoke up soothingly and said with a smile:

> Don't be so harsh on my Greek friends. I taught them sabotage, how to steal, disassemble, and hide automobiles and trucks when I was an intelligence officer, flown into German-occupied Greece for work with the resistance. They learned their job well. I am proud of the boys. They just can't stop.

On another trip to Athens I discussed with top-level UNRRA officials the political ramifications arising from the detaining of a farming population in overcrowded cities because of the lack of shelter in their home villages. I urged the full utilization of a law under which farmers' cooperatives could receive building material and do their own repair with the advice and under the supervision of government engineers. I was referred to the Chief of Mission, Mr. Buell Maben, to whom I gave a complete picture of the northern border areas. After listening to my description of conditions in Macedonia, he proposed that I expound the matter with the acting prime minister of Greece, for which conference his office made the necessary arrangements. At this audience I gave not only a report on shelter rehabilitation work completed, but also on the difficulties of transferring the huge stocks of supplies from the ports' warehouses to the areas where such material was needed. I developed fully the possibilities of self-help by farmers under the existing law governing farmers' cooperatives. The prime minister was a patient and seemingly interested listener. He made no commitments, gave no encouragement. However, four days before the next election printed letters from the acting prime minister were posted at all government buildings, stating in effect: "I am deeply interested in your shelter problems. If you write to me, I shall see to it that shelter supplies will be made available to you."

Then there was this incident, which gives an insight into the trading and bargaining mentality of the near past. Five hundred mules had been unloaded at Kavala, veterans of the American Army's Italian campaign, a gift to the Greek Army for use in the mountainous terrain of Macedonia. My observation established that the mules were not being used, and I saw an opportunity to speed the building of dwellings in mountain villages by using a score or two of them for the transportation of lumber, tiles, roofing paper, etc. This plan was thoroughly discussed with the engineers of the prefectures and enthusiastically endorsed by them. On my trip to Athens I sought and received an introduction to the Chief of Staff of the Greek Army. I presented my plan to him, stressing the population vacuum existing in the strategic border areas facing Yugoslavia and Bulgaria. He listened with apparent interest and patience, then asked me this question: "Now supposing I *lend* you the twenty or more mules, how many jeeps will you *give* me?" Nothing became of this plan, as the army held on to its mules, claiming that the animals were foot-sore and required training and conditioning.

It may be noted that work in rehabilitation has many satisfactions and many disappointments. When I secured a quantity of tarpaper and an appropriation for labor for the repair of a shed at Serres station, and found on inspection a month later that refugees were still sleeping under the open sky, I confronted the Prefect with those facts. He acknowledged receipt of the material and funds and explained that he had "temporarily applied" the money to salaries, because his staff had not been paid for three months.

In spite of many setbacks, we were able to report in the spring of 1946 that 10,500 dwellings had been built or repaired in Northern Greece. A new, elected government had come to power in Athens. It debated its organization and its policies for three months, thus wasting valuable time of building weather. In this period I did my best to feed pertinent information into Greek technical and political channels, stressing particularly the necessity to populate the fertile, yet empty border areas.

I staged my own, private campaign to convince technical and political officials of the importance of including sanitary facilities in the building program. Our nurses had reported that typhoid epidemics occurred on an average of one per month. The usual cause was water contaminated by human feces. Plans for shelter construction or rehabilitation had never included the building of latrines. In the town of Servia in Kozani Prefecture, for instance, we had constructed 876 new family dwellings, yet not a single toilet. I took my plea for the inclusion of sanitary facilities via the minister for Northern Greece to the minister of health in Athens, submitting to him personally blueprints of designs which stressed low cost and simplicity for self-installation under the supervision of government engineers. The views of technical personnel at all levels had been favorable but seemingly I could not convince the politicians. A man seasoned in "the art of the possible" took me aside and gave me his discouraging prognosis that I would not succeed. "You see," he said, "a latrine is not a good platform for a politician to stand on." He was so right.

However, my plea to build in the border regions succeeded; in fact, the whole national budget for shelter rehabilitation was allocated to Macedonia. Yet, instead of continuing at the annual rate of 10,000 dwellings, the new budget called for only 3,000 units for the ensuing year.

I enjoyed the work, was assured that my services would be needed for at least two more years; therefore I asked my family to join me. I made arrangements with an educational institution at Baltimore to supply me with study material for my son, then nine years old. Shipping arrangements were made by UNRRA, and my family arrived on a military transport early August 1946. Their arrival coincided with the receipt of news that UNRRA was to be liquidated at the end of the year, not later than March 1947. All prior agreements were null and void. For my private treasury, this was bad news indeed, as it had involved an expenditure for my family's travel of nearly $1,500. My wife and son joined me at my station and headquarters at Kavala, one of the most beautiful and favorably situated towns in the world. They accompanied me on a few, rough field trips and were thus able to absorb some of the atmosphere of the region, its natural beauty, and the warmth of its people. They were able to see the ruins of Philippi and later of Corinth in the south, dream about Saint Paul's travels and the epistles he preached there and, henceforth, they were able to read with something more than understanding:

> And a vision appeared to Paul in the night; there stood a man of Macedonia and prayed him, saying. "Come over into Macedonia and help us." (Acts 16:9)

It was a most satisfying task to come over and help the people of Macedonia at a time of their greatest need. We, messengers of the United Nations, arrived to bring them food, clothing, and shelter when they thought they had been forgotten and abandoned. They showed their gratitude in their eyes and their demeanor. In one mountain village a farming couple went into their storage bin to offer us from their winter reserves – a handful of walnuts. At another occasion a young man walked about a mile to bring my wife a chair, probably the only one in the village. Several of my hardy co-workers in field offices said: "I'd rather shake the corny, callous hand of a Macedonian farmer than the oily, slippery one of an Athens politician."

We, UNRRA field workers, were persona grata in royalist, as well as left-wing villages. We saw to it that food and other donations were given out equitably, without regard to political affiliation. We were, more than we realized at that time, a true peace-preserving force in that area. As soon as we left, civil war erupted in Northern

Greece. Upon our liquidation all functions of distribution were assumed by Athens' royalist government, which determined to withhold rations from leftist-oriented villages. "Why should I feed those fellows who shoot at me?" was the way a royalist politician put it.

In February 1946, Stalin had broken with the policies of his former Western allies, and he then encouraged the creation of a Communist-dominated Macedonian state, carved mainly out of Greece. It was another effort in the Pan-Slavic expansion southward toward the Aegean Sea. The method used for the realization of this dream was Communist agitation and propaganda by infiltrated armed forces linked to dissatisfied and disgruntled villagers. Starved-out villagers went to the mountains, from which they waged a civil and ideological war against Athens' royalist government, with arms and ammunition supplied by Soviet Russia and Yugoslavia. It was this development and the threat to the balance of power which brought bi-lateral American aid under the Truman Doctrine to this area. Signs of revolutionary activities in Greek Macedonia were visible during the months before our departure. There were raids by Andartes – the old Greek resistance fighters – from their mountain strongholds upon farms and villages. Some police stations were destroyed and sections of roads mined. My counterpart in shelter rehabilitation operating in the province of Thessaly, south of Western Macedonia, was killed when his jeep ran over a mine. The waiter of a village restaurant which I had visited just one hour before was "arrested" and killed by Andartes because he was an alleged royalist informer. This was the political atmosphere at the time of our leaving Greece in November 1946.

The international staff of UNRRA was deeply concerned about the efficacy of the Greek national administration taking over the manifold duties of our United Nations operations. We thought we knew the needs of the farmers and of the working class in industry; we knew that the warehouses at port cities were full of supplies donated by the nations of the world. Furthermore, we knew how the governments in Athens had delayed the distribution of needed supplies, uncertain when such acts would yield maximum political benefits, i.e. "our party did this for you." There was also the suspicion that the absence of international supervision might encourage bribery, corruption, and theft. Yet, as guests of the government of Greece, we had to defer to their policies and also yield to the dictates of our United Nations administration.

45. Athens, October 1946 – the front page of *The Nation* newspaper. Harry Edward appears in full UNRRA uniform to talk about his year as director of housing and his work in rebuilding life in northern Greece and providing shelter for the thousands left homeless after the war. The journalist was clearly impressed: 'a sympathetic person – this famous Olympic Games athlete – and for a moment I was taken aback. But he was tall and forceful, with dark eyes and he looked ten years younger than his actual age of forty-eight.'

At headquarters, some Greek personnel had told the Athens press about our work in shelter rehabilitation in Macedonia, as they had learned it from written and verbal reports. Four newspapers printed brief comments, and following a press interview *Ethnos* [*The Nation*], Athens' largest paper, ran a front-page feature story about me as an Olympic athlete and my contribution in Greece's rehabilitation in two of its issues. It was good to have such a closing chapter of one's efforts.

15

PASSING THE STATUE OF LIBERTY
ONCE AGAIN

Our family, together with many other departing UNRRA workers, boarded the SS *Vulcania* at Piraeus and reached New York City nine days later. Again I passed the Statue of Liberty. Again many questions agitated my mind. Will I become, henceforth, again black, treated as a sub-human, relegated to second-class citizenship? In the United Nations organization I had been able to walk tall, as a full man. I had been treated as a human being; the position I had held and my person had been respected. How much had the United States changed in the two years of my absence, during those first two years of the United Nations, so full of hope and promise? The USA had emerged from World War II unscathed, its huge industrial plant intact. It possessed the secret of the atomic bomb and stood strong and respected in the family of nations. In the eyes of the world, the United States was the unchallenged leader of the universe, technically and morally. Mrs. Eleanor Roosevelt, as chairman of the United Nations Commission on Human Rights, labored diligently then on guidelines for universal human relations and conduct.

Sir Hersch Lauterpacht, who had been one of Britain's delegates to the formulation and signing of the United Nations Charter and who was subsequently elected to the International Court of Justice, wrote at that time:

> These provisions (human rights and freedoms) are not mere embellishments of an historic document; they were not the result of an afterthought or an accident of drafting. They were adopted, with deliberation and after prolonged discussion before and during the San Francisco Conference, as part of the philosophy of the new international system and as the most compelling lesson of the experience of the inadequacies and dangers of the old.

Had the "compelling lessons" been learned? How new and better would the United States be after its bloody struggle against Hitler's ideology? Again I would learn the hard facts upon setting foot on American soil.

After staying in a mid-town hotel for two weeks and eating in restaurants, our family transferred to a furnished apartment at the periphery of Harlem, where we were obliged to live doubled up for a full year before we were able to locate a vacant, unfurnished apartment. Construction activities for housing had practically stopped during the war years, because steel had been rationed subject to government priority licenses. Housing was extremely scarce. Finding a suitable job was even more difficult. Again I had to resort to menial bread-and-butter jobs, while my wife pitched in as a typist in the Municipal Civil Service.

The education of our son William became a real problem in that period and gave us some concern. He had lost recorded school time by his travel abroad. We found the Harlem Public School he attended very poor in quality, the teacher using our son as a tutor of other children. In a conversation with the school's Principal, I insisted on a test of my son's abilities, because a prior test had revealed a relatively high and satisfactory rating. The Principal complied; the tests confirmed my assertion, and the initiative of the Principal made possible my son's transfer to an IG (intellectually gifted) school. Subsequently I applied for my son's admission to the highly respected Fieldston School of the Society for Ethical Culture, which accepted him as a scholarship student. The six years he spent there became a significant chapter in his life and his development.

My own efforts to enter the private business sector of our economy proved unsuccessful. I endeavored to find a niche in pre-fabricated housing. In Greece I had been favorably impressed with the speed with which we had set up pre-fabricated hospitals and orphanages. I felt that America's enormous post-war housing need could and would be filled by the application of America's mass production technique, so clearly demonstrated by the war-time output of vehicles, tanks, ships, and planes. It took me a few months to learn and observe the obstacles thrown into the path of such possible achievement by vested, local interests, such as lumber merchants, plumbers, electricians, bankers, by organized labor and the various restrictions written by them into thousands of local building codes. I found a drift in the United States in the pattern of the historic post-war isolationist trends with a strong anti-foreign sentiment, especially in trade unions, while government and business were pre-occupied with the conversion of industry from war to peace-time production, with blacks as the last to be hired.

16

BACK TO GERMANY WITH
THE UNITED NATIONS

I communicated with friends abroad in international organizations and learned of a vacancy in the International Refugee Organization in Germany. I applied through United Nations channels in New York, was accepted, and proceeded to IRO headquarters at Bad Kissingen, Germany. Thus, I returned to another agency of the United Nations after a lapse of two years. In reality the work of the IRO was a continuation of the displaced persons phase of the UN Relief and Rehabilitation Administration. However, it had gone through several stages of growth. After the liquidation of UNRRA, the International Refugee Organization began operation on July 1, 1947. Its focus was, as the name implies, on refugees, because it was realized that the presence of millions of unsettled and dissatisfied people in the occupied zones was creating dangers which threatened the political stability of Europe and constituted a menace to the security of the whole Western world. However, even preceding the demise of UNRRA and the creation of IRO, the governments of Belgium, Brazil, Canada, and Venezuela had formed the Intergovernmental Committee on Refugees (IGCR) to regulate and assist in the migratory movement of refugees from Central Europe. The contractual agreements entered into by IGCR and the migration channels they had established were taken over by the Preparatory Commission for IRO, which developed further emigration under government selection schemes and emigration under normal consular procedures. After these growing pains, the IRO took over the existing functions and added another category, namely placement of individuals with prospective employers or sponsors on the basis of their qualifications or needs.

Having acquainted myself with the history and growth of my employer organization, I presented myself with my credentials of a former UNRRA displaced persons officer to the Chief of Repatriation and Resettlement Services, US Zone of Occupation, at Bad Kissingen. Lo and behold the official had been a member of our demonstration team at UNRRA's Training School at College Park almost four years before. I was assigned to the nearby IRO Area headquarters for Franconia, namely Würzburg, for training and observation of displaced persons activities. This included a one week's stay at the staging center at Schweinfurt, where IRO assembled the selected and documented DPs for transportation by rail to shipping points. Because of the illness of the regular transport officer, I was called upon to supervise the dispatch and transport of about 500 displaced persons, one full trainload, from Schweinfurt to Bremerhaven on the North Sea, one of IRO's embarkation centers. Usual procedure involved a brief stay for refugees of from three to fourteen days in the converted German Army barracks there to effect coordination with sailing schedules of chartered IRO ships. It was an interesting experience. One little incident on that trip stands out vividly in my memory. A young man, a displaced person from Lithuania, who worked as a clerk in our IRO offices, had been assigned to me as a transport aide. After all displaced persons on the transport had been housed, all documents safely transferred, I invited the young man to the officers' mess, where we ate and relaxed. At the end of the day, as we both boarded the train for the return journey, he turned to me and said: "I thank you for

46. September 1949, Harry Edward in Strüth, Ansbach, southern Germany, at a farewell event for Swedish officer Margret Törnell (right). He became resettlement officer, responsible for thousands of displaced persons trying to find homes and lost families.

your kindness. It means so much to be treated as a person instead of a unit of an impersonal group." I fully understood his language and the feelings that prompted his remark.

My stay in the Würzburg Area was brief, less than three weeks, when I was ordered to take over the duties of resettlement officer for the Ansbach Area, with its many assembly centers housing about 20,000 persons at that time. Many centers were scheduled to be liquidated and consolidated over the next months. There were, therefore, two main phases to my work: 1) the moving out and into channels of migration the selected and documented persons, and 2) the transfer of thousands of displaced persons from centers to be closed to larger assembly centers. The area of Franconia containing the many centers extended from the border of Eastern Germany, with Coburg and Hof at the northern-most points to the Danube at the south, the Taube river in the west and the Naab in the east.

It was the custom to keep nationals together. Thus we had Polish, Ukrainian, Czech, Hungarian, Yugoslav, Estonian, Lithuanian, and Latvian assembly centers. We also had assembly centers for Jews where dietary laws were observed. In the Hindenburg Kaserne of Ansbach, a former German Army barrack, where our area head-quarters was located, we had Estonian, Lithuanian, and Latvian nationals, and in the courtyard three flagpoles of equal height for the flags of those countries. Such national groups maintained their own schools, in an attempt to perpetuate their language and their culture. They also kept alive former parishes and their church organizations. Certified pastors of such congregations were placed on IRO payrolls, as were other DPs performing useful and needed community services. There was much home rule in the various camps, and it was inevitable that the international staff was drawn into many phases of "local politics," while outside of the assembly centers we had obligations to effect harmonious working relation-ships with the US Authorities of Occupation (in the US Zone) and with agencies of the German Government. In Ansbach we had a hospital for displaced persons, staffed by qualified physicians from many countries and supervised by an international medical officer. This institution was but a phase of the whole range of social activi-ties, which are the basis of every normal community. Facilities were provided for the education of children and the vocational training of adults. Health and rehabilitation services were organized for the ill, undernourished, and physically handicapped. Special child welfare services were provided for the great number of unaccompa-nied children and orphans. The aim for which these activities were designed was to rehabilitate the displaced persons and make it possible for them to become useful citizens in new countries.

Resettlement became the principal goal of International Red Cross operations. It was estimated that there were about 7 million persons displaced by actions of war in German-occupied areas at the end of hostilities. Most of them streamed back to their homeland by all kinds of transportation, some of which I described under my UNRRA experiences. There was, however, a large group, estimated at 3 million, who refused to return home, declaring that life there would be intolerable to them. Most of them came from the western-most border states of Soviet Russia, namely the Baltic states, Poland, Ukraine, Hungary, Yugoslavia. It was that group of refugees which became the main concern of IRO.

Our international organization had to focus on:

1) opening of resettlement opportunities,
2) establishing procedures of documentation and clearances,
3) arranging for transportation to countries of immigration,
4) setting up procedures in countries of immigration.

As some countries of immigration were far away, like Australia and New Zealand, the creation of one long, connected chain of clearly established procedures was no small task. In the months of September and October 1949, IRO moved to new countries about 28,000 each month and had under charter thirty-five ships plying to North and South America, as well as to Australia. Besides there was emigration to many European countries, such as Belgium, France, the Netherlands, Sweden, and the United Kingdom of Great Britain. This, then, was the framework of my activities as resettlement officer in which I worked three years until IRO had solved the most pressing part of its work by an orderly migratory process, the transfer of nearly 1 million persons – and we, IRO workers, had worked ourselves out of our jobs at the end of 1951. As already inferred, those days of 1949 were very busy ones. The schedule for the liquidation and consolidation of assembly centers called for the concentration of refugees in centers in and around Munich, locale of the new head-quarters of IRO operations in the US occupied zone, a city which had also a modern airport. A number of missions arrived from countries seeking immigrants, and schedules were set up for the transfer of refugees from assembly to resettlement centers for interviews with selection officers of visiting missions. The criteria varied with the needs of each country of immigration and we, resettlement officers, had to publicize and clarify the various requirements to inquiring refugees. The power given us, international officers, was quite enormous. The goal of our joint work was, of course, the speeding of migration to immigrant countries. Thus, should we find and determine willful and capricious sabotaging of our effort, we were authorized to withdraw all privileges of food and shelter from such persons. I do not know of a single instance where this rule was invoked. We were all too familiar with the anxieties and thoughts of refugees, who had to make the important decision to pull up sticks in Europe and venture forth to unknown places in America or Australia.

At a time when the United States quota was filled and an Australian Mission was in the field actively recruiting, I repeatedly called attention to the opportunities in that young country, only to be rebuffed. The overwhelming majority wanted to go to America and the letters from previously migrated fellow countrymen were eagerly read and carefully studied. They were, no doubt, a factor in the refugees' reluctance and decision to wait for possible, favorable action by the Congress of the United States of America. Their faith was justified and rewarded when Congress passed an amendment to "The Displaced Persons Act of 1948" allowing an additional 108,000 refugees and displaced persons into the country beyond the previously stipulated 200,000.

The motivation behind the Displaced Persons Act was humanitarian in essence, but it had also political aspects. It was recognized that the presence of well over a million restless displaced persons in the US occupied zone in Germany contained potential, dangerous, social dynamite. In the United States, a Displaced Persons Commission coordinated the resettlement work and sponsorships undertaken by thousands of church groups and social-minded individuals throughout America.

Canada, on the other hand, based its immigration policy solely on the nation's economic needs. They had a Rockminer Scheme and a Beetroot Workers' Scheme, among others, under which they sought young, suitable workers. After such workers had become established, the Canadian Government would assist such immigrants in bringing their families over.

The Australian immigration policy was motivated by the government's wish to populate a relatively empty continent with white people. Families were kept together, but when over forty-five years of age were classified as "dependents" in family units containing younger workers. New Zealand followed a similar policy.

Among European countries of immigration, national economic needs were prime considerations, for example coalminers for Belgium.

The outstanding feature of immigration laws in Central and South America was the stress laid on manual labor. They wanted no intellectuals and no Jews. Jews faced also some restrictions in Anglo-Saxon countries. Australia stipulated a quota of 5 percent, of which hardly one-fifth was filled, while Canada stressed nominated cases, which means that Canadian residents would indicate and sponsor the immigration of specific displaced persons. From the vantage point of an international resettlement officer I could appreciate the need of a country which would welcome Jewish immigrants. Israel answered that need.

All IRO assembly centers were open and people were free to come and go as they pleased. A few displaced persons found jobs in the German economy and became "free living." Some restless and adventurous young men went to the French occupied zone and joined the French Foreign Legion, which was then actively recruiting for their colonial war in Viet Nam. There was also some Communist-directed infiltration and propaganda in assembly centers.

When I took over the administration of the large Augsburg assembly center, located in the housing project of former workers of the Messerschmitt factory, I made two job changes: namely that of Chief of Camp Police and Chief of the Post Office. I found among the unclaimed mail many copies of *Pravda* wrapped in German newspapers. An active cell had operated in the camp, with the post office as its base. A fresh look at matters of security was also most desirable. International assembly centers were outside the jurisdiction of the German police, and such shelters were sometimes used by elements sought by the police. There was a small camp police to settle inevitable disputes and to discourage rowdiness. However, matters of greater seriousness were dealt with by the US Military Police and the Provost Marshal's Office.

The administration of assembly centers was similar to that of a municipality. Problems of food, shelter, protection, garbage collection, sanitation, etc. had to be solved. Education of children, care of the sick had to be attended to. Some people sought divorce, others wanted to get married. Oftentimes there was a time factor introduced, namely the departure for a new land.

Once I received a telegram from Naples, one of the embarkation centers for transports to Australia. A young man of seventeen years did not reach Naples, yet I had certified the nominal roll in Augsburg that he was on that transport. His mother alleged that she did not know where he was; other children reached Naples safely. A quick response with clarification was requested, otherwise the family would not travel on the ship to Australia. We worked quickly and feverishly on that puzzling case. What actually happened was the following. After her divorce, the German mother had remarried and the new husband from a Baltic country had decided to take his family to Australia. When the divorced German husband heard about the departure, he had come to the railway station to claim and kidnap his seventeen-year-old son. The mother was afraid to disclose the story lest she displease her new husband and spoil the emigration to Australia. It was simple after unraveling the story, but most disturbing before finding the live body of the son.

The documentation for emigration varied from one country to another. In general, however, it included our IRO form with all personal information; added was a "Good Conduct Certificate" by the German authorities, a CIC (Counter Intelligence Corps) certificate stating that no derogatory information existed, a "Berlin Check" verifying that the Nazi records held nothing deemed unfavorable to the immigrant's character. Then there would be photostats of diplomas or German trade union certificates showing that the bearer had passed certain tests and was found qualified in a trade or profession. Added would be a medical statement on the refugee's health, certifying also immunization, etc., and, of course, the Temporary Travel Document [TTD] in lieu of a passport. The last mentioned document was issued by the Tripartite Combined Travel Board in Germany, which on request by the IRO also granted the necessary exit permits. The TTD would have also the necessary visas for transit through or entry into certain countries.

The formalities for migration to the United States were a little more complex. Besides preparing the above-stated documents, applicants had to appear before a representative of the Displaced Persons Commission who would check on US sponsorship; then before the US consul for a visa; then before an official of the US Immigration and Naturalization Service. In all cases they had to swear to the truth of the statements made in the documents, doing more swearing in one day than they had done in their whole life.

The documentation procedures just described were the final steps before emigration. Most displaced persons had lived for many years in two to six assembly centers in a camp-like fashion, uncertain what their future would hold. Whenever lists of accepted refugees went up on the bulletin boards in the centers, a wave of excitement would ripple through the camp; friends were leaving, and vacant places were left in houses, churches, clubs, and schools. There was constant change, continued uncertainties. This nervous tension would carry over into the office of the resettlement officer.

Anxious people would constantly inquire about the status of their emigration possibilities. In some instances they wanted their departure delayed to go with friends. In some cases we had to postpone departures – as in the case of pregnant women or when epidemics of measles occurred.

Early in our operations it was mandated that all clerical and maintenance work in assembly centers be done by displaced persons. The best educated and most adaptable people were hired first. They were also the first to find opportunities for emigration. And so it happened that our office staff changed often and the functions of the international staff in the closing stages began to resemble those of a teacher, training new staff continuously. We received permission to hire Germans and engaged a number of *Reichsdeutsche*, the group of Germans previously resident in the Baltic states, Transylvania, or on the Volga, those who had heeded Hitler's call to come back to the German homeland. Such persons were usually from a former privileged middle class, well trained, and proficient in several languages. German was the lingua franca of displaced persons. Most of them were forced to learn it as impressed labor, in order to survive. There were many older people who just refused to study another language and made no attempt to adjust themselves to new, changed situations. They became a part of the "hard core" and hard to place. For them, IRO established old-age homes and transferred jurisdiction over them to the German Government's Welfare Department. There were also many abandoned, unattached children and orphans, which we gathered at an institution in Bad Aibling. For the care of the chronically ill, a special wing of a German hospital in Munich was dedicated. The transfer of jurisdiction to German authorities was a somewhat painful matter. When I was faced with that situation upon closing the Augsburg Center, I decided to make it as frank and direct as possible. After discussions with my supervisor in Munich, I called an open meeting at the center's recreation hall, to which I invited also officials of the German

47. January 1951, cocktails before a multinational farewell dinner for one of Harry Edward's directors.

Government's Departments of Labor and Welfare. They sent their senior civil servants. I presented the assembled displaced persons to them as human beings, not abstract statistics, people who had been forcibly brought to Germany against their will by their preceding government. I, on behalf of the International Refugee Organization, entrusted their future to their care. There must have been many heavy hearts to see IRO leave. Many must have felt truly left behind in a hostile Germany. Hundreds of displaced persons and their families moved into public housing projects offered by the German Government. They became "free living" in the German economy. As it happened, the German economy improved during the following years, and it is hoped that the DPs left behind became firmly established and integrated in Germany.

17

A NEW EUROPE

During the three years of my service with the International Refugee Organization I had taken part in many happy leave-takings of my international fellow workers and participated in many parties. However, after handing over all the documents to the Munich headquarters and all the buildings with their equipment to the German authorities, my departure seemed sad and gloomy. I was the last person to leave the Augsburg installations, looking dark and desolate, in the first week of December 1951.

Instead of returning home by air, I had booked passage on the *Île de France* from Le Havre to New York. This was considerably cheaper, and the margin saved I applied to an overland trip through Alsace Lorraine, the battle areas of Verdun, and the Aisne. It was a good decision, because it enabled me to attend a session of the Council of Europe at Strasbourg on the historic day of December 10, 1951. That day was the second anniversary of the Declaration of Human Rights, chosen for a special gathering of Europe's post-war leaders under the auspices of the Council of Europe.

My status as an ex-UN employee helped me to obtain a hard-to-get pass to the gallery of "The Orangerie," the Assembly's meeting hall. All proceedings were conducted in French, under the firm yet

48. On the back of this photo, Harry Edward wrote,
'Fleet foot in Zoot suit!' – caught by the camera when
rushing out of the billets.

benign chairmanship of [Paul-]Henri Spaak. Alcide De Gasperi, Premier of Italy, pleaded in fluent French for an early political union of the free democratic nations of Europe. "What we are doing," he declared in essence, "is the result of pressure from the East." "However," he added, "what we are doing is also good and desirable for itself." France's Foreign Minister Robert Schuman also urged a United Europe, but laid greater stress on the evolution of economic arrangements. It may be recalled that the Coal and Steel Community had come into existence just nine months earlier. Dr. Konrad Adenauer, Chancellor of Germany, tall and ramrod-straight, came to the speaker's podium. His opening phrases, spoken in German, seemed harsh and jarring on the ears, after the smooth-flowing French oratory. Although he had complete command of the French language, one could understand after a moment's reflection why he had chosen to address the Assembly in his native tongue. After all, this was Strasbourg, which the Germans had claimed for centuries and about which they had sung: "O Strassburg, Du wunderschöne Stadt!" (You beautiful town!) His speech had been awaited with much interest, because Dr. Adenauer had just returned from a visit to London, where he had had conversations with British political leaders. His comments reflected Great Britain's hesitation to join in the structuring of a United Europe, because of her commitments to her dominions and colonies. Dr. Adenauer referred to similar obligations carried by West Germany, desirous of keeping options and channels open toward the East for a possible return of her lost eastern provinces. Paul van Zeeland, Foreign Minister of Belgium, argued in a most lucidly knit speech in impeccable French that plans for a political approach be deferred but that approaches to an economic union be diligently explored.

When listening to the dreams of Europe's political leaders on that memorable day, about six years after the cessation of hostilities, many thoughts seemed visionary and unreal. Yet, looking back over the two decades which have elapsed since then, one is impressed with the solid accomplishments of that group of dreamers and those who followed in their footsteps. During my brief sojourn at Strasbourg I made some notes on the agenda for the first meeting of the Consultative Assembly held in 1949, four years after the guns of World War II became silent. This document provides a glimpse of the post-war concerns of delegates:

1) Changes in the political structure of European nations to achieve greater unity.
2) Social security, non-discrimination of workers because of differences of nationality.

3) Creation of a European Patent Office.
4) The introduction of a European passport.
5) Extension of human rights and the securing of fundamental freedoms.
6) European refugees.
7) Scientific research and development, pooling of material resources and technical manpower.

When comparing the hopes of 1949 with the realities at the beginning of the 1970s, we may briefly note:

1) Many changes in the political structure of European nations have taken place, many policies and institutions tending toward greater European unity have been established.
2) Non-discriminatory social security laws have been enacted.
3) Conventions on patents were passed in 1953 and 1954.
4) Unhampered travel without need of visas and customs checks exists today practically throughout Western Europe.
5) In the field of human rights, Europe has made the most significant gains. The first important convention passed by the Council of Europe was the one on human rights.
6) Displaced persons and refugees were a serious problem in 1949. In the Augsburg area, the Bezirk Schwaben of Bavaria, where I was working, 26 percent of the population belonged to the aforementioned categories.
7) As to scientific research and technical manpower development, the following organizations sprang from the deliberations and actions of the Council of Europe:

1950   The European Coal and Steel Community.
1953   European Conference of Ministers of Transport.
1954   European Organization for Nuclear Research.
1955   European Civil Aviation Conference.
1955   Ministerial Committee for Agriculture and Food.

1957   The European Economic Community.

1957   The European Atomic Energy Community.

The last twelve years have seen these significant milestones established on the road to European unity and international understanding:

1958   First session of the European Parliament.

1960   European Free Trade Association (EFTA) convention signed.

1963   Yaoundé Convention, associating eighteen independent states of Africa and Madagascar with the European Community.

1964   First meeting of the European Parliament with parliamentarians from the Yaoundé states.

1967   Merger of Community Executives and Councils into a single Commission.

One has here an impressive picture of then and now.

When reviewing the efforts European statesmen have invested in building machinery for a United Europe, I am invariably depressed by the relative absence of will and determination in building unity in the United States of America. It was on May 17, 1954, when the Supreme Court of the United States declared unconstitutional the separation by race of American citizens in schools. Yet today, over sixteen years later, hundreds of school districts have failed to comply with the court's directive and the country has drifted more and more into disunity.

When Robert Schuman launched his plan for a Coal and Steel Community on May 9, 1950, his declaration included this significant sentence:

The uniting of the European nations requires that the old opposition between France and Germany be overcome; the action to be taken must, first of all, concern France and Germany.

188

Here was bold and courageous facing up to realities and the assigning of a high-priority rating to the solution of that problem. The problem was an extremely complex one. There were thousands of French and German graves which silently argued against a union; many wars had been fought. There were different languages, different cultures, many vested national interests, economic rivalries, nation-oriented and divergent laws, customs rooted in the deep, deep past.

How simple seems in comparison the solving of America's racial problem. Here is a common national history, common language, common economy, even similar culture and culture values. Required is, of course, a strong, national will to accomplish unity and to assign to this goal the high priority American national unity deserves. Paraphrasing Robert Schuman's speech to apply to the American scene:

> The uniting of the races of America requires that the old prejudices of the white, agrarian South, of racial exploitation by business and industry and of racially divisive practices by organized labor be overcome; the action to be taken must, first of all, concern the leaders of American Government, business and labor.

As can be seen, my short stay in Strasbourg evoked many reflections and led to some research and studies on the birth and evolution of the European idea. After leaving the historic capital city of Alsace, I traveled through the Vosges Mountains, Saarbrücken, Metz, Verdun, and passed through many rural settlements made famous by battles which raged over this terrain in World War I. The memories which those names awakened formed a poignant juxtaposition to the hopes of European statesmen attempting to build a new integrated Europe on the ruins of World War II.

18

REUNITED WITH THE STATUE OF LIBERTY

The voyage on the *Île de France* from Le Havre was a truly rough one. For four days we passed through the two hurricanes which had capsized the *Flying Enterprise*, the ship that floated on its side for several days with the captain clinging to it. In mid-ocean our ship answered the distress call of the SS *Bristol*, a British tramp steamer with a crew of forty-one men. We "stood by" – or more correctly circled – the sinking ship for twelve hours in rough seas, when the ship would often disappear in the many valleys of the rolling waves. During the whole time, a rescue crew of the *Île de France*, dressed in heavy clothing and life-preservers, stood ready to launch a boat to go to the aid of the crew on the sinking vessel. While watching them prepare the lifeboat, I developed a profound respect and admiration for those men of the sea. The white-capped waves of the heavy sea, with a canopy of low-hanging clouds in the grey dusk turning into night, did not look at all inviting. Suddenly there were loud blasts by our ship's whistle and we steamed off, resuming our course, leaving the sinking ship behind. I inquired later about the story of our rescue attempt and learned that the ship had been actually in distress, but that the crew could not abandon ship, because the water in its hold was not high enough to bring the protection of marine insurance into operation. In the meantime, the SS *Bristol* had received news by radio that a sister ship of her company was on the way and due to reach her in twelve hours. The captain of the sinking ship had assured the captain of the Île de France that he could hold out till the arrival of that vessel. To this landlubber it seemed somewhat cruel to toot this cheerful goodbye to the crew on that sinking ship and leave her to wallow through the stormy night. We learned that the ship eventually had to be abandoned, and that she sank in the stormy North Atlantic without loss of life.

The last two days of the voyage were smooth, and upon entering the harbor of New York I passed once more the Statue of Liberty. Again a mixture of thoughts, of apprehensions entered my mind. Will I, anew, be assigned to a second-class citizenship, or will I remain "me," the international worker, the man?

This time I did not attempt to locate a job in American private industry. The doors appeared to be still securely locked, barring the entry of black men to office positions. Opportunities to low-level civil service jobs seemed to be available. I submitted my dossier of studies and experiences to the United States Civil Service Commission, which listed me as eligible and qualified as an administrative officer GS 13 and as a foreign affairs officer GS 12. By mail and personal calls I made contact with many international organizations and Federal Government departments. Then I had to wait for the result of security checks. This was the era of Senator Joseph McCarthy and his aggressive Communist smear practices, which had the personnel departments of federal agencies almost paralyzed. While waiting for the development of my application efforts, I enrolled in a number of courses in political science at the New School for Social Research and kept the home fires burning by a temporary job with the US Treasury Department, namely the processing of Federal Government tax refunds. My job rating was "Clerk, GS 2." It was an experience worth having, because in none of the civil service set-ups with which I had become acquainted, here or abroad, have I seen the human element consciously so downgraded and degraded. All absences of employees were checked by home visits made by sleuth-playing, favored foremen (GS 6), no conversation between employees or even humming to oneself was permitted on the job while executing the many monotonous tasks. When leaving this temporary, depressing job I requested an interview with the official in charge of these New York City operations. He was a former colonel of the US Army, who received me coldly. I submitted evidence of my relatively high Federal Civil Service rating and touched upon my international experience. Thereupon I conveyed my impression on the depressed morale of his staff. "What do you expect from GS 2 clerks?" was one of his comments. As I could not share his views, he became even colder and sharper, accusing me of having hummed a tune while working. To this I pleaded guilty. He had made inquiries from my forelady (GS 6) who had apprised me previously of that rule. This experience afforded an interesting glimpse into the atmosphere and leadership of an old-line Federal Government department.

19

ASIA AND THE SPECTER OF MCCARTHY

Among the many applications I had sent out was one to the Committee for a Free Asia, whose directors gave favorable consideration to my international experiences. I was invited to their head office in San Francisco, in California, where I was interviewed by the heads of the various departments during my one week's stay there. A position was offered me, and I was delighted to embrace this opportunity, to work again in the international field. In 1952, the Korean conflict, then two years old, and the French colonial struggle in Indochina occupied the front pages of newspapers. It was a time of nationalist stirrings throughout Asia, and the program of the Committee for a Free Asia providing educational support to developing nations seemed to have the germ of tremendous possibilities. There were other phases of international relations in which the committee was interested and active. Its basic philosophy was, however, to reach out to Asia, to seek and develop common interests, and to establish cultural bonds across the Pacific. The majority of its policy-making executive committee were Californians, with economic and cultural interests rooted in that west-coast state. They regarded their home state as America's window on the Pacific, and the Golden Gate as the natural door to the Far East, which is, however, westward from San Francisco. Aware of the changing post-war relationships of the United States toward Asian nations, they had sponsored the organization of the committee and its Radio Free Asia, the latter patterned in many ways after the activities of Radio Free Europe.

The radio programs consisted of news and comments on cultural activities by Asian groups in the United States and abroad, music, and historic reviews. They filled four hours each day and were conducted in English, Mandarin, Cantonese, and Hakka, diffused by short wave over a station on Guam. In these early years of the 1950s, many Asian leaders came to the United States on brief visits in response to invitations by the Departments of State, Agriculture, and Labor, as well as by private organizations promoting cordial international relations. This was the post-war period when the United States of America and the Soviet Union bid for the mind of the uncommitted world, a struggle openly waged in the forums of the United Nations. The Asian visitors to our shores were shown around our country by their hosts, and the Committee for a Free Asia was often instrumental in greeting them on arrival and sharing their impressions of the country upon their departure. In this manner we were able to place at their disposal many media of communications, for example newspaper publicity, articles reflecting their views, radio and television interviews. We also learned to listen most carefully to the cautiously phrased words of adverse criticism with a view to correcting our approaches to other distinguished visitors and their countries.

For instance, the editor of the renowned Indian English-language magazine of opinion *Thought* commented at the end of his American tour: "I have been to numerous cocktail parties, but was never invited into an American home." When I asked him whether I should hail a cab to take him to his hotel six blocks away, he declined and related to me this story:

A Hindu diplomat, amazed at the constant use of automobiles by Americans, asked politely: "Don't you ever use your feet?" There came the American's quick response: "Sure, I do. The right one is for the brake and the left one for the clutch."

A senator from Ceylon told me about the friendliness of Americans. On his cross-country journey by train he made the acquaintance of an American couple. They prevailed upon him to break his travel at Denver, to spend a few days at their home. During these days they showed him the scenic splendors of their environment, which proved to be a memorable experience for the Asian visitor. He turned to me in the re-lived delight of that visit, saying: "You know, this would never happen in Ceylon."

A Thai judge, when giving me his address with his verbal invitation for a visit, said to me:

When you come, please stay with us a while. Do not just rush through our country. We enjoy visitors and like to know them. True, we have many formalities which we observe, yet, they may also serve useful functions. Like enjoying the eating of an artichoke we peel the outer layers of ceremonial conventions to reach in time the inner person fully revealed.

The Committee for a Free Asia was aware that many national movements had been started by young patriots resident in this country, often inspired by our own Declaration of Independence. To mind would come: Sun Yat-sen, Syngman Rhee, Ignacy Jan Paderewski. A public relations program was, therefore, developed to establish and maintain liaison with existing groups of Asians in the United States. It became my assignment to visit a Sacramento group clustered around a Hindu temple, a Pakistani community living near a Stockton mosque, Filipino organizations, etc. Before embarking on those contacts, I deemed it advisable to call upon the consuls of the various Asian nations located in San Francisco to acquaint them with our programs and activities. Their reception was generally very cordial. However, one visit deserves a detailed description.

An Asian consul received me at the appointed time and launched immediately into a recital of unpleasant contacts he had had with American military personnel. I listened patiently and with interest and said at an appropriate moment that I did not represent the military nor the United States Government but a private organization concerned far more with the future than with the past. He then disclosed that he had spent over twenty-five years in the United States, especially on the West Coast, and that he remembered vividly and with strong feelings the many signs he had seen at the approaches to several towns and cities: "Orientals not welcome here!" Or sometimes more tersely: "Orientals keep out!" or "Orientals move on!" Thus, I was obliged to listen to the mental hurts suffered by a prominent representative of an important Asian nation.

This conversation took place in 1952, when the still existing racial segregation in the United States armed forces was being severely criticized by our Asian and European allies in the Korean War. This armed conflict was legally an action by the United Nations, and the separation of soldiers by the color of their skin within units of the United States as part of the United Nations forces was an insulting example before the eyes of Asian fighters, who had just concluded their anti-colonial struggle.

Asian racial sensitivity also surfaced at another occasion. I welcomed to the United States the Mohammedan advisor to the Ministry of Education of a large Asian country. I wanted to present him to my directors, but learned that they had scheduled a board meeting. They proposed, however, to call at my office on their way to the conference room. The directors spent five to ten minutes with the visitor and thereupon excused themselves. After they had left, the Asian educator turned to me and said with embarrassing frankness: "Now I feel more comfortable; now we can talk."

With the turning of the calendar to the year 1953, I was instructed to give my attention to youth activities. I welcomed this focus, as I saw a great possibility to involve the world's youth in international relations using the many branches of sports as a lingua franca. Since our Olympic Games at Antwerp, all subsequent Games had successfully nurtured and developed the social side of the Olympics and, furthermore, Asian youth and the Asian press had become very sports conscious. Plans were under discussion at that time to launch the Second Asian Games in 1954 at Manila, and the real worldwide Olympics were scheduled to be held for the first time in the Pacific area, namely at Melbourne, Australia, in 1956. The time seemed opportune. I was asked to submit a tentative plan of approaches and contacts for my directors' consideration, and upon their approval was sent to New York and Chicago to develop those contacts and to invite the opinions and suggestions of those experts.

In this endeavor, the committee's office in New York and my friends and former associates in the United Nations proved to be most helpful. In the United Nations I acquainted Mrs. Eleanor Roosevelt and Mrs. Edith Sampson, members of the US Mission, with our hopes and plans, which I also discussed with specialists in Community Development and Education. I procured lists of key officers and addresses of the Asian offices of UNICEF (the UN's

49. Self-portrait taken in February 1953. Harry Edward wrote on the back of the photo: 'The flash didn't go off, battery dead. Taken in my lodgings.'

Children's Fund), UNESCO (the UN Educational, Scientific, and Cultural Organization), and WHO (the World Health Organization). The directors of the International YMCA and of the UN Associations provided me with similar lists. The ever youthful and dynamic Roger Baldwin, Secretary of the International League for the Rights of Man, whom I had greatly admired as the founder and secretary of the American Civil Liberties Union thirty years before, was a seemingly inexhaustible source of information. Leaders in the field of International Labor, such as Messrs. [Jacob] Potofsky, [Jay] Lovestone, and [Arnold] Beichman, were encouraging and liberal with advice. Vera Dean, author and director of the Foreign Policy Association, as well as the executives of Olympic Associations such as Avery Brundage, Asa Bushnell, and Ted McGovern were interested and generous with information. At the end of my three weeks' trip I had accumulated an impressive file of source material and much data about ongoing programs in Asia.

Upon my return to San Francisco, I dove enthusiastically into the amassed information with a view to separating facts by subjects and geography, and correlating them into a meaningful pattern. We at the Committee for a Free Asia had also much useful knowledge and valuable contacts which had to be meshed into the newly acquired information. I became deeply absorbed and greatly excited about the feasibility of utilizing the enthusiasm generated by the 1954 Asian Games and the 1956 Olympics at Melbourne for the building of bridges of common interests, namely sports, across the Pacific. I saw possibilities of American athletic coaching, talent assisting and encouraging Asian youth in the furtherance of Olympic sports. The Olympic code seemed to provide a sound, juridical basis upon which equitable sports relationship with tolerance and good sportsmanship could be built. In sports, I reasoned, there is acceptance of basic rules by all participants, a recognition of the principle of equality, and of Olympic ideals and traditions. Briefly, in sports the world's youth speaks the same language, devoid of semantics. Furthermore, competitive sports provide a controlled outlet for combative tendencies, satisfying youth's sense of adventure by travel and public acclaim, while stimulating the imagination of thousands of non-participants.

I discussed the plan and its implementations with members of our organization, and the general approach with interested people outside. There were few critical challenges. I had seen in my own time the great development of international sport in many branches, and had also witnessed the social side of the Olympic Games become an established characteristic. Could these positive features be consciously nurtured and expanded? Simple, crude statistics seemed to encourage my optimism. In the Olympic Games of 1920, only Japan represented Asia, whereas in the 1948 Games there were twelve nations from that continent. In the Olympic Games of 1952, seventeen Asian nations sent 504 representatives to far-off Helsinki, Finland, where one out of every eleven competitors was an Asian. The growing interest in Olympic sports in Asia was to be rewarded and further stimulated by holding the Games for the first time in the Pacific area. To me, the evolution of events seemed to be the realization of dreams which had agitated the minds of a small group of us, athletes, at the Olympic Games thirty-three years before. I was greatly keyed up. I added constantly to the accumulated fund of information for the proposed trip to Asia, and had hopes that I might accomplish as thorough an organization job as had been my fortune to accomplish in Fuel Oil Rationing during World War II.

The spring brought political storm clouds from Washington DC. Congress became impatient with the stalemate of the Korean conflict and reviewed with critical eyes all USA–Asia relations and cooperative efforts. Thus, Radio Free Asia's programs received much adverse criticism: not the quality of programs, but the assumption that it reached a mass audience, which was doubted. Denied the free or low-cost use of the broadcasting facilities on Guam, Radio Free Asia was obliged to close down, forcing the dismissal of one-third of the committee's highly trained staff. I was not affected, but the separation of so large a number of co-workers was demoralizing.

Six weeks later, when working in the depressing atmosphere of a greatly denuded office, I was called to the executive suite and informed by the directors that "we are unable to continue with our plans to send you overseas, . . . home office was reorganized." "We have no position to offer you here which is commensurate with your abilities." It was a shock – perhaps no greater than the shocks which my co-workers had suffered two or three months before.

In the economic recession of that period, partly resulting from the war expenditures of the Korean conflict, jobs were scarce, specially at the 1953 summer vacation time. I took a part-time job as a stock clerk at Macy's, enrolled in a summer course at the New School for Social Research, and made a few trips to Washington to locate job vacancies at levels and categories in which I had been found eligible. I continued this plan of studies and work-search in the fall, but extended my work from part-time to full-time. The advantage I perceived was that the flexible work schedule allowed me to work on Saturdays, while giving me Wednesdays off for occasional trips to Washington. However, our federal capital suffered in those Eisenhower years not only from the war-induced economic squeeze, but also from the spiritual paralysis of McCarthyism and an influx on federal payrolls of retired army officers. The finding of a job vacancy at GS 10 to GS 13 levels proved to be an impossible task on my trips there approximately every six weeks. It was a most discouraging experience.

After one year of fruitless efforts to get out of the rut, I decided to get my academic background evaluated in American terms by heads of department at City College and the Baruch School of Business Administration and do some studying in a structured manner. I felt spiritually crushed when Dean Emanuel Saxe of the Baruch School informed me that no credits could be granted me for studies and examinations in England toward the professionally accepted title of "chartered secretary," a parallel status to that of the better-known chartered accountant, certified by the Institute of Chartered Accountants. Excluding those studies, I was given credits for a year and a half's work for the various classes I had taken at accredited institutions in the United States. Dr. Saxe helped me to face up to the harsh reality that I had to give up any hope of a job abroad to "stay in residence" for my studies at the school. Tied to a menial routine job because of economic need, I decided to apply my scarce spare time to studies toward an American degree. These were difficult days in our family, long hours of uninspiring work and long hours of studies and homework. My wife helped to balance the family budget with her earnings from the New York City Housing Authority. Our great concern was to give full support to our son in the opportunities offered him by the Fieldston School of the Society for Ethical Culture.

Suddenly one of the many applications I had filed with Federal Government agencies bore fruit. The United States Army inquired about my availability for a social worker's position, GS 9, for the handling of refugee problems under their command in Korea. I replied in the affirmative and the slow-moving "processing" procedure began operating. From time to time I inquired at the army's New York office for civilian personnel about the progress of my application. A white-haired, sympathetic lady of the office staff assured me several times that the papers had been approved at the various levels and were progressing in routine fashion. When the final stage had been reached, she asked me to get my passport with a recent photo affixed. This document was then sent to the US Army Washington. Unexpectedly came Washington's response that I was not accepted. I went to the New York office, spoke to the white-haired clerk, who gave me a sad, compassionate look. She shrugged her shoulders upon my inquiry regarding the reasons. I made two telephone calls to the US Army's Washington office handling civilian applications, only to be told that the reasons for administrative decisions cannot be divulged. This left me truly angry, bewildered, helpless, and frustrated. I felt upon my person the impact of McCarthyism, so widespread in those years with its innuendos and veiled reflections on persons' character and reputation. It caused me to speculate what reaction the sight of my photo must have aroused.

When I discussed my experience with friends, I learned that many university professors and scientists had been similarly treated by arrogant government officials, and that many of their friends and acquaintances had declined to work on government-sponsored programs. One may well reflect how much our space program had been set back by McCarthyism in the Eisenhower period. We only know that the first Sputnik took us unawares and proved to be an enormous, psychological Russian success. This period was a trying time for one's spirit.

As I attempted to be continuously busy, my disciplined efforts were also wearing down my physical strength. Nature had blessed me with a good physique, which I had tested in competitive sports. I had also learned that the application of a determined will could overcome flagging physical strength. Somehow I had discounted or even disregarded the lapse of time since those sport events in my youth, and therein I had made a very serious and grievous error. In the mid 1950s I had been under excessive stress, both emotional and physical for many, many months. Such stress had been caused by unrelieved, suppressed emotional tensions, far greater than I had realized.

20

BREAKING POINT

Each person has a breaking point, and I discovered mine on April 14, 1955, when I suffered a massive heart attack.

I was home at that time, having been ordered to stop work by the physician whom I had consulted upon my complaint of chest pains. On that day I was sweeping the rug, and the movement to and fro of the vacuum cleaner was the immediate cause bringing on the attack. I was alone in the apartment. Fully aware of my throbbing, laboring heart, I stopped sweeping, walked the 22 feet to the bed and stretched out on my stomach, fully conscious. I knew what had happened. I controlled myself to be calm, absolutely calm. Awake and fully conscious, I stayed in that position for six hours. In that time I reflected what the situation of my family would be if I were to die. However, I was not in a pessimistic mood, but was considering plans to summon medical help. I walked the 40 feet to the kitchen telephone, called the doctor, reported what had occurred. He said he would be on his way immediately. I left the apartment door unlocked to enable the doctor to enter. Then I walked back to the bed to await his coming. Immediately upon his arrival he took a cardiogram, which confirmed the fact of a thrombosis. The doctor arranged by telephone for hospitalization and summoned an ambulance, whose arrival coincided with my wife's return from work. The scene she encountered was an unexpected, unwelcome surprise.

While the doctor explained to her the facts of the occurrence, I observed and was impressed by the quick and efficient work of the ambulance attendants, the manner in which they lifted me onto the stretcher, strapped me in it, stood me up like a mummy in the elevator, then rolled me into the ambulance. My wife accompanied me to the New York Hospital, where day and night nurses watched closely over my blood pressure and other medical indices during the first critical twenty-four hours. I knew that I passed a feverish night, felt, however, quite good and certainly still alive in the morning. Nevertheless, I was astonished to be told not to lift my arms and that I would be fed by a nurse. This was a novel experience, which was, however, dispensed with on the following day. So it seemed I was getting better. Confined to bed and inactivity as I was, I decided to make the best of my stay in bed. The nurses were solicitous, cheerful, and pretty, and I found it easy to reciprocate with cheerfulness and wit. During the first week, the nurses and student nurses had to wash me. On one occasion a graduate nurse forgot in our lively conversation to wash my face, and I felt compelled to teasingly ask her how she could ever forget my face. The superintendent of nurses came to me and said that I proved to be the best therapy for nurses' morale they had ever had. Later on, in the third week, when nearly all the nurses had been withdrawn because I could do all the necessary hygienic tasks for myself, I had occasion to speak again to that stern-looking superintendent of nurses. At that time I filed my "complaint" with her, stating that there had been a decided decline in the quality of nursing service, especially of TLC (tender, loving care).

Confinement in hospital or in prison offers an excellent opportunity for introspection and for an analytical review of past and current events. One's visual world has then suddenly shrunk to the unaccustomed hospital room with its occupants. Our room accommodated six beds, which were occupied by male patients with coronary difficulties or stomach ulcers. During my three weeks' stay, there were, of course, a number of changes caused by the discharge of patients; yet, in these long hours in bed one had an opportunity to become acquainted with one's fellow sufferers and their visitors. The hospital staff focused its attention on the medical problems discovered and to be mended, but my layman's mind kept on speculating how much of the physical damage had been caused by anger, fear, worry, and frustration, often bottled up inside ourselves. To what extent was and is our materialistic-oriented society to blame for this human cost, a cost usually hidden from our eyes and of which we become aware only on occasional visits to hospitals, mental institutions, old-age homes, courts, and prisons? Although this philosophizing is a highly subjective mental exercise, nevertheless some deductions and real values will emerge if one can be courageously honest with oneself and ready to learn from experience. Lessons which I learned were to value and respect my good health, to listen more carefully to the body's signals of over-stress or impairment, and to maintain a sound outlook on life, in which respect for the dignity of the human being holds a central place.

Visits by friends afforded great pleasure in those days of physical incapacity. My son, then in his final weeks of his senior year at the Fieldston School, brought me a specially welcome surprise, namely the news that he had won a New York State Regents scholarship, in addition to the NROTC (Naval Reserve Officers Training Corps) scholarship previously awarded him. It seemed that he, himself, derived great pleasure from bringing me this surprise. My physical setback and the realization that some responsibilities had been shifted onto his shoulders appeared to have made an impact on him, affecting in some way his maturing. However, the greatest burden in that trying period was carried by my wife, and carried uncomplainingly. Not knowing the certainty nor extent of recovery made for a bleak, beclouded outlook into the future.

The stay in the hospital was a relatively short one, barely three weeks. I left that institution to the tune of the then popular song "You've got to have heart, lots and lots and lots of heart!" Convalescence was normal, but to me surprisingly slow. I had the pleasure of seeing my son graduate from high school in a colorful, open-air ceremony on Fieldston's Riverdale campus. An important chapter of his life had closed and four years of studies at Rochester University, NY were before him. All parents will know the financial commitments involved upon their children's entering college. Thus, I, too, had to give serious thoughts to a somewhat adjusted vocational career. I took a number of civil service examinations and accepted the first job offered, namely that of employment interviewer in the New York State Employment Service, the same functions I had performed twenty-four years before on a temporary basis.

This looked hardly like any progress in my life's vocational history. Yet, every human benefit and every prudent act is founded on compromise, and I hoped that the future would reveal that this step was both prudent and beneficial in the circumstances. In this new job as a trainee I was told there was much to be learned, as I followed the lecture courses prescribed as part of the in-service training. Much of the subject matter was not new to me, because my United Nations work had involved me in numerous contacts with European labor exchanges, their regulatory procedures, and underlying labor laws. Still fresh in my mind was also my experience in the service during the days of the New Deal, when Mrs. Eleanor Roosevelt and Mrs. Rose Schneiderman, President of the National Women's Trade Union League, kept the doors of their Lexington Avenue offices open to the public, and the director of the Employment Service was accessible at an office on East 28th Street. The atmosphere in this New York State service had changed considerably in a quarter-century which had seen a growth in the number of employees, a greater diversity of functions, and an expansion of civil service regulations. With the introduction of a multitude of rules and new features, it seems, something valuable had been lost that had made "the whole world kin" in the days of the great depression. A civil service had grown up with a rigidity of structure and frigidity of attitude, similar in many ways to that of class-conscious Europe – at least, so it seemed to me when observing the service as a new trainee. I was assigned to the Professional Placement Service, namely their Social Work Unit, where I was given some small latitude in the organization of the files and the introduction of a cross-index system indicating specialization and location of residences.

21

KOREA AND VIET NAM

In my study and analysis of job orders, I came across a job vacancy in far-away Viet Nam. In the year 1956, little was known about that country – except, perhaps, that it was part of former French Indochina, where French troops had been decisively defeated at Dien Bien Phu in 1954, in their unsuccessful struggle to retain control of their colonial empire in the Far East. An international child welfare agency, namely Foster Parents' Plan Inc., sought a director to establish an office and organize their services there. Command of the French language was a requirement. Again, all the challenges of such a job excited my mind. My health had been very good over the preceding two years, and I did not harbor the slightest doubt that I could satisfactorily discharge the duties connected with that assignment; yet the separation from the family, with my son's going through his second year of college, gave me reasons for careful reflection. After submitting my application to the agency's headquarters in New York City, I was called to a number of interviews with several directors. Upon their reaching a decision regarding my employment, quick action was requested in the obtaining of the necessary passport, visas, inoculations, and "post reports." I complied with their wish for swiftness and found myself en route to Asia three weeks later, namely in the first days of February 1957.

The directors had proposed my visiting their long-established agency at Seoul, Korea, to acquaint myself with the organization there, its structure, procedures, forms, and adaption to social needs. Hence, after a two days' stop-over at Tokyo, I flew to the Korean capital, where I landed on their coldest day in fifteen years (-15 °F). The sky was blue and clear, and I was informed that the cold blasts came from the plains of Manchuria. Customs inspection was held in an unheated building, and on that cold day the service was unusually quick and courteous. Reservations had been made for me in Seoul's modern, government-owned Bundang Hotel, where I stayed during my four days' sojourn in the Korean capital, filled with programed visits to several orphanages, refugee settlements, with many hours shared in the inspection and performance of office functions. I learned to take my shoes off at the door, which was not an easy task on those cold days, when the fingers were numb, stiff, and frozen, but such was the custom of the country. Taboo was the handshake, the friendly custom of Europe, which I found later equally acceptable in Viet Nam. In Seoul, however, when greeting Korean women, the oriental bow took the conventional place. Being obliged to walk barefooted or in thin paper slippers in the Korean house, I became interested in the construction of such dwellings, because I found the floor of the office and of the adjoining director's dwelling comfortably warm. I learned that the kitchen was built approximately a half-floor below the level of the office and private quarters, and that the flue of the kitchen fire was laid underneath the floor, warming it and the airspace above it, allowing people to sleep on straw mats laid on the floors. It was the same house construction the Romans had used in their early settlements in cold and damp Britain. In my brief stay in Seoul, I was also introduced to the Korean manner of eating, namely the assuming of the cross-legged, squatting position before a table about eight inches high. Initially it was hard on the leg muscles, the buttocks, as well as on the hands and fingers when attempting to convey the delicious food to a hungry mouth by means of two wooden chopsticks. But with persistence, and finally with the use of a spoon, my plate was emptied in my desperate endeavor to do just honor to my host and to the cook.

My flight from Tokyo to Seoul had taken me over the length of Korea. From the air, the country had looked rocky, rather harsh, partly snow covered, forbidding. Yet, I knew from descriptive material and from my experience in Greece that among the mountain ranges there were many fertile valleys; but in the month of February they had not been visible from the airplane. When I traveled through Seoul, a city of nearly a million and a half people, I saw hundreds of war-damaged buildings, some being repaired and reconstructed, and I sensed the pulsating energy of its residents. I wondered what the basic resources of the region were, and directed my questions to the American director of Foster Parents' Plan in Korea and his Korean senior assistant. They smiled, and the director, who had spent many years there, responded: "The Korean miracle." It seemed that many visitors, impressed by the vitality of the Koreans and having made similar observations, had asked the same question before. Since the partition at the Thirty-Eighth Parallel, access to the rich natural resources to the north had been blocked. Yet, a people with an ethnic homogeneity and a high educational level had applied its imagination and energies to the country's reconstruction with remarkable results. The single-minded and often ruthless regime of Syngman Rhee undoubtedly contributed to the harnessing of Korean energies in the post-war period. American aid, both military and economic, also contributed substantially. These surface observations practically invited further study and inquiry, but this was not possible because my itinerary called for my return to Tokyo and a flight to Saigon via Hong Kong.

The air approach to Saigon contrasted sharply with that to Seoul. There was a lush green below, an undulating, seemingly endless carpet of verdant vegetation, broken only by multi-colored geometric patterns of tended fields as the plane neared its destination. Ahead, beyond Saigon one could see a huge expanse of lowlands, watered by meandering, snake-like rivers, many rivers – the huge delta of the Mekong, Bassac, and Saigon rivers with some of their tributaries and connecting canals. The plane landed at Saigon's Tan Son Nhut airport, with its small but modern structure and conveniences built with American economic aid. When leaving the airplane, one felt engulfed by humid, hot air, a reminder that Saigon is just 10° latitude north of the equator. When going through customs I had my first problem case with Viet Nam's civil service bureaucracy. The official inspected the Japanese camera given me in New York by my employer and demanded a customs fee for the camera which, he suspected, had been purchased in Japan. He insisted on the submission of a bill of sale, which I did not have. I explained in French my mission and my intention to see the President of Viet Nam. I pulled out of my pocket a letter of introduction to President Ngo Dinh Diem, which had been given me by a French-speaking American who had befriended Diem in the days of his lonely exile at Maryknoll College and Seminary at Ossining, NY. This was too sudden a turn of events for the conscientious customs officer, who dropped any further discussion relating to the camera and let me pass. I, together with other passengers planning to stay in Viet Nam, had to surrender our passports to an immigration and security official at the airport. We were asked to claim our documents at a given government office two to three weeks later, an extraordinary procedure.

At the Majestic Hotel, where I checked in, I met a large group of Americans: engineers, draftsmen, and administrators of engineering companies constructing highways and bridges under contract with the US and Vietnamese governments. There was also a sizeable group of actors following a posted schedule of filming scenes for *The Quiet American*. I also shared a few pleasant moments of interesting conversation with the representative of *The New York Times*, Mr. Foster Hailey.

Prior to my leaving New York I had called upon many members of the American Friends of Viet Nam. They were a group of people who had worked in or visited that Southeast Asian country, hence had a first-hand acquaintance with many phases of social conditions. Some of them had given me letters of introduction to friends and acquaintances then resident in Viet Nam. In this manner I got to know many persons in key positions and learned from them much about this strategically situated nation. In those early days in Saigon, the public relations director of *The Quiet American* and I were invited to a dinner in the home of Monsignor Hartnell, Regional Director of Catholic Charities. There the quick-witted, verbose, and "bouncy" Jewish PR director asked me whether I was Catholic, to which I responded in the negative. Thereupon, with gleaming eyes and malice aforethought, he smilingly introduced me to the assembled Catholic guests as the newly arrived director of Planned Parenthood.

The assignment given me as director of Foster Parents' Plan activities in Viet Nam was 1) to obtain a signed contract with the government, 2) find office space, 3) equip offices, 4) engage and train an office staff, 5) initiate the specialized social services rendered by this international child welfare agency. The procuring of a signed contract and, with it, the legalizing of our status and work seemed to me the most important phase of my initial work. With this in view, I set up an appointment with the minister of health and welfare. In a two hours' conference, he insisted on many changes in the previously submitted draft contract, changes to which I consented. However, I could not yield on the point that the determining of eligibility of each case of American sponsorship of a Vietnamese child was to be at his discretion. Such an arrangement would have made our service an extension of the Vietnamese Government. The draft contract had been drawn up in harmony with the basic agreement of August 31, 1954, entered into by former US Ambassador Donald Heath with the Government of Viet Nam. Under that umbrella agreement, voluntary agencies were given the right to import relief supplies without imposition of customs dues, and to obtain free transportation to inland points of distribution. Representatives of such agencies were to have freedom of movement to supervise the distribution of supplies. With the mentioned point left unresolved, the minister proposed his discussing the terms of the contract with President Ngo Dinh Diem.

A few days later, on February 22, 1957, I was shocked and shaken when Foster Hailey, the representative of *The New York Times*, hailed me at the Majestic Hotel: "Oh, Edward, guess what happened today? President Diem was shot at Ban Me Thuot!" In the fraction of a second following that statement it seemed that hundreds of thoughts raced through my mind. I glanced at the street, there was calm, no crowds there. I wondered why I had not heard anything on the radio. If the president was killed, that would mean a revolution. I was tense and eager for more news. Mr. Foster Hailey continued calmly:

> I just flew in from Ban Me Thuot (some 190 miles north east of Saigon) where the president had met in the stadium the assembled leaders of the Montagnards, the tribes of the hill country. I stood about 15 feet from the president when a man came out of the crowd and opened fire at President Diem, wounding the minister of agriculture, standing at the president's side but not injuring the president himself. The assailant was overpowered and arrested. Immediately on arrival at Saigon I submitted my dispatch to the Ministry of Information. The officials told me that this occurrence was none of my business and that they could not pass it. Thereupon I told them that I would be obliged

to fly to Singapore and file it there. After a hurried conference they approved it for immediate dispatch by cable.

With the mind of a newspaper man, he reflected: "This will make the front page of the *Times* for two days."

We discussed at some length the probable impact of this incident, the attitude of the Vietnamese news services, and speculated on the motivation and the possibility of a conspiracy. On the following days the Vietnamese newspapers reported the attempt on the president's life, but played it down to the bare outline, as reported by the foreign press.

I learned that some of the acquaintances I had made in Saigon, thanks to the letters of introduction, had spoken to the president about the work Foster Parents' Plan was planning to launch in Viet Nam. He was, therefore, in possession of fragmentary side lights of my mission when the minister of health and welfare submitted to him the draft contract with the proposed changes. It appears that the president had asked the minister to leave the contract with him and had indicated that he would discuss the matter with me directly. I learned many months later that the minister of health and welfare was greatly offended by the president's decision to take the negotiating of the contract into his own hands, and that the minister thereafter gave up all welfare functions of his ministry, having them transferred to a newly created Ministry of Welfare.

In the second week of March 1957 I was informed by a government official that the President of the Republic of Viet Nam wanted to see me at the Presidential Palace on March 25th. The expression of such a presidential wish is, of course, the equivalent of a "royal command," to be promptly accepted. I ordered a white suit, which is practically a uniform *de rigueur* for such occasions, arranged with the US Operations Mission for the loan of a limousine, and thus felt prepared for the day as it approached. The limousine took the Vietnamese Government aide and me to the Presidential Palace, where the Chief of Protocol received us and conducted us to the Ambassadors' Reception Hall. After a while, we were informed that the president would be available in a few minutes, and the Chief of Protocol then led me to a room reserved for presidential audiences. The president arrived some minutes later with a rather hurried step, in the company of his official interpreter. He appeared, however, quite relaxed and affable, greeting me with a ready, warm smile. I knew that he was about 5 feet 3 inches tall, yet he seemed even shorter and more rotund than I had judged from photographs. His face was round and smooth, belying his age of fifty-six years. As soon as he had learned that I was quite fluent in the French language, he dismissed his interpreter and invited me to partake of the aromatic, Vietnamese tea served to us by waiters. I presented the letter of introduction I had brought from the American acquaintance of the president, and after a few formalities the president asked me to tell him the story of our organization and of my mission in Viet Nam.

I described the organization of a committee of philanthropic Americans under the impact of the early days of the Battle of Britain, when many British parents were concerned about the safety of their children and sent them to the United States and Canada. This committee assisted in the reception and placement of thousands of British children. With the turn of events, when Great Britain was no longer a beleaguered bastion but became the base for the invasion of Europe, British parents sought the return of their children, and the committee was able to render again a useful, needed social service in assisting in the children's transfer. After the Allies' landing on Normandy's beaches and the retreat of the Nazi forces, thousands of orphans were found in distress and need in many Allied lands. The committee, then organized under the name of Foster Parents' Plan for War Children, raised funds for the care, maintenance, education, training, and well-being of children orphaned, destitute, and distressed, and provided means for the

50. April 1957, the French-language *Saigon Gazette* prints on
its front page a picture of Harry Edward's meeting with Vietnamese
President Ngô Đình Diệm. The headline quotes Harry: 'I can say with
respect and sincerity that the President is a man who really knows the
problems of his people.' Diệm's tenure was a short one.
51. Harry Edward sharing tea with Ngô Đình Diệm.
52. Harry Edward in Saigon, in 1958, with some of the
orphans assisted by the international child welfare agency
he headed in Vietnam.

transmission and expenditure of funds. The organization stressed the purely humanitarian character of its work, free from any connection to any group having a political or propagandistic interest. Offices were opened in London, Paris, Brussels, Rome, Athens, and later in Seoul and Pusan, and tens of thousands of children and their families benefited from the unique personal services rendered by Foster Parents' Plan, Inc., the name of the then almost twenty-year-old international child welfare organization. The unique feature lay in the person-to-person relationships encouraged and established across national borders. The children benefiting from the generosity of their American, Canadian or other sponsors would write monthly letters to their foster parents, describing their home, school, living conditions, and their sponsors would acquaint them with his or her homelife, vacation trips, and other vignettes of life. In such a manner, many windows were opened from one land to another, and international, cultural understanding enhanced, all through the eyes of children and their philanthropic friends.

President Ngo Dinh Diem listened with evident interest. He said that he had experienced difficulties in organizing and enthusing the wealthier groups of Vietnamese in participating in relief work, in the transport and settlement of refugees from the north. He praised the ready assistance provided by the poor people residing in villages along the highways. His mind seemed to be on the great exodus of 1954, when about 800,000 refugees left North Viet Nam and went south, while about 140,000 traveled northward to live in North Viet Nam. He appeared to become quite absorbed in memories of the past as he rushed on in sketching the transplanting and settling of whole villages in many parts of the Republic of Viet Nam. I attempted to make some comments pertinent to the points he described, but failed to arrest his attention. When I realized that he did not seem to hear my respectful: "Oh, Monsieur, le Président!" I ceased making any attempt to interrupt what became essentially a monologue, an exposition of his philosophy of welfare, of ways and means of assisting the refugees.

I learned later that President Ngo Dinh Diem was a compulsive talker, who often lost himself in a theme which not only absorbed his mind, but also shut out his senses of hearing and seeing. This characteristic distressed many of the presidential advisors, who were anxious to submit their own thoughts and contributions only to find themselves dismissed at the conclusion of the president's exposition. However, in his talk – it seemed clear to me – he made these points: 1) he did not want to have Viet Nam portrayed as a poor country, and 2) he did not wish to have his country shown as begging for help. When I stated that a government official had brought to my attention a family in Hué badly struck by a series of misfortunes, the president offered the use of a government plane to take me to the old imperial capital in the northern part of South Viet Nam. Thanking him, I pointed out the necessity of first carefully organizing our operations in the Saigon area, before expanding our services into the provinces. Thereupon he reached for the telephone and called the governor of the Delta Region, one of the three governors representing the president in the three regions of the country, which were the northern provinces, the central highlands, and the delta provinces. At that point, the audience had lasted over one hour. While awaiting the arrival of the governor, I was able to add some pertinent information to the data originally given and comment on certain rights and privileges usually accorded social service organizations in the international field. I mentioned that such terms were provided for in the draft contract which I had discussed with the minister of health and welfare.

Upon the arrival of the governor, the president explained the substance of my mission and expressed his wish that I be taken to Phu My, the government's old-age home, and to Thu Dau Mot, the school and shelter for deaf and mute children. Both institutions were serviced by Sisters of French Catholic Orders. I expressed my thanks for the audience with which the president had honored me, as well as for his interest in the work to be launched. I assured him of our agency's sincere efforts to bring assistance to the children of Viet Nam. The audience had lasted one hour and thirty minutes. My conference at the Presidential Palace was reported by the Vietnamese press, and I was inwardly hopeful that this publicity would speed the formulating and concluding of the contract. The draft contract was on the president's desk, one of hundreds of documents accumulated there awaiting action. To pry it loose with a notation of approval was the politically delicate task to be accomplished.

The New York headquarters of our agency had difficulty in understanding the delay in procuring a signed contract. The executives were anxious to set in operation the Vietnamese program at an early date and were preparing publicity material to give it a successful send-off in the United States. Steve Allen, the popular television and radio personality, had consented to sponsor the first Vietnamese child. I was fortunate in getting an interview with the minister of foreign aid, who was not only sympathetic with our program but also sensitive to the American approach and method of organizing such a promotional plan. He was able to speak to the *chef du cabinet de la présidence*, the chief administrative officer of the presidency, a position similar to that occupied by Sherman Adams in the Eisenhower Administration. That high official, an able lawyer and chief drafter of the Vietnamese Constitution of 1956, reviewed the draft contract, made a few minor changes, and signed the document on May 3, 1957, for and on behalf of the Government of Viet Nam, avoiding thereby any jurisdictional disputes among ministries.

While my main efforts were focused on the finalizing of the contract, I was able to recruit four Vietnamese employees who became the nucleus of a larger staff later. All were able to speak French, three of them also spoke English. The accountant had, besides, fluency in Chinese, acquired when he was a resident of Hong Kong. The government provided us with a room in one of their government office buildings, and I "raided" the USOM (US Operations Mission) warehouse for surplus desks and typewriters, an effort which was most rewarding. Thus, we were in business less than three months after my arrival. I was most fortunate in having as my senior assistant a graduate social worker from Saigon's School of Social Work, organized in 1947 under French auspices. The school's entrance requirement was a graduation certificate from a school of nursing or school of midwifery. Studies in the discipline of social work extended over two years, including six months of field work with some recognized social welfare agencies. The background in health services and hygiene proved to be most useful in the Vietnamese setting.

Our small staff set to work with much enthusiasm. They contacted orphanages, nurses, district chiefs, Catholic Sisters and Brothers, teachers, and social welfare organizations. We stressed that we were an international, private organization dedicated to child welfare, working under a contract with the Government of Viet Nam. I placed photostatic copies of the contract document into their hands to counter any challenges as to the authenticity of our statements. The public response was most favorable. We were put in touch with genuine cases of hardship and distress, which we investigated and documented in the prescribed form for submission to our headquarters in New York. We administered our humanitarian service equitably, on the basis of need, without regard to political factors. Catholic Sisters brought to our attention families which they had kept from starving after the disappearance of the head of the family. After verification, we documented children of such family units for adoption, i.e. sponsorship. Our New York office informed us after a while that the list containing cases in which the father had "disappeared" had not reached them. An inspection of our copies revealed that the group of cases sent with the lost list included two cases in which the father had been sent to a camp for political prisoners. The families had heard of their fate only after a long period of silence. This was the first indication that our mail was being tampered with and censored. Thereafter all mail was sent "registered," which assured delivery, but was no guarantee of freedom from censorship.

By reliable grapevine-telegraph I was informed that the newly appointed minister of social service or *action sociale* had held a meeting with his staff. At that gathering the staff had challenged the minister by raising the question why the government service could not be as effective as the new American-sponsored international child welfare organization. I do not know whether the minister suffered a "loss of face" in this confrontation. However, we soon felt the dead hand of government clamping down on our work. Unbeknown to us at that time, letters had gone out from the Ministry of Welfare that all proposals for "adoption" or sponsorship under the Foster Parents' Plan be sent to the Ministry for approval. Almost immediately the free and frank communication we had enjoyed with nurses, teachers, and district chiefs disappeared.

In December 1957 I received an invitation to a conference at the Presidential Palace from the *chef du cabinet de la présidence*, who had signed our contract. I prepared myself thoroughly for that conference and drafted an aide-memoire in case I would find it impossible to cover verbally all important points. I was taken to the palace by a senior officer of the Welfare Department who was, I learned later, a secret service officer on Mme. Nhu's staff. Mme. Nhu was the sister-in-law of the president and the official hostess at the Presidential Palace. I explained to the senior minister in a forthright manner our operations in compliance with the terms of the contract to which he had attached his signature. I developed in detail the method and standards we were applying to our humanitarian work in the spirit of our agreement and the knowledge we brought to it because of our long experience in Europe and Korea. He was an engrossed listener who asked challenging questions. The animated half hour of our conference sped by, ending with a cordial handshake and his comment: "Ah, c'était une bonne conférence!" ["That was a good meeting!"]. He was in complete agreement with our application of the contract terms. During those thirty minutes, the representative from the Ministry of Welfare sat by silently like a dark shadow in the background.

Anxious to develop our work, I was not sufficiently detached at that time to see the political maneuvering of the palace guard, desirous of bringing our work under the domination of one of their ministries, in this case the Ministry of *Action Sociale*. Wherever foreign aid was involved, this tendency could be observed. My effort was to deal directly with the beneficiaries, affording no opportunities for bribery or extortion of tributes. Our staff was scrupulously honest, all money transactions were witnessed by two members of our staff, documents countersigned, and all our records were audited by the world-renowned firm of Price, Waterhouse & Co., chartered accountants. In the early days we accepted as evidence of receipt the fingerprints of the illiterate parents. Later we insisted on a written signature, forcing them thereby to learn the writing of their name as the first step toward literacy. It was heart-warming to watch the children teach their parents and to see the glow of satisfaction and pride in the parents' eyes upon their accomplishment. Our staff was liberal with praise for their progress and thus we gave encouragement to further studies. No longer would those parents be obliged to ask officials of the government to sign for them – a long step was taken toward personal independence.

For the proper evaluation of each case of distress, our social workers or I would visit the homes of the prospective beneficiaries, which took us into the slums and shanty towns of Saigon. In this respect we were most unorthodox in the eyes of Vietnamese officialdom and even suspect of Communist sympathies. Social workers of the Ministry of *Action Sociale* never left their offices, handling only paperwork and compiling reports and statistics. Home visits and the recording of home conditions were delegated to the police. The attitude of government officials high and low toward us, as people deeply concerned with the welfare of slum residents, paralleled in many ways the suspicious views and prejudices registered in America toward those who identify themselves with the struggles of ghetto dwellers. Labels, such as the Vietnamese equivalent of "n----- lover," usually "Communist," were easily attached to those who refused to recognize the social chasm that was supposed to separate them from the dwellers of shanty towns. This attitude and the desire to establish and to extend quickly the authority of the Saigon-based government to the Seventeenth Parallel over and above the heads of the population created an emotional and political vacuum brutally exploited by Hanoi-based infiltrators. For centuries, the village had been the center of Vietnamese life. It represented the enlarged family and provided social security to its members. It was the administrative center, and the economic and social life of the villagers revolved around it. People referred proudly to their home village where their ancestors lay buried, although they may have migrated to other parts.

The revolution against the French colonial masters was engineered and led by the "intellectual" middle class, i.e. the lawyers and physicians, who had the freedom to move among their countrymen by virtue of their profession. They were strongly represented in the government of Ngo Dinh Diem, whose commitment upon taking office in 1954 was: 1) to gain national independence from the French, 2) to preserve national territorial integrity, and 3) to stave off the Communists. Ngo Dinh Diem was spectacularly successful in the first three years of his regime, but then the weaknesses roughly sketched became visible. In place of increased freedom had come increasing repression; Diem governed, but did not lead.

American policy strongly supported Ngo Dinh Diem, who had an impressive background as a brilliant administrator, and who was, in the eyes of friends and foes alike, regarded as incorruptible. However, from 1958 American diplomats found the manipulations of Diem's younger brother Nhu and his articulate wife, the malevolent Mme. Nhu, beyond their reach and power of influence. Ngo Dinh Nhu held the position of presidential political advisor, but had no government status. Yet he moved commanders and military units around the country to prevent the formation of any coalition of officers that might threaten the regime. Madame Ngo Dinh Nhu organized her own Women's Solidarity Movement, with uniformed cadres and intelligence apparatus. The minister of welfare was her attorney and, in retrospect, it seems to me that Mme. Nhu regarded all Vietnamese welfare activities as her exclusive, private domain. At the opening of the School for the Blind in Saigon, organized by Miss Genevieve Caulfield at the invitation of the government, this blind American leader, renowned for her work for the blind of Thailand and Japan, was brusquely brushed aside and disregarded by Mme. Nhu, who appeared at the inauguration as the guest of honor. The presiding minister of education did not offer any recognition to Miss Caulfield who, a few years later, received from President Kennedy America's highest civilian award.

I had enjoyed a cordial relationship with the minister of education in planning the distribution of 100,000 wooden shoes to the school children of Viet Nam. Such shoes, produced in the Vietnamese economy, had been underwritten by American donors. When noticing my presence in the group of many visitors to the inauguration of the School for the Blind, the minister of education insisted that I take a seat on the row of chairs reserved for dignitaries, namely the second chair at Mme. Nhu's left, while the minister of welfare, to whom I always reported our activities and plans, was assigned the fourth chair at her right, probably to his resentment, all of it to my utter dismay. It was my intention and endeavor to keep away from politics, yet one becomes involved and ensnared by occurrences such as these.

In the year 1958 the air of intrigue and repression grew thicker. No organizations whether for purposes social, cultural, educational, sports, etc. could be formed unless licensed by the Ministry of Information and Youth. The investigation of charter members and the issuance of a license would consume many months. Outside Saigon no group in excess of four could meet unless prior notice had been given to the local police, such was the announcement posted in hotel rooms. Our work also felt the impact of the government's repressive measures. As already mentioned, the Ministry of Welfare had sent out letters to teachers, nurses, district chiefs, and organizations, who had cooperated with us. I had initially submitted the list of our contacts to the minister. The communication said that needy cases were no longer to be referred to our agency, but to the Ministry. I was informed to apprise the minister of welfare of any journeys outside the Saigon area at least forty-eight hours before my intended departure. All of these restrictions were quite contrary to the terms and the spirit of the contract we had concluded. The Ministry then sent us long lists of recommended cases, which we investigated only to find that the lists were laden with government employees. We were obliged to decline most of them as being outside the guidelines which we had formulated, a copy of which we had previously mailed to the Ministry. By means of conferences with the Ministry of Welfare, I hoped to bring our operations back to the spirit which had animated the discussions leading to the signing of our contract. It became clear, however, that only complete submission to the dictates of the minister, implying a dissolution of the contract, was the aim. In the meantime, the government's signer of our contract, the *chef du cabinet de la présidence*, had broken with the regime and had resigned. All my efforts to reach his successor were futile.

My relations with the Ministry took a turn for the worse when I discovered that a few hundred cooking stoves, a gift of Foster

Parents' Plan to the most needy families of a burned-out village, were being sold by a committee organized by the Ministry of Welfare. After bringing this to the minister's attention he explained that his administration aimed to be "fair" to all the citizens of the burned-out village. As there were not enough stoves for all the families, those who got them had to pay for them and the money was then placed into a community fund for the benefit of all. Such was the story of the minister of welfare. I pointed out that under this arrangement the best situated received the gifts intended by the donors for the families in greatest need. The minister was furious about my discovery and accused me of having distributed gifts without his knowledge and consent. He referred to twenty stoves of various sizes and styles which we had previously distributed with the cooperation of the local priests and village chiefs, in order to determine which size and style might be most acceptable and suitable. What had apparently piqued the minister were the queries by villagers why American gifts distributed by an American welfare organization were free, whereas when distributed by a Vietnamese government agency they had to be paid for.

The directors of Foster Parents' Plan had placed at my disposal a Letter of Credit in the amount of $1,000 earmarked for relief of families of the burned-out village. The amount had been sent me in response to my documented report of the disaster which had befallen the four parishes making up the village. After some planning with local leaders, we had thought that stoves, replacing the open hearth, would introduce a new safety measure and be also a symbol representing the center of family activities, around which a new life would be built. However, after observing how the government's deliveries of the first batch costing $250 had been handled, I withheld the further development of this plan.

Frustration seems to have been – and still is – an in-built feature of work in Viet Nam. There were several heads of voluntary agencies who shared with me the disappointments they felt resulting from the blocking of their endeavors, to which they had dedicated their thoughts and strength. Such stories came to me especially when I was the chairman of ICVARV, the International Committee of Voluntary Agencies in the Republic of Vietnam, in 1958. However, we members of ICVARV, cannot say that we had not been forewarned. I recall that at a 1957 meeting of that organization the lady chairman of the French Red Cross had said that we, the new members of that committee, would become disappointed and frustrated with the results of our work. At that occasion I had commented that I was an eternal optimist and had hopes. Subsequently I repeatedly invited the representative of the French Red Cross to our meetings, but the mentioned 1957 meeting was her last attendance. It was obvious to many of us that the government of Ngo Dinh Diem was playing off American influence against waning French influence, and the lady's discontinuance of cooperation with international social welfare work presaged, in effect, the subsequent withdrawal of French scientists attached to the Pasteur Institute and other French institutions. Their resignation was a serious blow to Vietnamese health services. In 1958 there were only 369 licensed physicians for South Viet Nam's population of 15 million. Several provinces were without a medical officer. To alleviate the need, the US Operations Mission proposed the introduction of qualified Filipino doctors, the cost to be underwritten by American foreign aid. The politically organized medical profession of Viet Nam first balked at that suggestion and then insisted that the Vietnamese Medical Association would reserve for itself the sole power to assign such Filipino physicians, presumably to areas to which the Vietnamese doctors would not go. This was deemed unacceptable to the medical director of USOM, hence the plan fell through, and the poor people of Viet Nam were the losers. The constant attempts of acquiring, holding, and exercising veto power over American aid, economic and military, runs through most of our relationships with that Southeast Asian country.

From the first days after my arrival in Viet Nam, I used every opportunity to learn the Vietnamese language. Initially I attended classes organized by the Vietnamese–American Institute, later I pursued such studies at the University of Saigon. My aim was to acquire the fundamentals of the language, to enable me to communicate adequately and freely with the people of the soil. In order to improve my thinking in that language and to exercise the difficult tonal inflections, I arranged for two exchange lessons weekly with our chief English translator. I also sought opportunities to speak to children, hoping to master thereby their basic thinking and expressions. I had been most favorably impressed by the language abilities of the Brothers of the Catholic Order of Don Bosco, devoted to the welfare of orphan boys. Several Brothers had arrived from European and Latin American countries without any knowledge of Vietnamese, yet after a year they had mastered the language sufficiently to freely communicate with their charges. I realized that behind such an accomplishment was much disciplined work, but I was determined to make a valiant attempt to acquire such knowledge. I tried to move freely among Vietnamese. On occasions I attended some social affairs, e.g. a family gathering or wedding. However, before accepting such invitations, I took the precaution of discussing the advisability of my attending with my trusted chief social worker.

As my relationship with the minister of welfare became strained, staff members and Vietnamese professionals brought me the news that they had been approached by government officials speaking disparagingly of our work, implying the advisability that the Ministry of Welfare supervise closely our work. I urged our staff to conscientiously pursue our efforts for the benefit of the poor people of Viet Nam in the spirit of our contract with the government. I expressed the belief that there were more people of goodwill than of ill-will. To strengthen the hands of our social workers in their public contacts, I supplied them with our guidelines and photographs of our original contract. I became increasingly aware of the monitoring of our telephone conversations, the censoring of our mail, the screening of all persons coming to our offices in the government building. I learned that a Vietnamese civil service acquaintance had been "promoted" to a better-paying security service job, admittedly to report on my views and actions. The setting in which I found myself reminded me of a passage in *The Rape of the Mind* by Joost A.M. Meerloo, MD:

> By forcing a man to betray his inner feelings and himself, we actually make it easier to betray the larger community at some future date. If the law forces people to betray their inner moral feelings of friendship, even if these feelings are based on juvenile loyalties, then that very law undermines the integrity of the person, and coercion and menticide begin.

I saw the integrity of many persons violated, coercion practiced, and menticide, the rape of the mind, committed. A few years later, the above dictum was vindicated by events in which President Ngo Dinh Diem and his brother Nhu lost their lives and the minister of welfare narrowly escaped with his own. In 1958, with no political bargaining power in hand, I was obliged to yield to coercive maneuvers of the welfare minister; our agency had to accept the screening and selections by the Ministry of *Action Sociale*. The change in the political climate between early 1957 and late 1958 was great, indeed. In 1957 there was optimism in continuing political and economic improvements, land distribution, government reform. President Diem visited Korea, Taiwan, India, the Philippines, and the United States of America, raising the prestige of South Viet Nam. The conference of the Colombo Plan nations was held in Saigon. President Diem made a few trips into the provinces, but his austere personality did not exude the warmth and empathy for which the people of the soil were yearning. He was unable to strike emotional roots into the hearts of the peasantry, and remained to most people a distant Mandarin image. His political following was mainly in the armed forces and the civil service. He knew intimately intrigue and treachery, which he had exploited in his rise to power. Plagued by suspicions of revolutionary coups, he relied more and more on members of his family in the execution of his policies. The Ngo family exerted considerable political power and influence as ambassadors, political advisors, governor, Catholic bishop. However, these circumstances also earned for the regime the accusation of nepotism.

The year 1958 saw the replacement of many civilian chiefs of provinces by military men, the shuffling of military commanders, declining activities in land and civil service reform. The revolutionary thrust of 1954–55 seemed spent. A reaction to the authoritarian rule of the Ngo family set in, spawning intrigues and counter-intrigues. That period marked the decline of the Ngo Dinh Diem era. It also ushered in the era of North Viet Nam's renewed political penetration into villages of South Viet Nam, with increased infiltration of armed gangs murdering village leaders. The story of work in Viet Nam is somewhat depressing. It is the story of intrigue, bribery, and corruption. It is the story of frustration to most who came to help the young national government. Yet, it was obvious that the people of the soil were deserving of a better fate. I met many sincere Vietnamese civil servants in high and low positions eager to uplift and serve their deprived fellow citizens yet entrapped in an antiquated civil service structure. They, too, suffered despair and frustration. In 1958–59 many critical comments about Ngo Dinh Diem's leadership found their way into the columns of the American press.

Thus, in October 1959, almost a year after my return to the United States, I was invited by the American Friends of Viet Nam to be a panel speaker on the topic of Social Welfare. The two days' conference was promoted by the public relations firm of President Ngo Dinh Diem, ostensibly to improve his image in the United

States. Before accepting the invitation, I made it clear to the president of the American Friends of Viet Nam that I might be critical on some aspects of the regime's performance. I was told that there would be no restrictions on my comments, hence I accepted. At the conference there were four English-speaking ministers of President Diem's regime, some of whom presented papers. Most speakers were, however, American specialists in agriculture, economics, health, education, and social welfare, who reported on their experiences in Viet Nam; nearly all of them avoided any criticism of the regime. It was at the luncheon session that Roger Baldwin, Secretary of the International League for the Rights of Man, speaking from the floor, boldly expressed his distrust of the Diem regime when the existence of internment or concentration camps for political opponents was disclosed. Later at the panel discussion on Social Welfare, Dr. John Dorsey of Michigan State University and I sketched some obvious infringements of human rights. In our audience was Viet Nam's minister of foreign aid, who, a year later, was obliged to flee his native land after breaking with the Diem Government – another story of frustration.

22

BACK HOME TO A SOUL-CRUSHING EVENT

When I returned to the United States at the end of 1958, I landed at J.F. Kennedy Airport in New York, then called Idlewild, which had become in the age of air travel the major port of entry. I could not help thinking about the Statue of Liberty now standing relatively forlorn in the inner bay of New York City and the part it had played on my returns to these shores. I mused that in time some individual or organization laying claim to fervent patriotic motivation would insist on erecting a replica of the Statue of Liberty at J.F. Kennedy Airport. Thoughts of the Statue always awakened memories of the past, reminding me of the need to steel myself for the change from Man to Negro in a racist society.

During the two years of my stay in Viet Nam I had received at my home address several letters from the New York State Civil Service Commission inquiring about my availability for vacancies as a business consultant in the NY State Department of Commerce. A reply was always demanded within forty-eight hours and my wife had always promptly responded with information that I was on a foreign assignment. Soon after my return, I made a trip to visit my son at Rochester University and combined with it a call on the Civil Service Commission at Albany, New York I learned from a clerk that I had passed the examination taken before my departure to Viet Nam, third highest in points, but that my standing on the list was fourteen out of twenty-seven listed as eligible. Most names ranked above me had veterans' preferences of ten points. Significant to me was the clerk's remark that my name was practically at the top of the list at that time, a list still active in its third year. I went to the nearby Department of Commerce and was informed that vacancies would occur, and that I would be notified. In a subsequent telephone conversation the administrative officer of the Commerce Department in charge of employment instructed me to see the Deputy Commissioner at their New York City office. This interview was made most significant by the continuous attempts by the Deputy Commissioner to down-grade and belittle my United Nations and US Government experiences. He kept on repeating: "I am looking for experience in private industry." My ten years' work in the private sector two decades before were brushed aside as too old. The Chief Commissioner came into the office, busied himself at a nearby desk and seemingly listened to our conversation. My documentation on conferences with the prime minister of Greece, ministers and governors of that country on economic and social matters, with the president and ministers of Viet Nam, laudatory comments by Governor Herbert H. Lehman as director-general of UNRRA, all were deemed as not pertinent. I knew I was up against a wall of racial prejudice, having also learned that this particular government department had not hired any black professional workers before. It seemed to me that the commissioners felt that behind a brown face there could not possibly be an accumulated experience in business and economics qualifying me as business consultant, although tested by examination. It may be also that in their view a black face would not reflect and portray the professional image of the department. Among several examinations held in that period I had taken also the one for employment interviewer, whose eligible list was promptly published. Rather than contest the discouraging responses elicited from the commissioners of the Department of Commerce, I accepted my former job in the Department of Labor, six grades below the title of business consultant. Four more times I was asked by the NY State Civil Service Commission whether I was interested in vacancies as business consultant; four times I replied promptly in the affirmative within the required forty-eight hours. Never was I called for an interview by the NY State Department of Commerce. These circumstances I brought verbally to the attention of the Commissioner of the NY State Commission against Discrimination in an attempt to adjust the apparent violation diplomatically. However, I perceived a strong reluctance on the Commissioner's part to bring a charge against his fellow commissioner, therefore he did not file an official complaint. While these happenings were dispiriting and disheartening, an event of soul-crushing magnitude occurred on December 19, 1959.

Our son broke his neck in an automobile accident. A telegram received on that Saturday morning from the commanding admiral in charge of Bethesda Naval Hospital informed us that Lt. William Edward, US Marine Corps, had suffered severe spinal injuries in an automobile accident. Upon our son's graduation in June 1959 from the University of Rochester, which he had attended with an NROTC (Naval Reserve Officers Training Corps) scholarship, he had been sworn into the US Marine Corps as a second lieutenant. In the months of severe training that followed, he had developed a strong, sinewy body and was credited with outstanding leadership ability. On that fateful day which changed the lives of our family, he was on the grounds of the US Marine Corps' training base at Quantico, Virginia, homeward bound to his quarters, a passenger in the car of a fellow officer. His friend nodded a moment at the wheel, causing the small car to go down an embankment, rolling over and forcing the rear seat into my son's neck. He remained conscious and directed his friend to seek help. That night he was transported the 50 miles to Bethesda Naval Hospital, at Chevy Chase, near Washington, where an emergency operation was performed the following morning. His friend, the driver of the car, required no hospitalization, having suffered only a cracked collar bone.

WILLIAM H. EDWARD
General Science

53. In 1959, aged just twenty-two, Harry Edward's son Bill had graduated as an officer in the US Marine Corps when he suffered catastrophic injuries in a car crash. As a quadriplegic, he rose to become Coordinator of Professional Services at Harlem Hospital and a member of the President's Council on Spinal Cord Injury. He died in April 1986.

My wife flew immediately to Washington, and reached the bedside of our son in the evening. The surgeon who had operated on him informed her that he would not walk again and would be confined to a wheel chair. My wife conveyed this sad news to me by telephone. She insisted on remaining at our son's bedside, a decision approved of and encouraged by the surgeon, who viewed the maintenance of his courage and of his hope as crucial at that critical medical stage. I visited my son on weekends, leaving it to my wife's judgment to call me at any emergency. The surgeon had instructed us not to divulge to our son the discouraging prognosis. It was painful to listen to his dreams and plans of leaving the bed and walking out of the hospital. I kept all friends informed of our son's condition and progress. Many traveled to Washington to visit him. One young lady, a former fellow student from Fieldston, the Ethical Culture School, organized a group of girl students working on a psychological research project in Washington into small groups to visit him daily, each day another group of girls – a tremendous morale booster.

I wrote a letter to Brigadier General James Roosevelt, who had stood at the side of his famous father after he became similarly handicapped. Congressman Roosevelt had served with distinction in the US Marine Corps, and I pleaded passionately that he give encouragement to this stricken junior Marine officer, my son. He responded promptly and magnificently, by mailing an inscribed copy of the book *Affectionately F.D.R.*, written by him with Sidney Shalett and a personal letter, which included this section:

> I have just heard of your bad luck and resultant problems which I know must be very hard to take. I thought perhaps you would enjoy the enclosed book which, with Mr. Sidney Shalett, I recently wrote about my father.
>
> As you may know, father, too, suddenly had to face life with almost complete paralysis from the waist down.
>
> Of course, no two people ever solve their problems in the same way, but from what I know of your fine record, I am sure you will find many friends, as well as those in the family, who will make the planning of a wonderful future much easier.

The receipt of this letter by a humble second lieutenant, written by a USMC general, son of a president, caused a ripple of excitement in the US Naval Hospital. Undoubtedly it strengthened the spiritual resources of our son at a trying time. I felt most grateful to Congressman Roosevelt, whom I kept informed by descriptive Christmas letters of our son's rehabilitation and progress over the years. In my life I had many reasons to be thankful to members of the Roosevelt family for their accessibility and democratic bearing. In 1932, when I worked on *The Crisis* magazine, I sought a full-page advertisement by the Democratic Party at election time and contacted Elliott Roosevelt, who was then working with an advertising agency. Mr. Elliott Roosevelt introduced me personally to the men handling the national publicity for the campaign.

In 1947, after my return from my United Nations assignment in Greece, I felt deeply concerned about the polarization of Greek public opinion. A large segment was then moving to the Royalist right, while another segment was drifting to the Communist left. The moderate, liberal center seemed to be torn asunder by those forces, and the political picture reflected that struggle. As mentioned previously, UNRRA, the UN Relief and Rehabilitation Administration, which had a comprehensive rehabilitation program in that country, had been a stabilizing influence, assisting all citizens irrespective of political beliefs. Upon UNRRA's withdrawal, a civil war erupted immediately between the extreme elements. Before the conflict became a grim reality, I expressed my anxieties, based on personal observations, in a letter to Mrs. Eleanor Roosevelt, then the active chairman of the Human Rights Commission in the United Nations, and requested an interview. She replied promptly and set a date in January 1947. The gracious lady received me warmly in her Washington Square apartment, listened with her usual concern and interest, and reminded me of her changed status when saying: "But Mr. Edward, I am no longer in the White House!" Often, so very often, have I reflected on the ease of approach to truly great persons, on their humility, their respect for people and their opinions, while contrasting those characteristics with the condescension, difficulty of reach or even unavailability of civil service employees sworn to serve the public.

At the time of my son's accident, I found myself in a civil service environment in which I observed daily unemployed persons, often troubled applicants, seeking job opportunities. Far too often they were not received by civil servants with that understanding attitude which strengthens faltering courage. Yet among the staff there were persons of sensitive disposition, and frankly I was the recipient of some eloquent evidence. While my wife stayed at our son's bedside during the six weeks of the critical, medical phase, I pursued my work at the Professional Placement Center of the New York State Employment Service. Upon hearing the details of my son's accident, the staff surprised me with a check, a donation of sixty dollars. I mulled over the most meaningful way to apply this gift and decided to place the amount to the credit of my son's telephone account. He was then confined to a Stryker's frame, a bed that is turned like a barbecue spit, and he was turned every two hours to lessen the accumulation of fluids in the lungs to avoid possible pleurisy. The telephone calls to his distant friends took his mind off himself, and the surprise element when hearing their voices cheered him as much as did his call to his acquaintances. When reporting this "investment" of the check to the generous donors, they shared in the joy and satisfaction that the gift was well spent.

The end of the sixth week brought the termination of the medical phase and the beginning of the rehabilitation process. This involved my son's transfer from the Bethesda US Naval Hospital to the Bronx Hospital of the Veterans Administration. The transfer, made by ambulance, airplane, and ambulance, proved rather strenuous to our patient, resulting in a week of anxiety, during which he was on the critical list with day and night nurses in attendance. After regaining some of his strength, the long and strenuous road of rehabilitation began: the discovery, development, adaption, and utilization of remaining muscular and nerve facilities. This process implied the involvement and coordination of many disciplines: corrective therapy, physical therapy, occupational therapy, educational therapy, psychiatric, psychological, and medical support. The family, too, played a part in the rehabilitation picture, in which the patient is trained to be independent yet also conditioned to freely accept help when needed. For sixteen months we were drawn into the many-faceted rehabilitation routines. My wife and I visited him almost daily in the hospital during that period. Toward the end there were regular weekend visits home, and after the delivery of a hospital bed and a rearrangement of furniture, the transfer to the home environment was effected.

Crises of such personal nature and dimensions provide food for introspection. In moments of meditation, I realized how the cosmos of my concern and efforts had shrunk from hundreds of needy Vietnamese children to one person – my son. I philosophized on the measure and value of one's contribution on earth. Who is helping more? The physician working in public health for millions of people or the specialist in heart valves? The community organizer or the social worker focusing on one troubled individual? The volunteer giving his strength to housing the many or the church worker visiting the sick? What are the values that society attaches to those functions? What are the true values? I found no satisfactory answer, but the speculation spawned many more questions.

Another set of speculations clustered around our son's future. Would he feel sorry for himself, drowning his sorrows in alcohol? Would he pursue studies and toward what goal? Blessed as he was with a nimble mind and tongue, I thought of a career in law. Desirous of exposing him to the atmosphere of the courts, I arranged with justices of the supreme and family courts to have him attend sessions and observe the work behind the scenes. However, he decided to take graduate work in psychology, partly for the reason – as he confessed some years later – to understand himself better, partly because US Marine Corps indoctrination had inculcated in him the goal and belief "to be a leader of men," hence psychology was a necessary tool. There followed three years of graduate studies in Columbia University's Teachers College, with classes arranged to allow me to take him to Morningside Heights after working hours. The culmination of these efforts came in 1965, when he received a Master of Arts diploma in Vocational Psychology, and also the higher-rated Professional Diploma in Rehabilitation Psychology. Thereafter he became briefly a counselor in the federally sponsored APEX Program, a support program for freshmen from underprivileged environments, under the auspices of New York University; then he spent three years in the rehabilitation of narcotic-addicted, before transferring to a modern hospital as a Coordinator of Rehabilitation Services. In the current position he can apply not only his studies, but also the lessons of his own experiences, while supplying a live, stimulating example to patients undergoing rehabilitation.

23

THE LIMITED HORIZON OF THE EMPLOYMENT SERVICE

With much of my time and effort going as an "investment" into my son's future, I deemed it unwise to reach out to new opportunities providing more elbow room. As a relative newcomer to the Employment Service of NY State, I brought with me a certain enthusiasm, grounded in the belief that my varied experience in the international economic and diplomatic fields could be put to good social use with personal benefits. In the first four years I supplied suggestions whenever invited to do so. Thus when the staff was asked to assist the personnel department in the recruitment of interviewers, I advanced the suggestion to invite back to active service former interviewers who had left because they wanted to raise a family. However, they would be asked to work on a half-time basis from 10 a.m. to 2 p.m., when the peak load of applicants had to be served. I believed I saw in New York City a good labor market for the utilization of married women's services on such part-time schedules, enabling them to see the children off to school and be home on their return. Bus and subway services would be speedy and pleasant in those periods. Claiming anticipated difficulties with labor unions and scheduling problems, the personnel department never vigorously explored such experimentation, which might have set a pattern in New York City. When submitting this suggestion, I had in mind the many children I had seen with their apartment's key hanging around their neck, playing in the streets after the closing of school, awaiting their parents' return from work. How many of those lonely, unsupervised children became addicted to drugs five to ten years later?

I mailed ideas to the Suggestion Box of the department, joined the International Association of Personnel in Employment Security, participated in their essay contests, garnered prizes and six Certificates of Award. The Manpower Report over President Lyndon B. Johnson's signature of March 1964 said: "to succeed . . . we must have: new willingness to experiment with fresh approaches . . ., new efforts to anticipate and prepare for future requirements . . ." However, I found that effective channels for communication up the ladder were practically non-existent. The discovery of this fact took me a few years. In face of overt, discriminatory hiring practices by business, I believed that a vigorous public relations effort by the NY State Employment Service would effectively implement the widely declared state and federal anti-discrimination policies. At a conference I heard Mr. Fred C. Fischer, [the New York department store] R.H. Macy's vice president for personnel, formulate in blunt terms a solution to problems presented by the State's Employment Service. He said: "You have a large staff. Go out into the field and sell your service!" Encouraged by this expert advice, I sought through administrative channels a conference with the division's public relations chief. It took six attempts over two months, five of them futile, to have a twenty-minute talk with that official. The cold and condescending attitude of that lady contrasted sharply with the gracious reception I had received from Mrs. Eleanor Roosevelt. My germinating ideas fell obviously on arid soil in the PR director's mind.

Early in the year 1960, the NY State Department of Labor had issued an excellent prognosis on manpower and technological changes to be expected in the decade from 1960 to 1970. In its conclusion, the report pleaded for the strengthening of many services touching upon manpower problems, i.e. youth counseling and guidance, active role with local communities, extension and improvement of employment services, research, training, special services for those technologically displaced, and elimination of barriers to employment of older persons, women, and members of minority groups "with utmost vigor." This report with its challenges for the decade of the 1960s gave fervor to my work during the early years. Pursuing some ideas, I sought to discuss aspects of the report with supervisors, only to find that this widely distributed document had not been read by most of the staff. In an effort to open up channels of communication, I addressed on June 1, 1963 a long letter (published in part) to the editor of the *Empire State Reporter*, saying:

> Great is the need for free unhampered communication from the grass-roots up through the crusty rigidity of the status quo.

And I pointed out from my own experience:

> In France civil servants are called "fonctionnaires," people who function but do not think. In Imperial Germany there existed also a supine, highly disciplined officialdom (Beamtentum), which Hitler took over for the implementation of his policies and without any difficulties.

When raising the issue of racial discrimination in employment and ways and means of handling it, supervisory personnel almost invariably turned their backs on me. The subject was deemed taboo in those circles. Yet the Kennedy Administration was developing at that time the positive and more aggressive phase of manpower training and management, with special attention to the population's deprived segment. President Johnson attempted later to solve the job problem of minorities by a combination of programs administered jointly and separately by the Office of Economic Opportunity and by the Department of Labor. Under OEO community action agencies came into being, filling a void left by the state employment services. The former charged that the state agencies were white, middle class-dominated, and filled with bureaucratic red tape that always worked against the poor and minorities. The general accuracy of that evaluation was conceded by Assistant Secretary of Labor Arnold R. Weber, of the Nixon Administration. Judged from the narrow base of my own former supervisory position in the New York State Employment Service, I cannot but agree.

Problems of education and jobs are at the core of America's human relations questions. Their solutions represent a measure of the effectiveness of our democratic society. During the last years, education has been wrenched from the moorings in middle-class values and from its entrenched, rigid, administrative structures. New foundations are being currently laid, allowing for greater flexibility and for easier access by all interested parties. Unchallenged thus far by critical public scrutiny are the public employment services, with their basic mission of maximizing employment, ascertaining what workers can do, locating jobs requiring such skills, and matching the two. True, the operating processes are complicated by many factors: personal, economic, industrial, even psychological; furthermore, the whole operation is set in a political framework. However, federal and state governments have recognized their public responsibilities in the field of manpower utilization by the issuance of numerous reports and directives, seldom followed up by vigorous action. New York State even financed a private research project. Its findings were summarized in The McKinsey Report, which stressed the importance of

a change from a passive role of meeting needs to which it (the service) is routinely exposed to an active role of meeting the needs it is able to discover.

In the ferment of the mid-sixties, the Federal-State Employment Services were on the defensive and the secretary of labor found it advisable to establish in 1965 a "Task Force" from among his staff and affiliated agencies. This Task Force brought in an excellent, well-documented report which failed, however, to get the needed implementation in the absence of a dynamic, politically based, supporting organization. Two years later, Dr. Eli Ginzberg, Chairman of the National Manpower Advisory Committee, wrote:

> The Employment Service ... has need to change further. The only question that it faces is whether it will take the lead and change itself or whether it will wait and be pushed into changes by others. The answer to this crucial question is the challenge that the leadership of the Employment Service faces.

Working as a supervisor in the NY State Employment Service, conscious of policy declarations and the highly useful social purpose to which our work was dedicated, I became aware of a sluggish, supine bureaucracy, which said to me: "Just do your work! We have no time to take on more! Don't upset the apple cart!" I often felt entrapped. Within the service I observed human beings become objects to be shaped by psychological tools into instruments of the organization, while small cliques manipulated groupings and associations in the furtherance of their private ambitions. The picture resembled in many ways the growth of the mammoth educational structure of New York City, with its intra-mural struggle for jobs and prestige between Jews and Negroes, a subject about which people are reluctant to talk.

When President Lyndon B. Johnson, in his 1964 State of the Union Message, addressed himself to the national problem of poverty, he said:

Very often a lack of jobs and money is not the cause of poverty
but the symptom. The cause may lie deeper in our failure to give
our fellow citizens a fair chance to develop their capacities . . .

Subsequent legislation and policy shifted the emphasis from
employment, the hiring process of matching men with jobs, to
employability, the manpower services encompassing education,
training, health services, etc. needed to make human beings employable. This approach required a thorough reorientation of thinking
by the staff of employment services. Hitherto their work had been
focused on the placeables, on the "advantaged," the well-motivated.
Schools had been concerned with those who made the grade, and
all techniques of testing and counseling were geared to that group.
Suddenly the employment services were asked to face up to the
plight of the "disadvantaged." Their staffs were unprepared to
reverse or redirect the lessons of their experience. In fact, the
director of the US Employment Service, addressing civil servants,
declared at that time: "In face of this national problem, experience
is often a liability. Don't point to the past!"

Today, five years later, it is clear that the employment services
have largely failed to adjust, that federal and state administrations
have down-graded the functions of those agencies. Instead of
bestowing prestige and authority on employment interviewers as
the voice, eyes, and ears of government, these civil servants have
become feeders of data for the computers. Another human link
between government and the people has been lost, and the concept
of government in the eyes of the public has become even more
impersonal and remote. Now, in 1970, the Hesburgh Report of the
US Commission on Civil Rights points accusingly at the seeming
inability of the federal bureaucracy to put national policy into
effect. The commission says unequivocally that there was a govern-
ment-wide failure in the enforcement in such areas as employment,
housing, and the use of government grants and services.

Aware of social conditions, sensitive to injustices, I felt often balked in my ten years' work in the New York State Employment Service, yet that period had not been entirely one of lonely frustration. I met many empathetic co-workers with whom I could share my feelings. I saw many devoted, hard-working civil servants. Among them were some who were just waiting for their retirement dates; there were several who worked in order to help their husbands build a profession, a home for their family, or some nest-egg for their children's education. I must confess that I, myself, sought a little time to gather strength, so that I might provide support for my son's rehabilitation. My civil service environment always reminded me of a United Nations story which is probably equally applicable to all bureaucratic settings:

> The Secretariat's chief administrative officer conducted a very distinguished visitor around the offices of the United Nations. The visitor, greatly impressed by the multiplicity and size of the operations, asked the administrative officer: "How many are working here?" Came the response: "Oh, about half."

24

INTERNATIONAL RELATIONS

Theory and Practice

In 1962, I was invited by the Mayor's Commission to the United Nations to assist in their work in greeting diplomats accredited to the United Nations and to help the newly arrived and their families in their adjustment to these often strange, metropolitan surroundings. Now active in my ninth year as a volunteer worker for the New York City Commission for the United Nations and for the Consular Corps, I can say that I have met hundreds of diplomats and consuls from almost all countries. This work, done on my personal leave time, provided some release from the confined activities of the employment service and strengthened my motivation to study political science. Thus, upon my mandatory retirement, I enrolled in full-time graduate work in international relations at the City University of New York, and one year later, at the age of seventy-one years, I was awarded a Master's degree, the oldest graduate at their commencement ceremonies.

The choice of my required thesis was provoked by the war in Viet Nam, my experiences in that country, and by the impressive growth and work of the Council of Europe. The topic was "The Mekong River Project, Taming Turbulence for a Serene Southeast Asia." In developing the theme, I traced the growth of the Mekong

River Project under the sponsorship of the Economic Commission for Asia and the Far East (ECAFE) to the grown, vigorous United Nations instrumentality it had become, supported by twenty-six sovereign nations, sixteen United Nations agencies, four foundations, and several private companies. Of the total investment of US$197.9 million, 45 percent was contributed by the riparian governments. Today, this joint endeavor is yielding visible dividends in hydro-electric power, flood control, irrigation projects, and in the training of technical manpower. The invasion of Cambodia by belligerent forces is undoubtedly beclouding the future. Nevertheless, the thesis that this regional development project, with its history of successful, international cooperation, may provide a framework for the post-war reconstruction of Southeast Asia may yet have some validity.

In my projection, I saw [the Burmese diplomat] U Thant as the director-general of an expanded Mekong River Authority. In his present position as secretary-general of the United Nations, he received a unanimous vote of confidence, given by all nations of the world, of the East and of the West. He is, therefore, best able to encourage the application of the Mekong's resources to the area's rebuilding on both sides of the ideological line. He is a native of Southeast Asia, a man of stature, prestige, and technical and political knowledge; hence he would be able to exact the best obtainable conditions from both East and West for the area's development and peace. In my international contacts I have been able to share this thesis and its implications with diplomats of the great powers, as well as those of Asia. I realize, of course, that much exploration and many discussions will have to take place before any tentative steps can be undertaken. U Thant's term as secretary-general of the United Nations will expire in 1971, and his possible availability may set some wheels in motion.

Like most of my fellow citizens, I became deeply concerned about US policy relating to Viet Nam. I perceived our national

interest lying in the stability of that strategic area after the destruction of French colonial power. With naval strength in the Pacific
seen as a key to success in the region, it was understandable that
countries would be drawn into the power vacuum in Viet Nam.
When anti-Communist Ngo Dinh Diem demonstrated strong leadership and considerable political strength in 1955, American support
was a logical consequence in the context of Secretary Foster Dulles's
policy in the Eisenhower Administration. Some of the rifts in our
relationship with the Diem regime have been touched upon. Now,
over a decade later and having the benefit of hindsight, we can see
the limitations of military power in wars against strong national-
isms in Viet Nam and in Czechoslovakia. In Viet Nam the clash of
ideology may be peculiar to that country. There are, however, many
evolutions and revolutions in progress simultaneously, similar to
our own domestic situation, as for instance: the mechanization of
farming, the expansion of education and of technology, migration
of population to urban centers, changes in the status of women,
protests by students and their participation in the political process,
court and prison reforms, access to and responsiveness by government. The changes in Viet Nam are even greater in the frame of
long-established Confucian concepts, with their orderly family
structure and in the face of pressing demands for nation building
requiring the modification of relationships between village government and the new national authority. All these changes were being
propelled by social and political pressures under the exigencies of
war at the very doorstep of the seat of government.

I found great difficulty in conveying a clear picture of those
circumstances to interested American groups. When explaining
those interlocked, confusing problems I seemed to perceive an
impatience to plough through those perplexities. "What do *you*
think?" was the question often posed. It seemed to me what people
really sought was a confirmation of their prejudices. They were
frustrated by the many, seemingly insoluble problems set forth by

the bloody conflict in which the United States had become so deeply involved. I felt often tempted to tell my friends that their temporary frustrations were minuscule as compared to those permanent ones faced by a person labeled black, Indian, Puerto Rican, or Mexican by a race-oriented society. I recognized that in both situations, at home and abroad, possible solutions would have to be explored. This realization was one of the reasons which prompted my investing time and money in the study of political science and international relations upon my retirement from active work. Of course, the *Weltanschauung* – or world view – from my Harlem residence and my experiences in the New York State Employment Service were other stimuli to my inquiries and research.

The study of political science is, of course, the study of the creation, use, and management of power, irrespective of any moral or ethical connotation. Power with its concomitant for adjustment, namely politics, are essential elements for the functioning of any society. Politics can be seen operative in the family in adjusting to parental authority and in the arrangements of privileges and obligations among its members. It can be observed in churches, business, and trade unions within their structures of delegated authority, in government with its checks and balances, and in the international arena with its balance of power. Essentially it is a method of keeping a social situation in equilibrium by voluntary or coercive accommodation. In the face of so many social changes, I felt I needed to sharpen the scientific tools for a better understanding of our times.

The awakening of my interest in the working of an industrial society goes back to the years spent in England, when hope filled the air for a brighter future after World War I, the war to make the world safe for democracy. In those days I read several books written by J. Ramsay MacDonald, who later became prime minister of Britain's Labour governments. His writings led to my discovery of the Fabian Society, that group of youthful, brilliant, socialist thinkers and writers, who rejected a Marxist revolution, but believed that social reforms could be accomplished by socialistic permeation of existing political institutions. Ramsay MacDonald was a member of that group, as were also H.G. Wells, George Bernard Shaw, Sidney and Beatrice Webb. The growth of the British Labour Party and the many political and social reforms of that era owe much to the literary contributions of that group, and especially to the works by Sidney and Beatrice Potter Webb. When in 1929,

54. Harry Edward achieved a degree in public administration and then, at the age of seventy-one, a master's in international relations.

Sidney James Webb was elevated to the House of Lords as Lord Passfield, his wife Beatrice, daughter of a wealthy industrialist and a pioneer social worker, refused to share in the title, allegedly saying: "And then I would be a Lady? Damn it!" When in 1932, Dr. William E.B. Du Bois introduced me to Herbert George Wells on his visit to the office of *The Crisis* magazine, I deemed it a rare honor to shake the hand which, by its voluminous writings, had so greatly influenced the world and had also left an impact on my growth. It was the Fabians who led me to Jean-Jacques Rousseau's *Le Discours sur l'origine et les fondements de l'inégalité parmi les hommes* [*A Discourse on Inequality*] and made me share Ramsay MacDonald's observation: "Today we are in the economic stage. Yesterday we were in the political stage. Tomorrow we shall be in the moral stage." In broad strokes, he thereby sketched the struggle for political rights and democratic structures in the eighteenth century, for property rights and economic reforms in the nineteenth century, and the moral challenges for the achieving of human rights in the twentieth century.

25

EXIT COLONIALISM

Enter a New Changing World

Since the reading of those works, I watched during the half-century of my working life the suicidal struggle among European empire builders for colonial possessions. Then, after World War I, I saw a revengeful Germany and a racially discriminated Japan challenge the big European powers for a place in the sun. During the resulting World War II, I witnessed the leaders of proud and arrogant empires plead with their colonial peoples to provide them with military and economic assistance for a joint struggle against the threatening forces of Nazi Germany, Fascist Italy, and Imperial Japan. Under the stresses of those times, the European empires were willing and ready to sign "promissory notes" assuring the colonial peoples of equality and freedom, goals for which they were asked to fight. At the end of the world conflict, the Asian nations presented those "promissory notes" to their colonial masters, and between 1945 and 1955 they received their independence, not always willingly granted, not always without bloodshed. The British Empire of dominions and colonies became a Commonwealth, loosely uniting independent, sovereign nations.

The call for freedom and the liquidation of colonial overlordships then swept through Africa from 1955 to 1965, practically completing the dissolution of the former British, French, Belgian, and Dutch colonial empires. In the United States, the post-war changes in its own colonial structure were less thoroughgoing. Here, too, America's colonial people presented for payment the "promissory notes" given by the government during the war, when assuring its darker citizens days of freedom and equality after the victorious conclusion of the war against Hitler's legions and their master-race concepts. Black America had answered the country's call by enlisting in segregated units of the armed forces. Black America had shared in the war's sacrifices. However, the change from the colonial status was slow in coming. Presidential Executive Orders, Supreme Court decisions, and some social legislation under the pressure of marches and demonstrations effected some modification; but the basic structure remained essentially undisturbed, causing the National Advisory Commission on Civil Disorders of 1968 to say:

> Just as Lincoln, a century ago, put preservation of the Union above all else, so should we put creation of a true union – a single society and a single American identity – as our major goal.

Almost thirty years ago – in 1944 – the broad spectrum of race relations was placed before the American public in a 1,500 page study in depth, titled An American Dilemma, by Gunnar Myrdal. The Swedish author pointed out: "The American Negro problem is a problem in the heart of the American." And he warned that: "The Negro problem is an integral part of, a special phase of, the whole complex of problems in the larger American civilization. It cannot be treated in isolation."

In the three decades since that scientific inquiry, American society has squeezed more and more Negroes and Puerto Ricans into decaying, urban ghettos, until this crowded, confined humanity exploded in anger, in a series of riots, into the face of the political power structure. A concerned President Johnson appointed in 1967 the Kerner Commission, which brought in a voluminous document in March 1968 called the Report of the National Advisory Commission on Civil Disorders, stating in its conclusion:

> What white Americans have never fully understood – but what Negroes can never forget – is that white society is deeply implicated in the ghetto. White institutions created it, white institutions maintained it, and white society condones it.

The ghetto mirrors the still existing colonial status of dark minority peoples in the American society. It portrays segregation imposed and freedom denied.

I listened over the years to many discussions on liberation, integration, separation, segregation, and other emotion-stirring topics among groups searching for freedom and full, unrestricted citizenship. To me, the goal seemed always very clear, namely integration into the family of mankind. Of course, *Realpolitik*, with its pragmatic base, may dictate many strategic, diversionary approaches. Nevertheless, this objective loomed particularly clearly before my eyes when I viewed our global universe through the cameras of our astronauts, seeing it as a richly endowed and pleasant star with limited, finite living space. Therefore, to enjoy our earth and its fruits it seems we have to find ways and means to wisely apply our best social and economic efforts and to get along with one another in relative harmony. I welcomed, therefore, international cooperation through the United Nations in outer space, the seabed, and the environment.

As has been seen, I remain enthusiastic about the feasibility of further expansion of regional development projects like the one on the Lower Mekong River. I still share the optimism of the founders of the Council of Europe that, by working together on common economic projects for joint benefits, mankind can slowly learn the manifold values of patient cooperation. For hundreds of years, rivalry among European nations spawned about four to six wars in every century. World War I and II in our century severely sapped the human, economic, social, and moral strengths of those countries, causing Sir Winston Churchill to appeal to them in eloquent terms in his speech of September 1946 at the University of Zurich:

> We must build a kind of United States of Europe ... a remedy which would, as if by a miracle, transform the whole scene and would in a few years make all Europe, or a greater part of it, as free and happy as Switzerland is today.

At that time a large part of Europe lay in ruins. Today, a quarter-century later, the European Common Market, the Coal and Steel Community, and Euratom, now merged into a powerful politico-economic structure is evidence that Churchill's advice was well heeded. Whereas in Europe nationalism is being harnessed and directed into European cooperative channels, in Asia and Africa nationalism remains a potent force, a force necessary for nation building and the creation of national institutions. Yet there, too, are many examples of regional, cooperative endeavors across national borders.

These and other changes in the world are being reflected in the deliberations of the United Nations and recorded in the minutes of its many meetings. Today, on its twenty-fifth anniversary, 127 sovereign nations claim membership of the world organization, which is an impressive increase from the fifty-one members who began operation in 1946. Unexpected by the founders of the United Nations were the political and ideological cleavage between East and West, the ramifications in power politics brought about by nuclear armaments, the extensive use of the veto in the Security Council. The United Nations was conceived as a vehicle for great-power collaboration toward peace and order in the world. However, the split between the two giants, the United States of America and the Union of Soviet Socialist Republics, caused both to settle many of their problems outside the framework of the United Nations, along the lines of balance of power and spheres of influence, encroached upon by the nuclear threat and by moral views and considerations as expressed by the smaller powers in the United Nations. The Assembly votes by the former colonial nations have acted as a restraining force on the political power moves by the two nuclear giants. Whereas in 1911 France could assuage the hurt feelings of Germany by ceding a slice of Cameroon to the latter's sovereignty without any recourse to world opinion or the population affected, such dealings are no longer possible in today's politics under the glare of the United Nations Security Council and Assembly.

In today's world, with its vastly improved communication systems, the status of race relations in the United States is of universal interest. The awarding of the Nobel Prize for Peace to Dr. Martin Luther King Jr. focused world attention on the long and difficult struggle of black America toward freedom and human dignity. Dean Rusk, Secretary of State in the Kennedy and Johnson administrations, was frank to admit that the unsatisfactory black–white race relations in America were the Achilles' heel of US foreign policies. The country's history shows the Negro thrust into the center of the nation's political arena. As a slave, he was a passive victim who, nevertheless, troubled the white man's concept of his nation as "conceived in liberty with justice for all." The Negro was an agent for violent change in the Civil War, and a strong force in economic, social, and political changes over the last one hundred years. Although he finds himself in a minority status in American society today, he is, nevertheless, exerting social and political pressures on many fronts in his efforts to achieve full citizenship. However, to repeat the words of Gunnar Myrdal: "The American Negro problem is a problem in the heart of the American ... It cannot be treated in isolation."

In the search for solutions in these days of confusion, many are trying to live in the past, while others are trying to project to the future. Overstatements are common on both sides, as if people are seeking strength and comfort in such declarations of group prejudices. People like to blame the politicians, the establishment, permissiveness, etc. But in the almost defiant words of the German psychologist Karl Jaspers: "The whole world will not change if I change. But the change in myself is the premise." This challenge to gain insight for changes provided another motivation to my undertaking graduate work in international relations upon my retirement, also for the continuation of my volunteer efforts in the New York City Commission for the United Nations and the Consular Corps, in which work I met diplomats of many former colonial nations. Often I perceived a kinship of aspirations: to live in dignity and walk the world with dignity.

I looked over the agendas of past Assembly sessions and found that from about 10 percent to 15 percent of proposed items dealt with the expansion of human rights and the elimination of discrimination, items usually sponsored by former colonial countries. If the process of acquiring liberties is through the joining of like-minded individuals to gain rights and privileges for themselves, surely here is common ground. It is an effort in which American blacks and other minority groups can join and thereby strengthen the United Nations. Resolutions of congratulations and support might be sent to the sponsors. Discussions and debates on the proposed agenda items could be encouraged in schools and colleges, interest in the emerging African nations stimulated.

The tourist dollars of American Negroes could be made to swell African economies. Surely, there is much to be learned, many more exciting discoveries to be made in that second largest of continents, now bursting forth on the world stage with its riches in resources, art, and hidden glories of past civilizations. Here is virgin soil for the scholar in history, archaeology, and in philology dealing with the origin, growth, and structure of hundreds of African languages. There are in the United States more black college graduates than there are graduates of British universities in Great Britain, a tremendous intellectual force which could exert beneficial influence in

US–African relations. Should Uncle Sam stray to paths of discredited colonial power politics in the future, a squeeze on the sensitive Achilles' heel may well bring his feet back to the broader road to adjustment and peace through a strengthened United Nations. The potentiality of political influence in the hands of the American Negro is tremendous. The key is "organization."

When I met A. Philip Randolph on a sunny day in 1931 on Harlem's Seventh Avenue, he greeted me with his usual warm, dignified manner and said in his sonorous basso: "Mr. Edward, I have good news for you. Last week we signed our contract with the Pullman Company." After I congratulated him, he added: "The signing of the contract was a mere formality. What is important was the organizing, the organizing."

Of course, the organizing must have a purpose, a short- or long-range goal, with the creation and use of power as the focus of organization. Varying conditions, myriad of challenges, resistance offered by entrenched interests, and the character of the emerging leadership, all will determine the goals on which to concentrate and the shape of the organization to be fashioned.

Today's younger generation, white and black, is moved by an urgent sense of crisis, and their perception and concern are well founded. The present crisis is real! Those suffering and deprived of the benefits of their societies, as for instance the writers and artists in the Soviet Union and the racial minorities in the United States, want better conditions and a change in the ground rules. The suppressed and deprived are voicing disagreement with the status quo and are propagandizing or organizing for a radical transformation. Their clamor is being opposed and resisted by those who have profited by the system and are entrenched in the seats of power, i.e. the Soviet bureaucrats in the USSR and "business" and "hard-hat patriots" in the USA. Social problems usually reflect conflicts of values between different sections of the community; often, however, also within the hearts and minds of the majority of individuals composing a community. James Weldon Johnson, the first secretary of the National Association for the Advancement of Colored People, a former US consul, poet, author of several books, composer of popular music, as well as of an opera, addressed this poem to the American heart and mind:

'We, to America'

How would you have us, as we are
or sinking 'neath the load we bear?
Our eyes fixed forward on a star
or gazing empty at despair?

Rising or falling? Men or things?
With dragging pace or footsteps fleet?
Strong, willing sinews in your wings?
Or tightening chains about your feet?

Those lines were written a half-century ago. At about the same time, a young West Indian by the name of Claude McKay, his soul seared by his American experience, wrote the following:

If we must die – let it not be like hogs,
hunted and penned in an inglorious spot,
while round us bark the mad and hungry dogs,
making their mock at our accursed lot.

If we must die – oh, let us nobly die,
so that our precious blood may not be shed
in vain; then even the monsters we defy
shall be constrained to honor us though dead!

Oh, Kinsmen! We must meet the common foe;
though far outnumbered, let us be brave,
and for their thousand blows deal one death blow!

What though before us lies the open grave?
Like men we'll face the murderous, cowardly pack,
pressed to the wall, dying, but fighting back!

Which path to follow? That was and remains the question before generations of blacks in America, and I confess that I, too, have wrestled with those alternatives. As I have shown, I have been fortunate in meeting many noble souls who left their imprint on my philosophy. Yet, as a resident of Harlem for more than forty years I have been exposed to many of the community's social problems. Thus, I am keenly aware of the grievous harm inflicted on thousands of my fellow citizens by the racial bigotry of the American society. I always sensed, as I recorded, the change from Man to Negro whenever I returned to these shores and passed the Statue of Liberty.

I am grateful to athletics and the contacts I have been able to make in my activities in sports. At the Olympic Games at Antwerp, an American Negro, when praising my performance, said: "Do you realize that you are the first Man of Color to stand on the platform of Olympic Winners?" I did not comprehend then the emphasis on color, nor did I ever check on the authenticity of that statement. However, I know that the press photo showing King George V of Great Britain congratulating me was given worldwide distribution in 1922, receiving space on the sports pages of many American papers. Those events made undoubtedly an impact on the imagination of youth in many countries and encouraged wider participation. When noting the broad representation in more recent international competitions, I confess to a feeling of satisfaction that my athletic endeavors had made a contribution to their growth. I hope that the story of my economic struggles in the face of racial obstacles may provide similar encouragement and inspiration, and contribute in some constructive ways to urgently needed reforms and changes.

55. The world at his feet. Spring 1920 and a young Harry Edward poses for a picture during a sprint-start training session with his Polytechnic Harriers teammates as they begin their preparation for a track season that will culminate in the Olympic Games.

APPENDIX

Harry Edward's Racing Career

Clubs
Verein für Volkssport (VfV), which became part of VfV Teutonia in Germany
Polytechnic Harriers, UK
Lyons Athletic Club, UK

Note
Mile medley relay – legs of 880, 220, 220 and 440 yards in that order, unless
 stated otherwise

Abbreviations

AA = Athletic Association	e = estimated time	YMCA = Young Men's Christian Association
AAA = Amateur Athletic Association	FC = Football Club	
	H = Harriers	
AC = Athletic Club	Poly H = Polytechnic Harriers	
ch = championship	VfV = Verein für Volkssport	
DNF = did not finish		
DNQ = did not qualify		
DNS = did not start		

Date	Meeting	Position	Distance	Time (mins:secs) or Distance	Notes
1912					
16 May	Verband Berliner Athletik-Vereine (Berlin Association of Athletics Clubs) meeting, Berlin	1st	50 metres (Youth)		
1913					
4 May	Verband Berliner Athletik-Vereine meeting, Berlin	1st	100 metres (Youth)		
18 May	Verband Berliner Athletik-Vereine meeting, Berlin	1st	400 metres	54.8	
5 July	Olympic Stadium, Berlin	1st	200 metres handicap		
20 July	Verband Mitteldeutscher Ballspiel-Vereine (Association of Central German Ball Game Clubs) meeting, Magdeburg	4th	100 metres		1st Schoulze (Germany) 11.2. Pouring rain

Date	Meeting	Position	Distance	Time (mins:secs) or Distance	Notes
3 August	Asseburg Memorial, Charlottenburger Sportplatz, Berlin	3rd	100 metres	11.5e	1st Richard Rau (Germany) 11.4; 2nd Schoulze (Germany). Beaten by a *Brustbreite* (a chest) and a further *Brustbreite*
5 August	International meeting, Berliner Sport-Club, Berlin	2nd	200 metres		1st Hans Skowronnek (Germany) 23.0
12 August	VfV meeting, Berlin	1st	100 metres (Youth)	11.8	
31 August	International meeting, Berliner Sport-Club, Berlin	DNQ heat	100 metres		1st Willie Applegarth
14 September Berlin Championships, Berliner Sport-Club, Berlin		4th?	100 metres		1st Schüler 11.4; 2nd Max Herrmann (Germany) One report said that in Rau's absence, Edward was favourite, but he was not in the first three
		2nd	200 metres	23.1e	1st Herrmann 22.8; 3rd Skowronnek. Beaten by 2 metres

1914					
17 May	Berliner Sport-Club meeting, Berlin	1st	100 metres (Youth)	11.3	
21 May	Verband Berliner Athletik-Vereine meeting, Berlin	1st	100 metres (Youth)		
27 June	Olympia-Vorspiele ('pre-Olympic meeting'), Olympic Stadium, Berlin	?	100 metres		1st Erwin Kern (Germany) 10.9; 2nd Rau. If Edward ran, he was not in the first four
28 June	Olympia-Vorspiele ('pre-Olympic meeting'), Olympic Stadium, Berlin	2nd	200 metres final	21.7e	1st Rau 21.6. Beaten by ¼ metre
		4th	4x100 metres relay (VfV Teutonia)		1st Turnverein München 1860, 42.6. Edward definitely ran the last leg (photo)
12 July	Berliner Sport-Club meeting, Berlin	3rd	100 metres	11.1e	1st Rau 10.9; 2nd James Patterson (USA). Beaten by 1 metre and ¾ metre (though a photo of the finish suggests the latter distance more like ¼ metre)
19 July	Leipziger Ballspielklub meeting, Leipzig	2nd	100 metres	11.2e	1st Rau 10.9. Beaten by 3 metres
		1st	4x100 metres relay (VfV Teutonia)		Team: Kuntke, Fahl, Edward, Grünberger (order unknown)

Date	Meeting	Position	Distance	Time (mins:secs) or Distance	Notes
26 July	Budapest	4th	100 metres		=1st (dead-heat) Patterson and Ágost Schubert (Hungary) 11.0
		1st	200 metres	22.0	
1919					
24 May	YMCA Empire Day Sports, Stamford Bridge	1st heat	100 yards handicap (off 5 yards)	9.6	
		1st final	100 yards handicap (off 5 yards)	9.8	2nd Harold Abrahams (off 6½ yards)
		1st	300 yards handicap (off 15 yards)	31.0	
9 June	Molinari AC meeting, Stamford Bridge	1st	100 yards	9.9e	2nd Billy Hill. Reported as 'a yard better than 10 seconds'. Strained leg at end of race
5 July	AAA ch, Stamford Bridge	1st heat	100 yards	10.2	

		4th final	100 yards	10.2e	1st Billy Hill 10.0. Edward eased up once beaten
		1st heat	220 yards		
		2nd final	220 yards	23.2e	1st Billy Hill 22.6. Beaten by 5 yards
		1st	Mile medley relay (Poly H)	3:37.8	Team: Albert Hill, Vic D'Arcy, Dick Burley, Edward
17 July	Poly H club ch, Paddington	3rd	440 yards		1st H.G. Jackson 53.4
31 July	Brigade of Guards Sports, Stamford Bridge	1st	Mile medley relay (Poly H)	3:39.4	Team: probably Albert Hill, D'Arcy, Edward, Jackson
4 August	Liverpool Working Men's Conservative Association Sports, New Brighton	1st	100 yards	10.5e	Time given as 10 7/16; 2nd D'Arcy
		1st	220 yards handicap (off 3 yards)	22.3e	Time given as 22 4/16
		1st	Mile medley relay (Poly H)	3:48.⌐	Team: Albert Hill, D'Arcy, Edward, Jackson

Date	Meeting	Position	Distance	Time (mins:secs) or Distance	Notes
9 August	Celtic Sports, Parkhead, Glasgow	1st heat	100 yards open handicap		
		DNQ semi-final	100 yards open handicap		There were four semi-finals with only the winner of each going through
		5th	100 yards invitation handicap (off ½ yard)		1st Billy Hill 10.2 (scratch)
		1st	220 yards invitation handicap (off 2 yards)	21.8	Beat Billy Hill (scratch) by a yard
		1st	Mile medley relay handicap (Poly H, off scratch)	3:32.8	Team: Albert Hill, Billy Hill (actually a member of Surrey AC), Edward, D'Arcy. Albert Hill ran the opening 880 yards leg; order of subsequent legs not known
16 August	London Fire Brigade Sports, Herne Hill	1st	Mile medley relay (Poly H)	3:36.4	Team: Albert Hill, D'Arcy, Edward, Jackson

Date	Event	Round	Race	Time	Notes
6 September	Wycombe Phoenix Sports, High Wycombe	1st heat	100 yards handicap (off 1 yard)		
		3rd final	100 yards handicap (off 1 yard)		1st H.M. Deeley 10.0
		1st heat	220 yards		
		1st final	220 yards	22.2	
		1st heat	300 yards handicap (off 2 yards)		
		2nd final	300 yards handicap (off 2 yards)		1st E. Burgess 33.0
		2nd	Mile medley relay (Poly H)		1st Surrey AC. Edward ran a 220 yards leg
1920					**In all his handicap races in 1920 and later, Edward started from scratch**
January – March					There were winter indoor Poly H meetings at the Regent Street Gymnasium in which Edward probably took part, but the *Polytechnic Magazine* failed to report the results

Date	Meeting	Position	Distance	Time (mins:secs) or Distance	Notes
15 May	Polytechnic Cycling Club 'After the war' meeting, Herne Hill	2nd	220 yards handicap	22.2e	1st E.M. Godfrey 22.2 (off 15 yards). Beaten by 'inches'. Photo of finish suggests the verdict might well have been given to Edward instead
22 May	London AC/Surrey AC/ Molinari AC meeting, Stamford Bridge	1st	4x110 yards relay (Poly H)	45.2	
24 May	England vs. Belgium, Stamford Bridge	1st	400 metres	52.0	The *Daily Herald* report that Edward also won the non-match javelin is surely incorrect. No other paper mentions it, and the *Polytechnic Magazine* states that D'Arcy took part, but does not mention Edward
5 June	South London Harriers meeting, Stamford Bridge	1st	100 yards	10.4	2nd Billy Hill (inches behind). Strong headwind
		Disqualified	Mile medley relay (880, 440, 220, 220) (Poly H)		Team: Albert Hill, J.H. Coxhead, Edward, D'Arcy. Crossed the finish line 1st, but Edward and D'Arcy took more than 10 yards to pass the baton at their exchange

Date	Meeting/Location	Place	Event	Result	Notes
12 June	Southern Olympic Trials, Stamford Bridge	1st	220 yards	22.0	2nd Bevil Rudd (South Africa). Run in a downpour. Edward had missed the 100 yards because of a delay getting through the entrance gate
12 June (later the same day)	Firemen's Sports, Herne Hill	1st	Mile medley relay (Poly H)	3:45.6	Team: Coxhead, Edward, D'Arcy, Tom Cushing, order uncertain – this is best guess, but Cushing could have run a 220 yards leg
16 June	Poly H club ch, Stamford Bridge	1st	100 yards		
19 June	Poly H Sward Bowl competition, Chiswick	1st	Pentathlon (individual events below)		Edward became the first winner of the Sward Bowl. Precise order of events uncertain, as long-jump result missing. Events scored 4-3-2-1 points
		3rd	Javelin	95ft (28.96m)	
		1st	Discus	93ft 10in (28.60m)	
		3rd	High Jump	5ft 3in (1.60m)	
		Unplaced	Mile		It is possible Edward did not start, if he already had enough points to win overall

Date	Meeting	Position	Distance	Time (mins:secs) or Distance	Notes
2 July	AAA ch, Stamford Bridge	1st heat	220 yards	22.8	
		2nd second round	220 yards	22.3e	1st Randolph Brown (USA) 22.2. Beaten by a foot. 3rd Abrahams
		2nd heat	Mile medley relay	3:37.1e	1st Achilles Club 3:37.0. Beaten by a yard. Team: Albert Hill, D'Arcy, Edward, Coxhead
3 July	AAA ch, Stamford Bridge	1st heat	100 yards	10.2?	The slowest heat winner ran 10.4
		1st final	100 yards	10.0	2nd Billy Hill
		1st final	220 yards	21.6	2nd Brown
		DNS final	Mile medley relay (Poly H)		Poly H withdrew from final, as Albert Hill was injured
7 July	Poly H club ch, Herne Hill	1st	440 yards	52.2	
17 July	Kinnaird Trophy, Stamford Bridge	1st	100 yards	10.0	2nd Abrahams; 3rd D'Arcy
		1st	4x100 metres relay (Poly H)	44.2	Edward ran first leg. Rest of team unknown
		1st	8x220 yards relay (Poly H)	3:06.2	Surely Edward would have run a leg? Abrahams ran last leg

Date	Event	Round/Position	Distance	Time	Notes
2 August	Liverpool Working Men's Conservative Association Sports, New Brighton	1st heat	100 yards handicap		
		Unplaced final	100 yards handicap		1st R.W. Sloane 10 3/16 (off 9 yards)
		1st	100 yards	10.4e	2nd Abrahams; 3rd D'Arcy. Time given as 10 6/16
		1st heat	220 yards handicap		
		1st final	220 yards handicap	22.3e	Time given as 22 5/16. Nearest opponent was off 18 yards
7 August	Rangers Sports, Ibrox Park, Glasgow	2nd heat	100 yards handicap		1st J.B. Bell (Queen's Park FC) 10.6 (off 5? yards)
		3rd final	100 yards handicap		1st Harry Christie 10.6 (off 5 yards)
		1st	220 yards handicap	22.6	
15 August	Olympic Games, Antwerp	2nd heat	100 metres	10.9e	1st Charley Paddock (USA) 10.8
		1st second round	100 metres	10.8	2nd Loren Murchison (USA)
16 August	Olympic Games, Antwerp	1st semi-final	100 metres	10.8	2nd Jackson Scholz (USA)
		3rd final	100 metres	10.9e	1st Paddock 10.8; 2nd Morris Kirksey (USA). A mistake by the starter meant Edward and Murchison (6th) were badly left at the start

Date	Meeting	Position	Distance	Time (mins:secs) or Distance	Notes
19 August	Olympic Games, Antwerp	1st heat	200 metres	22.8	
		1st quarter-final	200 metres	22.0	2nd Allen Woodring (USA)
20 August	Olympic Games, Antwerp	2nd semi-final	200 metres	22.5e	1st Murchison 22.4. Edward strained thigh when leading
		3rd final	200 metres	22.2e	1st Woodring 22.0; 2nd Paddock 22.0e
1921					
26? January	Indoor meeting, Regent Street Gymnasium	2nd	High Jump	5ft 6in (1.68m)	
		1st	Standing High Jump	4ft 4in (1.32m)	
9 February	Indoor meeting, Regent Street Gymnasium	1st	Shot Put	32ft 5in (9.88m)	
25 March	West End Hotels Sports, Stamford Bridge	1st	100 yards handicap	10.2	Injured foot

Date	Meeting	Event	Distance	Time	Notes
23 April	Poly H meeting, Paddington	1st heat	100 yards handicap	10.6	
		1st second round	100 yards handicap	10.2	
		1st final	100 yards handicap	10.4	
11 May	Poly H club ch, Stamford Bridge	1st heat	100 yards	10.8	
		1st final	100 yards	10.6	Adverse wind in final
		1st heat	220 yards handicap	22.6	Broke down at end of race and withdrew from final
14 May	Molinari meeting, Stamford Bridge	1st heat	75 yards handicap		
		2nd second round	75 yards handicap		Injured foot during race. Withdrew from final
1 July	AAA ch, Stamford Bridge	1st heat	220 yards	22.4	
		1st second round	220 yards	22.0	
		1st heat	Mile medley relay (Poly H)	4:24.2 (sic)	Team: R.C. Lightwood, Edward, G.E. Roe, Cushing. Only two teams started

Date	Meeting	Position	Distance	Time (mins:secs) or Distance	Notes
2 July	AAA ch, Stamford Bridge	1st heat	100 yards	10.4	
		1st final	100 yards	10.2	2nd Abrahams
		1st final	220 yards	22.2	2nd Abrahams
		1st final	Mile medley relay (Poly H)	3:35.6	Team: Lightwood, Cushing, Roe, Edward. Edward's split was estimated at inside 49 seconds: the 'lap time' was 49.8, and Edward took over 10–12 yards behind the leader. Edward ran with a large plaster on his right thigh
9 July	Croydon Sports, Wallington	2nd	100 yards handicap	10.5e	1st W.F. Casburn 10.4 (off 2¾ yards). Beaten by a yard
		1st	Three-quarter mile medley relay (probably 2x440 yards, then 2x220 yards) (Poly H)	1:53.4*	Team: Lightwood (440), Edward, G.L. Tozer/Tozen/ Tosen, Eric Nicol (220). *This time was given in all reports, but is clearly incorrect
14 July	Belgrave Harriers meeting, Earlsfield	1st	Mile medley relay (880, 440, 220, 220)		Team: Lightwood, Cushing, Edward, Roe

Date	Event	Placing	Distance	Time	Notes
16 July	Kinnaird Trophy, Stamford Bridge	2nd	100 yards	10.3e	1st Lancelot Royle 10.2. Beaten by inches
		1st	250 yards handicap	25.0	
20 July	Nelson Cottage Hospital Sports, Merton	DNS	100 yards short limit handicap		Lost his way en route to the meeting
1 August	Liverpool Working Men's Conservative Association Sports, New Brighton	2nd	100 yards	10.5e	1st Billy Hill 10.2. Beaten by 'a good 2 yards'
6 August	Rangers Sports, Ibrox Park, Glasgow	Unplaced	100 yards short limit handicap		1st Eric Liddell (off 1½ yards)
		Unplaced	300 yards short limit handicap		1st Christie 31.6 (off 10 yards) Very heavy ground. Travelled up overnight – out of sorts
13 August	Celtic Sports, Parkhead, Glasgow	2nd	100 yards invitation handicap	10.4e	1st Liddell 10.4 (off 1 yard). Beaten by inches
		1st heat	440 yards handicap		
		1st final	440 yards handicap	50.6	
11 September	Selected for England vs. France (100/200/Relay) but declined				

Date	Meeting	Position	Distance	Time (mins:secs) or Distance	Notes
1922					
1 March	Indoor meeting, Regent Street Gymnasium	1st heat	Relay (H.F.V. Edward's team)		Probably a shuttle relay, though a baton was used. Only two teams could compete at a time
		2nd second round	Relay (H.F.V. Edward's team)		1st T.J. Cushing's team
17 May	Poly H club ch, Stamford Bridge	1st	100 yards	10.4	2nd Fred Gaby
20 May	Brighton Railway Sports, Brighton	??	100 yards handicap?		Carrying a thigh strain
3 June	Lyons Sports, Sudbury	2nd	100 yards		1st Christiaan Steyn (South Africa) 10.5 (some reports said 10¼)
5 June	Molinari Sports featuring England vs. France, Belgium and Italy, Stamford Bridge	DNF	100 metres		Broke down – injured leg
22 June	P Division Metropolitan Police Sports, Herne Hill	1st	Mile medley relay (Poly H)	3:44.8	Team: Lightwood, Edward, Cushing, Gaby

24 June	Brighton Carnival Sports, Brighton	1st	Mile medley relay (Poly H)	3:42.4	Team: W.C.A. Chambers, Edward, Gaby, H.J. Witham Edward had fallen downstairs the evening before and had twisted his ankle
30 June	AAA ch, Stamford Bridge	1st heat	220 yards	23.6	Plasters on both thighs and bandaged ankle
		1st second round	220 yards	22.1	
		1st heat	440 yards	52.4	
		1st heat	Mile medley relay (Poly H)	3:39.4	Team: Lightwood, Gaby, Edward, Cushing
1 July	AAA ch, Stamford Bridge	1st heat	100 yards	10.4	Plasters on both thighs
		1st final	100 yards	10.0	2nd Royle
		1st final	220 yards	22.0	2nd Josef Imbach (Switzerland)
		1st final	440 yards	50.4	2nd Guy Butler
		2nd final	Mile medley relay (Poly H)	3:36.0e	1st Surrey AC 3:35.2. Beaten by 6–7 yards. Team: Lightwood, Gaby, Edward, Cushing
		Last heat	100 yards handicap		1st Deeley 10.4 (off 2½ yards). Eased off when could not catch the others. After the event, Edward caught an aeroplane (sic) to Paris

Date	Meeting	Position	Distance	Time (mins:secs) or Distance	Notes
8 July	Croydon Sports, Wallington				
9 July	'Prix Roosevelt' meeting, Stade Pershing, Paris	1st	200 metres (Prix Gaston Raymond)	22.0	2nd André Mourlon (France). Beaten by 1 *poitrine* (a chest)
		2nd	100 metres (Prix Maurice Boyau)	11.2e	1st René Lorain (France) 11.2 (photo of finish suggests margin very narrow indeed)
12 July	Poly H club ch, Herne Hill	1st	440 yards	51.4	2nd Cushing
13 July	Brighton Railway Sports, Brighton	1st	440 yards handicap	51.6	
15 July	Leeds Cricket, Football and Athletic Club Meeting, Headingley	2nd heat	100 yards short limit handicap	10.1e	1st F. Lomas 10.0 (off 4 yards). Beaten by ¾ yard
		3rd final	100 yards short limit handicap	10.1e	1st Lomas 10.0 (off 4 yards); 2nd Tom Matthewman (off 2 yards). Beaten by half a yard and by a foot
		3rd heat	220 yards handicap	21.8e	1st J.C. Harbron 21.0 (off 17½ yards). Beaten by 7 yards

Date	Event / Location	Placing	Event	Time	Notes
22 July	Liverpool Working Men's Conservative Association Sports, New Brighton	1st	100 yards	10.17 (sic)	Then travelled overnight to Paris – not by air this time
23 July	Poly H vs. Stade Français, Paris	1st	200 yards (sic) (Prix du Stade)	19.6	2nd Mourlon 20.2
		1st	100 metres	11.0	
		2nd	4x200 metres relay (Poly H)		Team: Edwards, C.B. Langley, Cushing, J.G. McColl. McColl, of West of Scotland Harriers, replaced the injured Gaby
3 August	Histon, Cambs.	DNQ heat	100 yards open handicap		
		2nd heat	100 yards short limit handicap		1st Bob Beazor
		1st final	100 yards short limit handicap	9.4	Downhill
5 August	Rangers FC Sports, Ibrox Park, Glasgow	3rd heat	220 yards handicap	22.9e	1st H.B. Anderson 22.6 (off 8 yards). Beaten by more than 2 yards
		3rd	440 yards handicap	49.6e*	1st G.T. Stevenson 49.0 (off 10 yards). * Estimated by historian Ian Buchanan

Date	Meeting	Position	Distance	Time (mins:secs) or Distance	Notes
9 August	Hibernian FC Sports, Easter Road, Edinburgh	2nd	120 yards handicap	12.2e	1st Liddell 12.2 (off 1 yard). Result described as 'close'
		2nd heat	100 yards handicap		1st A.J. Donaldson 10.6 (off 9 yards)
		2nd heat	440 yards handicap		1st Christie 53.0 (off 19 yards)
12 August	Celtic FC Sports, Parkhead, Glasgow	2nd	120 yards	12.4e	1st Liddell 12.2. Beaten by 4 feet
		2nd	220 yards handicap	22.6e	1st Liddell 22.6 (off 2 yards). Some reports say 22.4. Beaten by inches, though one report said 'comfortably'
		3rd	440 yards handicap		1st Stevenson 50.2 (off 8 yards). Well beaten
26 August	Metropolitan Police Sports, Herne Hill	3rd	100 yards handicap	10.0e	1st George Phillips 9.9 (off 4 yards); 2nd Nicol (off 4 yards). Beaten by 2 feet and by inches. 'Favourable wind'
		1st		4x220 yards relay (Poly H)	1:32.4

Date	Meeting / Location	Position	Event	Measurement	Notes
2 September	Wycombe Phoenix, High Wycombe	1st heat	220 yards		
		DNF final	220 yards	23.0	1st Billy Hill 22.4. Edward broke down injured (right thigh again?)
30 September	AAA relay ch, Stamford Bridge	DNS	4x220 yards relay (Poly H)		Arrived too late to run. Poly H finished 2nd
22 November	Indoor Gala, Regent Street Gymnasium	1st	Relay (H.F.V. Edward's team)		
4 December	Indoor meeting, Regent Street Gymnasium	=7th	High Jump	5ft 3in (1.60m)	Edward had done no training for the high jump at all
1923					
3 May	Inter-club meeting: Ashcombe AC vs. Lyons AC vs. Harrodian AAA, Barnes	2nd	100 yards		1st Edward Toms 10.4
		3rd	440 yards		1st Toms 51.0 'won easily'
12 May	Rover Sports Club, Coventry	1st heat	100 yards short limit handicap	10.2	
		3rd final	100 yards short limit handicap	10.1e	1st A. Davis 10.0 (off 6 yards). Beaten by 6 inches and by a foot
16 May	Poly H club ch, Stamford Bridge	DNF	100 yards		1st D. Crowley 10.6. Pulled up injured when leading (thigh again)

Date	Meeting	Position	Distance	Time (mins:secs) or Distance	Notes
9/10 June	Granted permission to compete in Paris but had not recovered				
6 July	AAA ch, Stamford Bridge	1st heat	220 yards	23.4	Legs copiously plastered
		3rd second round	220 yards	22.7e	1st Steyn 22.1; 2nd Billy Hill. Beaten by 5 yards and by a foot
		DNF heat	440 yards		1st J.V.S. Milne 52.2 (only two starters). Pulled up entering the final straight
7 July	AAA ch, Stamford Bridge	DNS heat	100 yards		
2 August	Histon, Cambs.	2nd heat	100 yards open handicap		1st G.W. Hardy (off 6 yards)
		2nd heat	100 yards short limit handicap		1st Hardy (off 5 yards)
		Unplaced final	100 yards short limit handicap		1st Hardy 9.8 (off 5 yards). Edward was not in the first four. Downhill
6 August	Liverpool Working Men's Conservative Association Sports, New Brighton	2nd	100 yards	10.6e	1st Billy Hill 10.46 (sic). Beaten by 1 yard

Date	Venue	Result	Event	Notes
8 August	Hibernian FC Sports, Easter Road, Edinburgh	DNS	440 yards handicap	Reported as having entered, but did not travel to Scotland
11 August	Celtic FC Sports, Parkhead, Glasgow	DNS	440 yards handicap	Reported as having entered, but did not travel to Scotland
8 September	Wilco Games, Yankee Stadium, New York	3rd heat	100 metres	1st Louis Clarke (USA)
		2nd heat	200 metres	
		4th final	200 metres	1st Murchison 21.6
15 September	Boston AA meet, Cambridge, MA	DNQ heat	440 yards handicap	
22 September	New York AC meet, Travers Island	1st heat	300 yards handicap	
		1st? semi-final	300 yards handicap	
		4th final	300 yards handicap	1st James L. Dalton (USA) 32.2 (off 12 yards)
1924				
12 February	Order of Elks meet, Thirteenth Regiment Armory, New York (indoors)	Unplaced?	100 yards handicap	Entered but not mentioned in results
16 February	Wilco Games, Thirteenth Regiment Armory, New York (indoors)	3rd	150 yards	1st Robert McAllister (USA) 14.8

Personal best times

100 yards	9.9e	London	9 June 1919
100 metres	10.8	Antwerp	15 August 1920
	10.8	Antwerp	16 August 1920
200 yards	19.6	Paris	23 July 1922
220 yards	21.6	London	3 July 1920
250 yards	25.0	London	16 July 1921
440 yards	49.6e	Glasgow	5 August 1922

Compiled by John Edwards
National Union of Track Statisticians (NUTS)

ACKNOWLEDGEMENTS

This publication began as a simple research exercise, undertaken for a completely different project, and then morphed into something far bigger and, frankly, way more wonderful and unexpected. Harry Edward's story captivated me and set me on the path to discover more. As I dug deeper, my liking and respect for the man grew immeasurably. It has been an immense pleasure to bring his remarkable story to the public eye, as he had so hoped to do himself.

I'm grateful to Harry's extended family in Germany (his sister Irene's family) who have also been so helpful, especially Lina Weiss, who provided me with the lovely early photographs from the family archive.

A pivotal moment was discovering Harry's papers – and of course his lost memoir – in the archives of the Amistad Research Center in New Orleans. The Center specialises in studies of African-American culture, and its staff could not have been more helpful or accommodating in making material available. I'd like to single out Head of Research Services Lisa Moore, Philip Cunningham and former Deputy Director Christopher Harter, as well as the new Executive Director Kathe Hambrick, for their support and encouragement throughout the project. When I visited the Center, a short tram ride from New Orleans city centre, I spent three days trawling through the boxes of Harry's papers, scrapbooks, letters and photographs.

While they were rightly proud of the Harry Edward Collection, the idea of actually publishing Harry's memoir was a new direction for Amistad. Once again, it could not have been more supportive, and it is my hope that the publication will lead more people to its door and even better recognition of this superb research facility.

Two other academic research centres require thanks – the University of Westminster, where all the Polytechnic Harriers archives are kept; and the Cadbury Research Library at the University of Birmingham, where the Amateur Athletics Association archives are maintained. Both could not have been more helpful. Special praise goes to Claire Brunnen, Anna McNally and Elaine Penn at Westminster; and to Mark Eccleston, the head of collection management, in Birmingham.

I'd also like to thank the staff of the Library of Congress in Washington, DC, who helped me navigate the vast archives of the Federal Theatre Project.

I have known for many years that there exists in Britain a wonderful camaraderie among sports historians, who are prepared to collaborate, help and propagate their passion. Nowhere has it been better illustrated than here. From Mel Watman, doyen of British athletics writers (who sadly died at the start of this project), to the likes of Peter Lovesey, Bill Mallon, Stuart Mazdon and John Edwards. They all instantly, happily and enthusiastically gave me their time and expertise. John's frankly extraordinary knowledge of early-twentieth-century athletics is matched only by his willingness to share it.

And, of course, there's the terrific Hannah Griffiths, the head of literary acquisitions at All3Media, with whom I shared the story and who then put me in contact with Yale University Press and its irrepressible editorial director, Julian Loose. His passion for Harry's story has been critical in bringing the whole project together. Big thanks also for the hard work, patience and gimlet eye for detail of Managing Editor Rachael Lonsdale, Production Editor Meg Pettit, Copy-Editor Clive Liddiard and Editorial Assistant Frazer Martin. Thanks also to everyone at All3Media and North One for their encouragement and support – and especially to my PA, Sally Westwood, for the painstaking hours of collating all my materials from the various archive visits into a comprehensive filing system that works. Truly above and beyond her day-to-day duties.

And finally, to a very special – and fundamental – member of the team, my wife Julie, who has lived the whole adventure with me, happily read and reread, and listened to every twist and turn of the project as it took me around the world. I couldn't have done it without you.

ILLUSTRATIONS